The Logics
of Globalization

The Logics of Globalization

Studies in International Communication

Anandam Kavoori

LEXINGTON BOOKS

a division of
ROWMAN & LITTLEFIELD PUBLISHERS, INC.
Lanham • Boulder • New York • Toronto • Plymouth, UK

LEXINGTON BOOKS

A division of Rowman & Littlefield Publishers, Inc.
A wholly owned subsidary of The Rowman & Littlefield Publishing Group, Inc.
4501 Forbes Boulevard, Suite 200
Lanham, MD 20706

Estover Road
Plymouth PL6 7PY
United Kingdom

British Library Cataloguing in Publication Information Available

Library of Congress Cataloging-in-Publication Data

Kavoori, Anandam P.
  The logics of globalization : studies in international communication / Anandam
Kavoori.
      p. cm.
  Includes bibliographical references and index.
  ISBN-13: 978-0-7391-2183-2 (cloth : alk. paper)
  ISBN-10: 0-7391-2183-9 (cloth : alk. paper)
  ISBN-13: 978-0-7391-2184-9 (pbk. : alk. paper)
  ISBN-10: 0-7391-2184-7 (pbk. : alk. paper)
  ISBN-13: 978-0-7391-3252-4 (electronic)
  ISBN-10: 0-7391-3252-0 (electronic)
  1. Mass media—Social aspects—India—Case studies. 2. Popular culture—India—
Case studies. 3. Globalization—India—Case studies. I. Title.
  P92.I7K38 2009
  302.23—dc22   2008035874

Printed in the United States of America

♾™ The paper used in this publication meets the minimum requirements of
American National Standard for Information Sciences—Permanence of Paper
for Printed Library Materials, ANSI/NISO Z39.48-1992.

To Mark Levy and
(the late) Michael Gurevitch
for beginnings

Contents

Acknowledgments

I would like to thank Nikos Kavoori for creating the chart in chapter 1 and for help in the preparation of the manuscript. I would also like to thank the following publishers and journal editors for permission to reuse material developed in prior publications.

CHAPTER 1

Kavoori, A. (2007). The word and the world: Re-thinking international communication/defining the IC prism. *Global Media Journal* (Mediterranean Edition), 2(2), 3–18.

CHAPTER 2

Kavoori, A. (forthcoming). Nation, song, film: The early films/songs of Raj Kapoor. *Global Media Journal* (Indian Edition).

CHAPTER 3

Kavoori, A. (Fall 2008). Gaming, terrorism and the right to communicate: A research agenda. *Global Media Journal* (American Edition).

CHAPTER 4

Kavoori, A. (fall 2008). Global music and Africa. *Global Media Journal* (African edition).

CHAPTER 5

Kavoori, A. (2006). International communication after terrorism: Toward a post-colonial dialectic. In A. Kavoori & T. Fraley (Eds.), *Media, Terrorism, Theory* (pp. 179–197). Lanham, MD: Rowman & Littlefield.

CHAPTER 6

Kavoori, A., & Chadha, K. (2001). Net tarot in New Delhi: Reading the future of the Internet in advertising. *Convergence: The Journal of Research into New Media Technologies, 6*(7), 82–95.

Kavoori, A., & Chadha, K. (2006). The cell phone as a cultural technology: Lessons from the Indian case. In A. Kavoori and N. Arceneaux (Eds.), *The Cell Phone Reader: Essays in Social Transformation* (pp. 227–239). Oxford: Peter Lang.

APPENDIX A

Fursich, E., & Kavoori, A. (2001). Mapping a critical framework for the study of travel journalism. *International Journal of Cultural Studies, 4*(2), 149–171.

APPENDIX B

Kavoori, A., & Joseph, C. (2002). Why the diasporic desi men cross-dressed. *Jump Cut: A Review of Contemporary Media, 45*, 1–22. Available at ejumpcut .org/archive/jc45.2002/kavoori/indianighttext.html.

Introduction

This book presents for students of international communication the theoretical language and methodological tools needed for understanding issues of global media representation. The book's origins lie in my own struggles in teaching international communication. I have struggled with existing "textbooks" which often reduce complex theoretical positions into banal propositions or take the opposite tack—assume that the student/reader understands (and agrees) with the jargon and theoretical/political position of the writer. I have struggled with the very nature of "textbooks" which remove the voice of the writer, leaving in place the (supposed) dispassionate presentation of "data," about "media systems," "globalization," and so forth. There is little evidence of the creative energy and intellectual engagement that goes into "deconstructing" a global text. Finally, I have struggled with textbooks that rarely examine issues of popular culture—that makes the study of international communication, so important and so central to understanding how the world works. Studies of journalism abound, but few address the texts of gaming, film, cell phones, sports, music, YouTube—all the things that surround the daily experience of global culture. To put this more informally, textbooks are just not fun.

This book is not written as a textbook (in the traditional sense of the word). Rather, it is an attempt to infuse the love that I have for teaching international communication theory (and interpretation) into print. It brings students into a conversation about global culture and communication through the presentation of a conceptual language (that is global in nature) and then a series of essays that take (part of) that language and apply it to one or more media texts in detail. It draws on my scholarly work in international communication over the last fifteen years, which has focused on a close reading of a range of media texts (film, journalism, new media). My primary goal has been to *present theory as a methodological tool* through which different media texts/performances and even lives can be deconstructed.

This is a personal book—I bring in different parts of my personal and professional journey—many of the specific texts I examine are from India (where I grew up and currently work on as a scholar). The choices of texts are eclectic—representing old and new media—they are chosen for the wider sociological/global condition (what I term "logics of globalization") they help animate. Equally crucial, they are drawn from popular culture.

The book engages students with ideas from a range of theoretical influences, all connected by a central concern—an understanding of the complexity of global media representations—at the heart of which I argue is the search for "identity." This is by necessity, an incomplete, partial journey—but one that is ambitious, it tries to make sense of the relationship between what I term "the word and the world." I would like this book to be about having fun—intellectual, creative and if possible, curative of what many textbooks offer: a straitjacketed, static, and banal understanding of communication.

The first chapter ("The Word and the World: The IC Prism") presents a "model" for understanding the role of communication in the world today. Drawing on a range of theoretical influences, it uses a visual device (the International Communication Prism) to orient readers to six "logics of globalization"—those of modernism, postmodernism, postcolonialism, nationalism, capitalism, and terrorism. These logics it is suggested are terms that represent cultural, economic, and social forces that are present on a global level. These logics are simultaneously empirical and discursive; they are frames for social action, and action themselves. These logics link with the world of media forms (such as television, film, Internet) in a noncumulative and nonlinear way. The chapter "maps" out the scope, range, and theoretical weight of each of these logics and then the connections between these different logics and popular media forms. The goal of this chapter is to provide a broad theoretical accounting of the terrain of the relationship between the "word and the world." It does not provide a detailed theoretical treatment of any single logic or media form (any of which could easily fill a book) but rather allows readers to have a "big picture" of the field of international communication—and orient them to the detailed readings of specific texts to follow in the rest of the book. The notes to this chapter provide guideposts to the literature in the field and the issues *evoked* (but not detailed) in this chapter.

Each of the chapters to follow undertakes a very narrow task—the deconstruction of a specific media text (a song, a film, a video game, etc.) using the wider theoretical lens that the first chapter sets up (taking up one or more of the logics of globalization and one or more of the media forms). In other words, the individual chapters provide theoretical detail by engaging with the literature in specific subfields associated with the text under examination (e.g., Bollywood studies in chapter 2, gaming studies in chapter 3, and so forth). Endnotes in each of these chapters provide a broader account of the field, referencing relevant literature—and providing students with a starting point for their own research.

The second chapter ("Singing of a (New) Nation: The Early Films of Raj Kapoor") examines how music encodes ideas about nationalism and national identity. Drawing on a close textual reading of songs from some of the films of an early Bollywood star (Raj Kapoor), it outlines the specific ways in which these songs manifest ideas about modernity in the immediacy of Indian independence from British rule. A concluding section, offers some thoughts about national identity in later time periods, focusing on other films by Raj Kapoor.

The third chapter ("Time to Kill: Gaming and Terrorism") focuses on how video games provide a narrative language through which to think about terrorism. It first outlines some key elements in how video games as a media form can be interrogated and then provides an auto-ethnographic account of playing *Counter Strike*, a popular video game focused on terrorism. A concluding section outlines the key elements in other video games, focusing on both American games and those produced in the Middle East.

The fourth chapter ("Tracking the 'Authentic': World Music and the Global Postmodern") examines world music, a genre that is synonymous with the discourse of "authenticity"—a key concern/longing in postmodern societies. The lives of individual music stars—Cesaria Evora (Cape Verde), Ibrahim Ferrer (Cuba), Ali Farka Toure (Mali), and Nusrat Fateh Ali Khan (Pakistan)—are examined to present different elements of the authentic. A brief concluding section outlines some of the conceptual issues not examined in the bulk of the chapter.

The fifth chapter ("Playing with Postcoloniality: Four Moments in Indian Cricket") looks at the role of sports in the postcolonial era, examining how (changing) ideas about masculinity becomes encoded in the body and performance of major Indian batsmen. Cricket it is suggested is a mediated discourse that allows for the playing out of ideas about performance, identity, modernity, and nationhood in a complex of ways, both in India and in the Indian Diaspora.

The sixth chapter ("Consuming Technology: The Discourse of Cell Phone Advertising in India") focuses on how advertising constructs new media technologies (like the Internet and the cell phone) into new cultures/markets. Focusing on issues of technology and consumer culture, it suggests that advertising provides a gendered set of codes through which these new technologies are internalized in the developing world.

Finally, in the appendixes provide a conceptual bookend. Appendix A is an essay on journalism—but not examining traditional news coverage, but "travel journalism" showing how this understudied genre is a critical site for thinking about the various logics of globalization. The second essay is a "research play"—a performative text that examines the role of identity in the dance culture of "India Night"—an annual student event at the University of Georgia. Please note that these last essays differ in format and structure from the rest of the book.

It is hoped that each of these individual studies (along with the introductory chapter) will provide students with the theoretical language and methodological tools to *begin* the study of global media representation—an exercise at the heart of the field of international communication.

1

The Word and the World: Defining the IC Prism

To see the world in a grain of sand . . . and eternity in an hour.

—William Blake

I write poetry in the spirit of joy. No one understands; so I just simply write.

—Mirza Ghalib

THE SETTING

International communication—a field at the interstices of a wider set of debates within/across its antecedent disciplines—comparative literature, sociology, international politics, anthropology (to name just a few) mirrors all of the anxieties that bedevil those disciplines.[1] These include concerns over globalization (as concept, symptom, and reality), identity politics (as a concept for understanding both experience and structure) and policy formulations (as an agent for determining global structuration and nation-state relations).[2] In addition it faces problems of its own making which include bridging an understanding between media structures and media use;[3] the place of media in constructs of global culture;[4] the imperfect relation between political economy(ies) and media cultures.[5] It has also remained largely derivative—global media and communication theories drawing on and retrofitting models from relevant theoretical frames—dependency and cultural imperialism; world systems and political economy; neoliberalism and media economics; transnational ethnography and reception analysis.[6]

1

To this laundry list of complaints let me add two more—*a theoretical ambiguity* emergent in borrowing from a wide set of transnational concerns (the geopolitics of violence, the use of popular culture, the media policies of global corporations to name three disparate concerns) without an overarching theoretical frame to locate them and a *epistemic ambiguity* emergent in often overlapping use of terms such as globalization, globalism, cultural imperialism, transnationalism, and so forth.[7]

This chapter is a summative theoretical/epistemic gesture aimed at restrategization; it is a critical engagement with theories of the past but *it is primarily an attempt at imagination*—blending the literature and ideas from a wide range of fields but more crucially centering communication at the international level (the *field* of international communication, so to speak) as the framework for thinking through the complexities and contradictions of our collective global moment (as experience, as strategy, and as structure). It also departs from the narrative axioms of the academic essay in two specific ways. One, it does not follow the usual divisions (introduction, literature review, data analysis, conclusion) in favor of a connected and developing theoretical argument. Two, the academic embedding is undertaken in notes to the chapter, leaving the narrative of the chapter itself free of citationary punctuation.

QUESTIONS AND DIRECTIONS

I would like to begin by asking some elemental questions about communication in the world today: How do we make sense of the word? And a related question—how do we make sense of the world? And the direct end point of such a dualism: how do we make sense of the word in the world?

In this paper I offer a theoretical construct that provides the vocabulary to examine the relation between the word and the world. The "word" (both the text and the communicative act) is difficult to pin down in a symbol-saturated, mass-mediated global society, operating in the liminal space between video and text, playing and gaming, living locally and interacting globally in real time. The "word" then is a term that we need to return to and examines its stability in the traditional realms of mass media (film, television, radio, etc.) but in the context of this chapter in how it takes definition via the "world." The "world" is of course not a homogenous, stable referent (if it ever was)—it is fractured, reanimated, rearticulated, and refashioned in new and unstable ways, where the boundaries of technology and humanity increasingly intersect, where resurgent forms of brutality coexist with the impulses of democracy, where the act of being and belonging are increasingly transformed by the realms of commerce and (hegemonic) communities.

How, in sum, do we arrive at an understanding of the relationship between the world and the word? I suggest quite simply: *by creating a vocabulary that centers communication at the international level in our understanding of the word/world. This communicative act then becomes the field of international communication, a destination for all of us—speakers, scholars, and practitioners of communication.*

This chapter attempts to provide such a vocabulary by engaging with five conceptual terms from the institutional history of comparative scholarship, relationally constructed into what I call the "IC Prism" (International Communication Prism). These are those of modernism, postmodernism, capitalism, nationalism, postcolonialism, and terrorism. I refer to these as "the logics of globalization." By "logic of globalization" I mean that these terms represent cultural, economic, and social forces that are present on a "global" level irrespective of where a speaker/text/practice is located in any traditional category of dividing up the world (the three worlds; developed/underdeveloped; West and the Rest; North and South). The logics are simultaneously empirical and discursive—they are frames for social action; and action themselves as seen across a range of representational sites. Parenthetically, I use the term "logic of globalization" as a replacement for the word "globalization" which has little analytical usability left given its use simultaneously by a range of interests (governments, activists, nonprofits), theorists (political economy, neoliberal, postcolonial) and contexts (music, fashion, food).[8] Instead, I offer the following definition of the "logics of globalization":

> The logics of globalization are global frames for understanding/locating cultural practice (including practices of mass mediated communication) that render visibility to social action; provide order to community formation; rationale for identity articulation. They provide legitimacy to the (global) social order of things and (simultaneously) the motivation to change them.

These logics of globalization (hereafter "logics") connect with the world of mass communication in a noncumulative and nonlinear way. I define forms of mass communication or "media forms" (such as radio, gaming, television, and film) as *institutionally structured patterns of meaning generation through which speak the logics of globalization.* To return to the dualism I began this section with, media forms (the word) and the logics of globalization (the categories that make up the world) are *co-constructed.*

Using the prism thus entails two simultaneous acts: a cross-referencing of the phenomena being studied through one or more of the analytical points of reference (nationalism, terrorism for example) and finding points of connection across media forms that may be appropriate. The point of departure can be anywhere on the prism—an analytical

LOGICS OF GLOBALIZATION

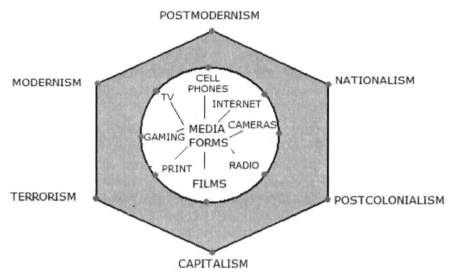

Figure 1.1.   The IC Prism

reference, a media form—with multiple points of arrival depending on the question being asked, which most commonly in the field of international communication have been organized around wider categories of the field of communication—those of content (quantitative and textual variants), intention (questions of "production," "auteur/authorship") and those of effect (framed under different paradigms as questions of reception, psychological responses, and ethnographic/anthropological insights).

DEFINING THE IC PRISM

I define the IC Prism in three steps (or sections). In the first section, I will provide a brief, thumbnail definition of each of the logics *as they relate* to the study of international communication followed by a second section in which I sketch the relationship *between* the logics. In the final section, I discuss the connections between each of these (interconnected) logics *to* various media forms.

Overall then, I begin by outlining the outside part of the prism and then move to the inside keeping in mind my goals of establishing the mobile nature of the relationship rather than assuming a theoretical and empirical fixity in any of these categories. In short they are *beginning* points for mapping the relationship between the word and the world.

Defining the Prism (Step One): The Logics of Globalization

- By *modernism*,[9] I mean the specific locus of institutional and cultural/communicative practices that emerge within the socioeconomic space of European industrial and urban growth and then become transmuted as a mediated vocabulary for cultural and economic development globally. The benchmarks of this development include those of industrial enterprise, economic valuation, political accountability, and personal freedom. Thus modernism retains its traditional use as a category of periodization and its wider use as a prescriptive for socioeconomic development.

- By *postmodernism*,[10] I mean the emergence of not only a new kind of social and economic accounting (culture as consumption) but a specific semiotic universe (a globally interconnected, rapidly mobile landscape of signifiers) and new vocabularies for cultural mediation (for example, hyper-tourism, micromedia, cybersex). Postmodernism's resonance with the articulation of identity politics (race, class, gender, sexuality) is retained and reflexively engaged with in the associated realms of technology, performance, cross-cultural transference, and regulated violence (across both state and non-state actors).

- By *nationalism*,[11] I mean both its traditional signifier as the communicative ethos of new states (and those yet to be born) and the emergent values of "renewal" in third world states as they grapple with current conditions of global capitalism (For example, the BJP inspired Hindutva movement in India which was unambiguously grounded in Hindu essentialism and an alliance with national/transnational capital) and global ethnicities and/or pan-nationalisms (the category of "Asian" or "Latino" for example). Nationalism functions as a discursive touchstone for state mobilizations over national identity (Iraq, Sri Lanka currently; the break up of Yugoslavia in recent memory) and regional "nationalisms" (in constructs like the "Arab Nation").

- *Capitalism*[12] is used both in the sense of a globally connected, historically contingent matrix of economic/cultural/mediated relations and its current "naturalization" by nation-states for social and economic development. Added to these are the multifaceted presence of capitalist values in a variety of contexts (the "marketplace" of both goods and ideas, for example) and guises (as state policy; as corporate strategy and belief systems—for example, the idea of "pleasure" in mass-mediated youth subcultures or "consumption" as a key value for the global middle class).

- *Postcolonialism*[13] is used in a complex of ways—as a category that signals communicative transference (between the modern and the postmodern) in the non-Western world; as a vehicle for the presentation of ethnic identity politics in the West. Most commonly, postcolonialism becomes the trademark of a global deterritorialization that moves people in search of jobs; trademarks in search of people; power in search of new locations and most crucially, the mobilization of "identity" in search of itself.

- Post 9/11, *terrorism*[14] emerges from a niche, regionalized (and narratively narrow) phenomena (Ulster, Lebanon, Oklahoma) to occupy the global center as both discourse and reality with multiple refractions across contexts of political action (the U.S.-led war in Iraq, Sudan's genocide, violence in Gaza), and institutional realignment (for example the changing role of the United Nations). In other words, there is a movement from terrorism to terrorism.

Defining the Prism (Step Two): Relationships between the Logics of Globalization

To complicate matters, each of these logics has a different set of meanings and contexts depending on which part of the world you are in. These include categorizations such as "Orient and Occident," "Developed and Underdeveloped," "West and the Rest," and "First, Second, and Third world." The bulk of international communication theory has been predicated broadly around the rubrics of theories developed in the "mother disciplines" of sociology, anthropology, literature, political science, and history. The two dominant approaches have been "development" theory and "dependency" theory, each field having an extended history. This history is in turn reflected in debates between political economy and cultural studies; globalization and anti-globalizationists; network analysts and cultural imperialism approaches, etc. In this chapter, I do not enter the shark infested waters around these categories, sidestepping them in favor of Trin-Min T. Ha's well-known reworking of the first and third world typology as a way to explicate the complex relationship between the various logics. Her formulation goes:

> A first world in every first world
> A first world in every third world
> A third world in every third world
> A third world in every first world

I prefer her reworking not only in that it centers issues of class (so central to the dependency approaches or world systems), social structure (important in development approaches), and identity politics (central to cultural pluralism/postmodern approaches) but that her typology is focused on *decentralization while maintaining a structural understanding of global relations.*

I now apply her typology to the relation between the logics using broad conceptual strokes:

- Modernism and postmodernism are categories of evolution (development) in the first world's of the first and third world's but categories of devolution (dependency) in the third worlds of the first and third worlds. Both modernism and postmodernism signal relatively complicated and new forms of identity politics (a break from religion in the case of modernism to democracy; and a break from science and national identity to micro/niche identity formations in the case of postmodernism). In the two first worlds, modernism and postmodernism often comingle relatively unproblematically, in the two third worlds, the relationship is often disjunctive.
- Post colonialism reflects agency and retributive justice in the third world of the first world, but national aspirations in the first and third worlds of the third world. Postcolonialism usually signals the mobilization of renewed modes of identity politics across all of the worlds.
  - Postcolonialism reflects a profound ambiguity in the two third worlds, a simultaneous acceptance and rejection of first world norms—the movement toward subalternity almost always marginalized by the project of capitalism (in both its national and transnational versions) and national elites.
  - In both the first worlds, postcolonialism reflects a movement toward the fetishization of micro-politics (especially gender and sexuality), a free imbrication with the workings of capital, and a reliance on a personalized politics as the vocabulary for identity articulation.
- Capitalism in both its national and transnational version echoes in complex ways in the various worlds.
  - For the first worlder in the third world it is an agent for national development, while for the third worlder in the third world it is simultaneously an agent of development and of alienation—created by the ethos of consumption—that intertwines aesthetics with identity (seen most fundamentally in advertising norms produced in the first world of the first world and disseminated to all the other worlds).
  - For the third worlder in the first world capitalism "naturalizes" national identity usually centered around a historically revisionist account of self (restricted to dominant conceptions of race, class, and gender).

- ○ For the first worlder in the first world capitalism is the unambiguous vocabulary for identity articulation whether uncritically espoused (for example, middle-class ethics of "work") or critically revised (for example, counter-cultures of suburban youth identity focused on corporate structured "revolutions") or structurally questioned (for example, the work of organized "labor"; the anti-globalization movement).
- Nationalism—that preeminent imagined community connects in multiple, often contradictory ways with the various worlds.
  - ○ For the first worlder in the third world, nationalism is synonymous with modernity (the unquestioned goal for postwar and post-liberalization nation-states) but is often accompanied by a class-centered ethinicism (Hindutva in India for example).
  - ○ For the third worlder in the third world, nationalism is the vocabulary of self-determination in the face of both national and global elites—this nationalism is often evoked through the lens of micro-nationalisms (Basque, Tamil, Croat) and that of pan-nationalism (African, Asian, Arab) interacting/reacting/working with the agents of local and global capitalism.
  - ○ Nationalism perpetuates its own reflexively constructed history— reiterated through the lens of national icons (flag, anthems) and their alter egos in the world of capital (cars, clothes, soft drinks). While nationalism is the face of modernism for the first worlder in the first world; for the third worlder in the first world, nationalism becomes a goal that their often hyphenated identity can aspire to but rarely achieve.
- Terrorism intersects in complex ways with the other logics of globalization. Terrorism can be seen simultaneously as an example of niche identity politics (so common to postmodernism) and as a rejection of modern identity formations (such as gender and sexuality). Terrorism can be seen as antimodern or as a new kind of modernity with the use of terrorist/state violence as its center. Terrorism can be seen as anti-national or as the determinative force for new nationalisms. Terrorism can be seen as anticapitalistic or as an intrinsic part of the global marketplace, drawing funding from nation-states and transnational money/arms/drug networks. In the context of different worlds, the contexts for terrorism are related to the discourse of the state and the kind of violence that the state predicates as legitimate:
  - ○ Terrorism for both third worlders is seen as commonplace when it is exercised by the state—much like the police violence they see in the streets, state intervention is a fait accompli, a relatively static, "normalized" set of discourses that they themselves are placed

within. This violence is often rationalized through modes of self-referencing via a capitalist logic that narrowly constructs any opposition to the system as violent (workers strikes, antiwar protests, cyber hackers).
○ For the first worlders (in both worlds), terrorism is an attack on the status quo, an assault on national identity and a system of economic privilege but it is equally a site where contestations between elites can morph "terrorism" into movements, ultimately absorbed into a global order organized by state elites, global corporations, and a institutionalized set of "publics" (education, media, religion).

Defining the Prism (Step Three): Connecting Media Forms and the Logics of Globalization

I now turn to a discussion of the inside of the prism by mapping with broad strokes how each media form reflects the co-construction between it and one or more of the logics of globalization (i.e., how the word and the world are connected in different mediated contexts). Before doing so I would like to provide a caveat about how I frame my comments about "media forms."

1. Rather than take the tactic of focusing on technology—"old" versus "new" media (e.g., radio vs. gaming), I would suggest that it is more fruitful to look at media forms as discursive agents for the logics of globalization.
2. Rather than seeing an unproblematic connection between single logics of globalization and single media forms (such as say television as the agent of high modernism; Internet as the symbol of postmodernity), I suggest a more useful way is to examine the complex and overlapping nature of media forms—this has as much to do with the interplay between media forms (radio on the Internet) and the fact that media forms have always been intertextually constructed (radio and television, television and film, gaming and television) but equally in that media forms intersect in complementary (and contradictory) ways across the logics. Hence, in the discussion that follows I do not map all the possible links between each of the logics and each media form but rather the important trajectories and connections between the two.
3. To keep things from getting too complicated I do *not* incorporate Trin Min T. Ha's four world's model in my discussion of each media form rather focusing on the more generic categories of first/developed/West and third/underdeveloped/rest in outlining how the logics and different media are co-constructed.

Television

Television can be seen as coterminous with a historically specific sense of the "modern," its technology inseparable from a key tenant of modernism, its self-reflexivity. Television is relentlessly intertextual, drawing from the representational history of other media forms (notably radio and film), and is complicit in the creation of its own history usually through the reduction of events into images—the last chopper out of Nam, the hostage crises, the challenger explosion—resulting in an effect where television *becomes* the event. Most crucially, television is concurrent with the emergence of modernity on a global scale. It could even be argued that television helped create the narrative topology of the postwar world especially its structuration around the three world's model. Nations in the second and third world were seen as facsimiles of the "real" modernity which was located within the cultural and media landscape of the West, specifically Britain (for the commonwealth), America (historically for South/Central America, the Philippines, and Korea and then the entire world), and France (for North Africa).

In its imbrication with the workings of national capital (in the industrial era) and then as a discursive agent of transnational capital (in the postindustrial era), television assumes a postmodern aura in the first world and a postcolonial echo in the third world. Here television is not just the platform for the arrival of postmodern/postcolonial programming (niche channels such as MTV in America; Aajtak in India) but provides both manpower and discursive sustenance to the construction of an entire cultural landscape (across contexts as varied as urban planning, fashion, political pedagogies). It needs to be emphasized that this relationship is neither arbitrary nor strictly developmental, it proceeds through the development of new modernities, (post-national in some cases such as Arab nationalism) or focused on a class centered modern identities (the global middle class).

It bears reminding that television is first and foremost a *popular* medium and its transgressive nature across genre and contexts (the political, social, cultural, and sexual) allows for it to be the engine that drives the daily life of national discourse. In claiming such a central place for television, one needs to spend just a little time examining the journey of Al Jazeera, over the course of the last decade, from its mutable relationship to the narrative construct of terrorism (framed variously as antimodern, postcolonial, and pan-national depending on the geopolitics of the speaker). Terrorism becomes through Al Jazeera both the language of jihadist terrorism and of its antithesis—an aggressive American imperialism as seen through the televisual eyes and ears of Arab national media (of which Al Jazeera remains the first and most vital instrument despite the mimicry of both Al Arabiya and Al Hurra).

Radio

Radio presents a wonderful paradox—its resilience and mutability is part of its own mythos, an institutional history that is embedded in the quintessential experience of modernity—traveling in a car (a vehicle for both transportation and discursive stimulation). This too has now become a symbol for identity politics in the postmodern first world and the postcolonial third world where radio appears at the margins (with print media and the Internet occupying center stage) but functions in a position that it appears to be best suited for—the creation of a contextual frame that sustains viewership *across* media. Today, radio is inseparable from the emergence of a global urbanity and urbanism (modern and postmodern, national and postcolonial in scope) and of the media that allows this urbanism. At the heart of this urbanism is the global neoliberal project and its model for economic/social development. A model based on the separation of work and home; pleasure and industry all made possible by the car. This journey (of cars and countries) is shaping contemporary China, India, Brazil, South Africa, and other frontiers of the global economy, writing a new cultural landscape (simultaneously similar and disjunctive from the experience of consumption in the developed world that it mimics).

It is no accident then that radio provides contextual placement at different points of modernity (first, as central to the emergence of a nascent national identity after colonial liberation, now as the manifestation of the cultural logic of global capitalism). In between these differing contexts there remain interesting divergences and appropriate contradictions such as *Radio Sawa* which is both an experiment in foreign policy and popular culture—making manifest that there is no direct correlation between the acceptance of the workings of one and an understanding of the other—rather it is their very difference that makes sense in the postcolonial context such as the Arab world, where the emergence of a new Arab nationalism strides successfully with global capitalism and Islamic radicalism.

In the case of terrorism, radio presents itself through the narrative presence of political speeches (the global fire chats of national/global leaders); the essentialist logic of speeches on terrorist tapes; the global imaginare of terrorism synodically represented by the voice and presence of Osama bin Ladin, known not just through file video but equally through voice and form, disembodied and intimate at the same time.

Internet

The Internet changes the equation both in/between the logics of globalization in some fundamental ways. Its effects post-dot-com (bubble burst) has perhaps been more important than in its gestation where the discourse about the technology far outstripped its institutional reach. The postmodern/postcolonial turn is frequently asserted through specific cultural/media formations as they reflect the effects of global capitalism. From the growth of niche consumer markets (with web based portals) to the public manifestations of niche identity formations (Kurds in Iraq, Chechnya in Russia), to the transference of terrorism from an antistate ideology to one of national identity-in-formation (with a revisionist account of history) we are seeing the Internet becoming not just a tool but an articulation of these tensions. Islamic fundamentalism of course uses the Internet as its mouthpiece—it is perhaps synonymous with the idea of a global jihad using a singular pan-national collectivism (Arab/Islam) and its multiple articulations across a range of state centered jingoism's (Russian, Indian, Pakistani, Nigerian) and global/ regional hegemonies (Israeli, American, Chinese). In each case, the Internet has emerged as the vernacular for fundamentalism—mainstream media focuses on terrorist use of the Internet for publicity (beheadings, terrorist video) but it is equally important in a more fundamental way— the building of community and diasporic identity. Issues of recruitment via Internet chat rooms and the reflexive consideration of hyphenated identities in western national spaces just scratches the surface of this relationship.

In sum, the Internet mediates a critique of modernity, an assembling of postmodern/postcolonial identity that has fundamentalism (and the idea of primordiality, based on religion or national identity) as its core consideration. The Internet's connection (on the face of it) with nationalism is much more tenuous—the use of the technology by states is largely heavy-handed and insecure (China and Iran are two obvious examples) but what is more interesting is perhaps the rearticulation (through the work of global capitalism) of a *consumerist nationalism* that mutates much more quickly through the Internet than it does through more established media. For example, this shows up in important ways around issues of identity politics—observe the mushrooming of the global sex trade in brides in the post-Soviet world (along prescribed lines of white sexual performance) and its intimate connection with the Internet as a form of cultural assembling.

While such consuming nationalisms are global, they are articulated through different national political ideologies (India and China are the ones that dominate media discussions of economic successes) where the role of the Internet is central. These global tensions are reflected in stories about economic deterritorialization (focused on metropolitan anxieties about outsourcing) and those of global cultural production.

Print

"Print" media is a complex of competing, transcending, and correlating texts—traditional media still dominate the international communication scene—from regional magazines and trade journals, to newspapers and special interest magazines. Print dominates the Internet too—e-mail is the most common use of the Internet. Convergence retains cache more as a rapidly emergent industry practice rather than as a form of public participation (even as this is rapidly changing). Print remains at the forefront of a rearticulated modernity—literarily, the idea of representation, the manifestation of identity through "word." The Internet makes this clear everyday with the birth of a countless number of blogs and websites which are overwhelmingly attempts at self-presentation through "print."

Global capitalism often realigns national media forms in interesting and often contradictory ways—state print and television dies an early death with the advent of satellite television but is resurgent in other ways—through the fostering of state-sponsored identity formations and practices (the use of state media for fostering the ideology of Hindutva in India is a notable case). The national and postcolonial imagination is rekindled primarily through the use of television (the recent elections in Venezuela, Chile, and Brazil are good examples) but print plays an important ancillary role—such as the creation of anticipation through advertising in the print media. It is here that the "cultural work" of establishing the discourse of consumerism is first established through performance/enactments of popular culture and conspicuous consumption. Print remains at the core a modernist convention—and one that embraces all the enactments of modernity—nationalism, terrorism, racism, feminism, and colonialism. In the beginning (of the modern world) is the word, but through its imbrication with writing on the Internet and texting on the cell phones, "print" is present at the end (or wherever we are) of the postmodern and postcolonial world.

Film

Film is critical—both in its role as an influential media industry; its central role as a semiotic network that feeds all other media forms (but especially television and the Internet) and in its sheer impact on the global imagination. Television might be watched by more people, the radio listened to more often (that long commute), and the Internet opened as a window on RL (real life) but it is film that dominates the space of cultural immersion that comes with entertainment globally—going to the movies, bringing them home, downloading them, receiving them via Netflix are only part of the question of its dominance—it is the role of film as the prime arbitrator of the moment of consumption that underlies its importance. Whether it's *Titanic* or Bollywood or the telenovela inspired film or the independent film (ranging across sub-ethnic and national inspirations), it is film that presupposes the moment of imagination—a self-reflexivity (that Paul Simon once referred to as "this is the way we look to us all") that lies at the core of the postmodern subject in the first world and the postcolonial subject in the third world. The idea of the national cinema remains at its heart both a modernist fantasy and a postmodern/postcolonial reality. It enters into the global marketplace simultaneously carrying the national imprint of the director (for example, Ang Lee or M. Night Shyamalan) and the use of that imprint to redefine and reassert the boundaries of the imagination—within the confines of the workings of global capitalism.

This cultural work is extraordinarily important as nation-states engage with both the discourse and practice of global terrorism—framing violence as within/against nation-states is a common leitmotif of filmic violence, but it is also in its centering of the individual (sometimes as victim but most commonly as hero—almost always a male) as an agent of social change. Film also frames terrorism as antiglobal with individual hero's/cultures upholding a specific construct of the national imagination but almost always upholding a global order constructed around ideas of individual humanity and the status quo (which is often predicated on capitalism as the natural order and a relentless individualism as the preferred natural state of being/action).

Gaming, Cell Phones, and Cameras

I will treat gaming, cell phones, and cameras collectively—they are part and parcel of a new postmodern/postcolonial sensibility that is at its heart anti-representational, with a strong reliance on post-reflexivity—they are also centered on a single idea: performativity. The performativity of gaming, cell phones, and the contemporary use of cameras (digital and disposable ones especially) are based on a commonplace assumption—this is how media should always be used, not passively (like television) but interactively. Children's immersion in gaming and cell phones are not just indicative of the use of the latest technology but the growth of a specific performativity. It is performative with a difference from earlier modernist/postmodernist modes in that they are not necessarily being used in a reflexive presentation of their identity politics (such as raves or retro-discos) but rather that the *presentation of daily life* (at work, at school, at play) is *performative*. On online games this may mean the adoption of both new roles and identities but more crucially in the adoption of a new set of rules about what matters and what governs the creation of self. In this articulation the non-Western world presents different conjunctures with these technologies—they are imbricated within the class matrixes of those societies and within the correlates that these technologies have within the framework of global capitalism (consumption, pleasure) but with some important differences—cell phones connect farmers, cameras make tourists accessible, and gaming exists as an antidote to television.

The effects of this technology are a little more difficult to predict—in a sense they are already following the paths of older media forms (such as the Internet and television), a gradual but firm path to the corporatization, the emergence and rapid dissolution of identity/niche identities, the centering of consumption, but there is also the possibility of a "tipping point" where the logic of postmodernity—the collapse between reality and fiction; image and policy is finally reworked to its logical extreme—the emergence of the next generation of modernities and their own sets of semiotic and real violence. The role of the cell phone in global terrorism certainly appears to be a harbinger of this social moment perhaps even the proverbial canary in the coal mine.

THE WORD AND THE WORLD: DIRECTIONS

To summarize, what I have tried to do in the above narrative is to map—with very broad strokes, a model for understanding international communication. This model, the IC Prism (a) framed an understanding of the world (structured through the logics of globalization) as inseparable (or to use my term, co-constructed) from an understanding of the word; (b) discussed these co-constructions by mapping out (again, with broad conceptual strokes) the logics of globalization and their interrelations with the different "worlds" (using Trin Min Ha's formulation); and (c) outlined how specific nodes of meaning production (media forms) correlate to the logics of globalization.

The rest of this book contains chapters that provide detailed looks at one (or more) logics and their "creative correlations" (see below) with one (or more) media forms. To use a cinematic metaphor, if this chapter has been a panoramic shot of the model, the chapters to follow are XCUs (extreme close-up's) of specific textual elements as they connect with the logics.

I would like to end this chapter with some general thoughts about why the international communication community should engage with the theoretical import of the IC Prism,[15] with the remainder of the book providing both theoretical detail and a methodological template.

1. Theoretical Voice and Complexity: The IC Prism signals a departure from the largely *determinative* nature of traditional international communication models (dependency, functionalist, effects, cultural imperialism, world systems, etc.) to one that I would broadly define as *creative and correlational*. By "creative" I mean the *act* of communication is simultaneously real and imaginative—the word exists in the world and the world through the word. This is the hermeneutic gesture taking a global bow, a shout heard around the world, but it is more—it is present not just in the nature of media events but in the very structuration of daily life, profoundly transformed from the vectors of imitation and refutation under the older paradigms and one that is "correlational" in its use of a globally encompassing narrative frame (the logics) drawing on local, global, and regional (using the idea of scales) elements and related discourses of identity (religion, race, national, gender etc). In subsequent chapters, this "hermeneutic gesture" will be evident in a variety of ways—the texture of a Bollywood song, a cell phone advertisement, a sports icon, a video game—as the sheer pleasure of negotiating with the texts of globalization is made evident.

   The IC Prism allows for complexity; it is multileveled in that it can be applied to a variety of discursive and empirical contexts—from television shows to fashion styles; from national media policies to technology protocols. It is this sensitivity to the idea/practice/context of communication that is often absent in macro theories that in the end insist on explaining the totality of the representational universe leaving out the very specificities of individual action (across a range of actors—states, social collectivities, corporations and yes the "individual"). This is not in anyway a return to the idea that "the universal I" or the nihilism of the postmodern project—it is rather an articulation of an idea—that the field needs a framework that makes sense as much in Denver or Dakar or Dare Salaam or Delhi—it straddles the individual and the collective in its phenomenological/structural certainty (and uncertainty) rather than in any absolutist framework whether derived from Marxist or neoliberal certainties.

2. Understanding Globalization: The IC Prism critiques the rationale behind the traditional use of the logics of globalization (nationalism breeds national subjects/media, terrorism breeds terrorists/terrorist media) and suggests that we understand globalization and media forms as co-constructed. In the above analysis, I have retained some sense of pedagogical unity behind the logics I have outlined (modernity and postmodernity, for example). In the chap-

ters to follow, the various analysis will reveal the "creative correlations" that *allow for communication* in/between the workings of the logics of globalization and media forms. My goal (in the rest of this book) is to show the complex set of both local and global frameworks that are embedded in the understanding of a single global music song or a piece of video or the graphical devices used in a video game.

3. Understanding Media Forms: The IC Prism decentralizes "media forms" from its stable referents as seen in fields like "television studies" or outlets like "the journal of radio studies" and replaces it with a movable frame, thereby keeping pace not only with technology but also the slipperier realm of cultural production (via media industries), cultural assembling (through the work of groups), and cultural reception (through the traditional category of the "audience" which now is fundamentally transformed through interpretative technologies like blogs and webzines). The IC Prism in this sense is a natural fit with contemporary debates about convergence and the creation of a new vocabulary for understanding the media forms of the future. The rest of the chapters in this book provide a detailed look *not* at narrowly constructed studies of "media forms" but in their creative correlations with the different logics of globalization—the chapter on Bollywood showing connections between nationalism, modernity, and cinema; the chapter on world music, the connections between video, music, Internet, (global) postmodernity, and nationalism; the chapter on cricket, an examination of sports icons (their media constructs emergent across media forms) animating the logic of postcolonialism and modernity; the chapter on video games illuminating the relations between play and terrorism and so forth.

These chapters are of course only a beginning. Much more needs to be done and the end of each chapter provides some suggestions for directions—ideas that students/scholars may wish to develop in their own projects. One specific task that is especially important is that of understanding *communication between* media industries and media discourses as they develop in different parts of the world (for example, the similar/different trajectories in China, Venezuela, and South Africa—would make up one important area for analysis). In a similar vein, the very nebulosity of future media forms should not allow for a nebulosity of understanding the questions that will always remain important—those of effects, of ideology, and simply, media use. These are questions without a bottom—but they have to be refashioned and reshaped by the nature of contemporary media forms.

NOTES

1. For a useful overview of the paradigms of international communication see Thussu (2000), Reeve (1993), and essays in various editions of Downing, Mohammadi, and Mohammadi (1995). Curran and Gurevitch's, *Mass Media and Society* (2005) provide similar narratives at different points in time in its four editions. Hamid Mowlana's pioneering work using a non-Western/Islamic frame is worthy of a paper all on its own. Rodriguez and Murphy (1997) provide a history of communication studies in Latin America while Sutz (2002) does a similar analysis of Latin American understanding of globalization. Frederik, McCaw, and Vasquez (1994) provide an important analysis of international communication education—a much-needed focus in communication schools and a concern addressed by the September 2006 Internationalizing Media Studies Conference at the University of Westminster. See the introductory chapter in Rantanen (2005) for a more updated version of some of the issues facing international communication education. For an important critical statement on the crises of communication education see McChesney (2000) and for a comprehensive and nuanced engagement of the future of interdisciplinary global media studies see Shome (2006).

2. "Globalization" as both a theoretical construct and an empirical process has been questioned, defined, critiqued, and rationalized by a range of theorists in fields as wide as political science, sociology, comparative literature, and anthropology (the "Borderlines" book series by the University of Minnesota is an excellent one-shop stop to see congruent/different trends across these fields—volume 23 on "The Politics of the Global" by Himadeep Muppudi is especially important for media studies in its detailed consideration in its analysis of "critical constructivism). The most influential theorists of globalization include Immanuel Wallerstein, Roland Robertson, Anthony Giddens, Manuel Castells, Ulf Hannerz, Arjun Appadurai, John Tomlinson, and Jan Nedervan Pieterse (and the numerous scholars who have interrogated different parts of their work—for example Giddens by Tomlinson 1994, Rosenberg 2000, among numerous others). The essays in King (1991) by many of these scholars remains one of the best collections on the subject. More recently, Holton (2005) has a cogent accounting of the first, second, and third wave scholarship on globalization as does the more contextual one in Hopper (2006). A range of global events from Darfur to 9/11 to the war on terror has animated the globalization debate in both the popular press (Thomas Freidman's *Lexus and the Olive Tree* is perhaps the best representative of this genre) and from a critical tradition in scholarship (see the essays in Freeman and Kgarlitsky [2004] of one such work) and on numerous outlets online, usually focused on political events (for example, opendemocracy.net and alternet.org).

3. Initiated by Hall's encoding/decoding model some of the key negotiations for audience research has been the career long work of David Morley and Ian Ang. For a recent summary of these debates see the introductory essay in Murphy and Kraidy (2003) and for a methodological reformulation of some key issues see Couldry (2000).

4. For an influential analysis of this see the collected essays of Appadurai (1996) and Hannerz (1992). For a more recent reframing of the conceptual and pedagog-

ical issues at hand see Tomlinson (1999) and Pieterse (2004). For a sustained debate on the issue of identities in a global context see Martin-Barbero (2002) and Schlesinger (2002).

5. The essays collected in Durham and Kellner (2001) are perhaps the best one-stop shop for understanding this debate with essays on the political economy of media (by Nicholas Garnham, Herbert Schiller, and Noam Chomsky) and media/cultural studies (with essays by Larry Gross, Jean Baudillard, Mark Poster, Raymond Williams, and Dick Hebdige). Thurston-Jackson (2003) reviews "cultural economy" approaches (books by Eric Louw, Richard Maxwwell, Paul Du Gay, and Michael Pryke) that draws elements from both approaches.

6. Thussu (2000, pp. 53–81) provides a useful summary of these connections especially the connections between dependency and structural imperialism theories and their devolution into cultural imperialism theory. Thussu's textbook itself is a good example of such retrofitting with an overall grounding in the political economy tradition which structures the narrative of his chapters on global communication infrastructure, marketplace, contra flows amongst others issues.

7. My essay is also a reaction to (and as a counterpoint to) three other issues:

- As an antidote to the kinds of theoretical/pedagogical divide that has become embedded in the study of international communication between practitioners and theoreticians; scholars and policy makers; creators and critics. This is not unique to international communication, but especially worrisome given the need of the hour—a critical engagement with the brutalities of the global moment: AIDS, endemic violence, genocide, hunger, and poverty.
- The kind of fixity that has "carved up" the field and practice of international communication into those of genre studies, policy studies, political economy studies, literary studies, and so on—the conversation between these is limited, often farcical, with little attention being paid to *internationalizing* media studies—rather the trend has been to refit existing subfields in communication with an international aspect—hence reception analysis becomes comparative reception analysis and so forth.
- As a replacement to understanding international communication processes as linear and evolutionary (from third to first, from developing to developed) which has little analytical value in examining the mutative nature of contemporary international communication, seen in the open and dialogic nature of media culture (Korean rap, Japanese anime, London Bhangra) and their placement within the strategies of global capital and local media elites.

8. The titles of two recent books, *Making Globalization* (Holton, 2005) and *Living with Globalization* (Hopper, 2006) are both focused on contextual analysis (drawing on network and third wave analysis) and have similar concerns (violence, terrorism, trade) but are evidence of the complex negotiations with the word "globalization." I am indebted to the late Marjorie Ferguson of the University of Maryland (where I went to graduate school) in pointing out the importance of examining the relationship between categories and processes of globalization—her essay *The Mythologies about Globalization* (1992) remains one of the most important benchmarks in the analysis of the term globalization. Mattelart (2002) engagement with "globalization" as a discourse is located in this critical tradition.

It is out of the scope of this chapter to give a sustained theoretical treatment of "globalization" as both process and concept; however critical junctures in the journey of this term can be identified. These include the context setting work focused on issues of global structuration (via states, institutions, markets, networks) of Roland Robertson, Anthony Giddens, and Manuel Castells, the reworking of their ideas in the context of culture by Tomlinson (1999) amongst many others; a move away from structuration to that of culture/deterritorialization in the work of Arjun Appadurai and Ulf Hannerz and the reworking of their ideas in the field of communication by Pieterse (2004), Rantanen (2005), and Kavoori (2006).

For useful summaries of the history of the term/theories of globalization see, Holton (2005, pp. 4–15), Hopper (2006, pp. 2–10) Pieterse (2004, pp. 7–21), Steger (2004, pp. 1–12). For a recent summary directly related to media/culture/communication see Rantanen (2005, pp. 4–8); Artz (2003, pp. 3–10); Tomlinson (pp. 1–31); Casey, Casey, Calvert, French, and Lewis (2002, pp. 111–115); and Chadha and Kavoori (2005, pp. 84–86). For a sense of where the debate stood in the early 1990s, see Robertson (1992), Freidman (1994), and Featherstone (1990).

9. Gidden's (1990) theory of globalization with modernity at the heart of it remains arguably the single most important theorization. Setting the context and scope of debate for years to come, it offered a rendering of the "institutional dimensions of modernity" (surveillance, capital accumulation, industrialism, military power) and argued that these dimensions were globalizing, creating what he called the "dimensions of globalization"—the world capitalist economy (from capital accumulation), the nation-state system (from surveillance), the world military order (from military power), and the international division of labor (from industrialism). While space does not allow for an extended discussion of how Gidden's work has been extended/critiqued, two books that have centered my understanding are Rosenberg's *Follies of Globalization Theory* (2000), which both critiques the institutional model, the historical reading, and theoretical consistency (on Marxist/critical lines), and Tomlinson's *Globalization and Culture* (1999), where (amongst other concerns) he links Giddens institutional model to what he calls "complex connectivity" in addition to issues of historical development, global reach, deterritorialization, and cosmopolitanism.

In the context of media and globalization, we can identify three separate insights/concerns/literatures that are focused on issues of modernity/modernism:

- A focus on transformed cultural dynamics from those of relative cultural coherence to those of fragmentation and the reflexive engagement with "tradition" (the literature on "development communication" remains rooted in this singular differentiation of societies, nations, and communities examined in a range of regional—Asian, Latin American, and developmental contexts (for a useful review see Fair and Shah [1997]).
- The creation of distinct social spheres under conditions of modernity—such as "work," "play" with *the crucial role of media* in the construction/placement of institutions, media practices, and texts within such spheres (this is the foundational directive of the literature on cultural tourism; pop culture studies; space/place research in fields like media anthropology, urban studies, and architecture.

- The development of media as a cultural technology first through photography, then radio and television—in each case birthing the modernist gaze focused on issues of authenticity, displacement, accumulation, segregation amongst others (see Fursich and Kavoori [2001] for a review).

10. Postmodernity as a framework for understanding globalization has been limited by the theories emergence and application to the mediated contexts of the developed world, especially the European and American experience. Having said that there are at least four major areas that examine how they (postmodern theory and globalization) connect:

- The reworking of Foucault's poststructuralist vision in a global context by Edward Said (and his heirs whose work has ranged across all areas of discourse).
- The emergence of postmodern values that work as an ideological anesthetic masking conditions of structuration and identity (as seen in the work of critical theory and transnational Marxist studies).
- The emergence of a global aesthetic and visual vocabulary that creates effects of simulation, dissonance, actualization, eroticization, and ideological affiliation (as seen in the work of the followers of Barthes, Baudillard amongst other semiotic/poststructuralist theorists).
- The reworking of identity politics (specifically issues of race, class, gender, and sexuality) in a global setting where they articulate issues of ethnicity, power, nationalism (in addition to those of race, class, etc.) and construct alternate/altered models of postmodernism/globalization(s). Some of the key ideas here emerge in the work of the subaltern school, postcolonial scholars, and transnational cultural studies scholars.

11. Benedict Anderson's notion of "imagined communities" has functioned as the key organizing principle for a considerable body of research on nationalism and national identity in relation to media (along with relevant ideas from the work by Ernest Gellner and Eric Hobsbawm). In the context of media/globalization we may identify three broad areas:

- The links between nationalism and ethnicity (or "ethno nationalism") in a global context articulating issues of cultural identity, nationalist hegemonies; the relation of nationalism to "modern" concerns of identity politics; the role of nationalism with concerns of immigration and multiculturalism (Conversi, 2004; Connor, 1994, 2000; Smith, 1998; Tambini, 1996).
- The connections between nationalism and nation-states in a global context examining issues of post-independence state formation on the basis of linguistic/cultural hegemonies; the role of state policy and regulated violence in constructs of nationalism; the links between nationalism and fascism (Billig, 1995; Smith, 1998; Hutchinson and Smith, 1994; Hosking and Schopflin, 1997; Appadurai, 1996).
- The connections between national cultures and cultural imperialism examining issues of historical and contemporary dominance in the cultural and economic arena by dominant nation-states (Mann, 2004); the role of language and media in that process (Barbour, 2000; Tomlinson, 1991) and the critical/subaltern reception of those processes in the non-western world (Appadurai, 1996).

12. The well-known (and worn) path from classical Marxist analysis to critical theory and political economy/dependency studies of mass communication provide the contextual frame for understanding the links between capitalism and issues of globalization. Two related sets of insights/concerns/literatures inform this understanding in the context of international communication.

- The usability of the classic questions of hegemony and ideology in a global context, where the issue is less one of the internal cultural/institutional mechanisms for the ideological work of media and more on issues of the intent and functioning of global capitalism. The question that has emerged with increasing frequency is the intimacy of global capitalism with local hegemonies (across a range of trajectories—national, religious, or using the cult of the leader); the postwar transference of national movements to national (usually based on a single political party) ideologies using a range of economic rationales (from capitalist to socialist to mixed economies); globalization and capitalism have become synonymous with economic integration, cultural (the "ideology" question) affiliation, homogenization (the "cultural imperialism" question).

- The usability of questions of global capitalist structuration around the classic questions of dependency and political economy where the debate has centered around questions of political agency (of both corporations and nation-states at the center) and economic effect (in the creation of markets/products along lines of center/periphery); questions of the role of communication in the economics of political life and inversely in the politics of economic life—the key issue has been the steady erosion of the public sphere by the forces of corporatization (in the media and in the academy), the emergence of vocabularies of neoliberalism (such as the field of media economics whose theories reify the marketplace) with one single overwhelming consequence: The role of the social formation (especially the question of class) is ignored and replaced by the omnipresence/ naturalization of the marketplace.

13. "Postcolonialism" remains controversial both as a descriptor for contemporary processes of globalization and as a theory with internal consistency and external (global) validity but we can identify two key areas that provide a new/ nuanced understanding of issues of globalization and media (see the debate between Kavoori and Shome in *Critical Studies in Mass Communication*, 15(12), 195–212).

- The reframing of questions of identity politics taken to a global level. This has been manifest in work that examines issues of not just gender politics but in the global gendering of categories; the intimate ties between personal expression and global placement; the working of global capital in local identity formations and perhaps most crucially in taking the audience question and framing it in terms of subalternity and agency rather than a unreflexive domination (as in "cultural imperialism"). The cultural studies and the transnational cultural studies project (taken to a "postcolonial" context) leaves a more than visible trace in how these questions have been developed.

- The "stretching out" of the personal and the institutional by emphasizing the deterritorialisation of ideas, peoples, goods, markets, and values while reworking/retaining foucauldian and habermasian questions of discourse and accountability in the public sphere. To its credit, this has been more than just a reworking of questions of dependency and political economy on a global scale rather there has been a retheorization of the political and the cultural in multiple trajectories—seeing connections between the post-colonial contexts of the first and the third world as seen in concerns of immigration, trade (of people, goods, and services) and the imagination.

14. Post 9/11 there has been a plethora of published work on media and terrorism. For example, the essays in Kavoori and Fraley (2006) provide both contextual embedding of issues of terrorism in a comparative context (across genre and region) and a range of theoretical perspectives (political economy, cultural studies, postcolonial studies) and methods (textual analysis, institutional analysis).

Kavoori (2002) outlines some of the theoretical issues around terrorism and globalization, focusing on notions of "mediated terrorism," and suggests three important contexts to problematize the relationship:

- Historical context: "To see the discursive placement of a specific form of violence—terrorism—within older standards of international reporting . . . these include notions of antistate insurgency, religious fundamentalism, tribal violence" (pp. 93–94).
- Corporate context: News about violence/terrorism is "validated or decried through the set of economic, political, and cultural vectors . . . western corporate coverage of news is usually referenced through issues of internal (state/cultural) failure or of inert tradition" (p. 93).
- Global context frame: "What we have been witnessing for years in the western media is not just (coverage of) terrorism but something grander—an 'ism,' to wit 'terror-ism.' The problem for people inside this 'ism' (the nations, peoples, cultures where terrorism begins) can be summed up as the problem of the 'double reflection'—where those looking in, look the same as those being looked at" (p. 94).

15. The tone and intent of this chapter is along the model building/critiquing exercises (for international communication) articulated in the early 1990s by Waterman (1990), Chitty (1994), Tehranian (1994), Mowlana (1994), and more recently by Kavoori (2006) and Shome and Hedge (2002). I have drawn elements from four key texts in developing the IC Prism—Tomlinson (1999), Appadurai (1997), Pieterse (2004), and Rantanen (2005), taking parts of their arguments to construct what I sometimes jokingly refer to "The unified theory of international communication."

REFERENCES

Appadurai, A. (1996). *Modernity at large: Cultural dimensions of globalization*. Minneapolis: University of Minnesota Press.

Artz, L. (2003). Globalization, media hegemony and social class. In Lee Artz & Yahya Kamalipour (Eds.), *The globalization of corporate media hegemony* (pp. 3–10). Albany: SUNY Press.

Barbour, S. (Ed.). (2000). *Language and nationalism*. Oxford: Oxford University Press.

Billig, M. (1995). *Banal nationalism*. London: Sage.

Brown, D. (2000). *Contemporary nationalism: Civic, ethnocultural, and multicultural politics*. London: Routledge.

Casey, B., Casey, N., Calvert, B., French, L., & Lewis, J. (Eds.). (2002). *Television studies: The key concepts*. London: Routledge.

Chadha, K., & Kavoori, A. (2005). Tracking the national in processes of globalization. In J. Curran & M. Gurevitch (Eds.), *Mass media and society*. Oxford: Oxford University Press.

Chitty, N. (1994) Communicating world order. *The Journal of International Communication, 1*(2) 100–119.

Connor, W. (1994). *Ethnonationalism: The quest for understanding*. Princeton, NJ: Princeton University Press.

Conversi, D. (Ed.). (2004). *Ethnonationalism in the contemporary world*. London: Routledge.

Couldry, N. (2000). *Inside culture: Re-imagining the method of cultural studies*. London: Sage.

Curran, J., & Gurevitch, M. (2005). *Mass media and society* (4th ed.). London: Hodder Arnold.

Damian, T. (1996). Explaining monoculturalism: Beyond Gellner's theory of nationalism. *Critical Review, 10*(2), 251–270.

Downing, J., Mohammadi, A., & Sreberny-Mohammadi, A. (1995). *Questioning the media: A critical introduction* (2nd ed.). London: Sage.

Durham, M., & Kellner, D. (2001). *Media and cultural studies*. Malden, UK: Blackwell.

Fair, J., & Shah, H., (1997). Continuities and discontinuities in communication and development research since 1958. *Journal of International Communication, 4*(2), 3–23.

Featherstone, M. (Ed.). (1990). *Global culture: Nationalism, globalization and modernity*. London: Sage.

Ferguson, M. (1992). The mythology about globalization. *European Journal of Communication, 7*, 69–93.

Frederik, H., McCaw, M., & Vasquez, R. (1994). The future of IC education in the United States. *Journal of International Communication, 1*(2), 41–56.

Freeman, A., & Kagarlitsky, B. (2004). *The politics of empire: Globalization in crises*. London: Pluto Press.

Friedman, J. (1994). *Cultural identity and global process*. London: Sage.

Fursich, E., & Kavoori, A. (2001). Mapping a critical framework for the study of travel journalism. *International Journal of Cultural Studies, 4*(2), 149–171.

Hannerz, U. (1992) *Cultural complexity: Studies in the social organization of meaning*. New York: Columbia University Press.

Holton, R. (2005). *Making globalization*. London: Macmillan.

Hopper, P. (2006). *Living with globalization*. Oxford: Berg.

Hosking, G., & Schopflin, G. (Eds.). (1997). *Myths and nationhood*. New York: Routledge.

Hutchinson, J., & Smith, A. (1994). *Nationalism: A reader*. Oxford: Oxford University Press.

Kavoori, A. (2002) The (news) value of violence. *Intersections, 2*(3/4), 92–94.

Kavoori, A. (2006). International communication after terrorism: Toward a postcolonial dialectic. In A. Kavoori & T. Fraley (Eds.), *Media, terrorism, theory*. Lanham, MD: Rowman & Littlefield.

Kavoori, A., & Fraley, T. (Eds.) (2006). *Media, terrorism, theory*. Lanham, MD: Rowman & Littlefield.

King, A. (1991). *Culture, globalization and the world system*. London: Macmillan.

Mann, M. (2004). *Incoherent empire*. London: Verso.

Martin-Barbero, J. (2002). Identities: Traditions and new communities. *Media, Culture & Society, 24*, 621–641.

Mattelart, A. (2002). Archaeology of the global era: Constructing a belief. *Media, Culture & Society, 24*, 591–612.

McChesney, R. (2000). The political economy of communication and the future of the field. *Media, Culture & Society, 22*, 109–116.

Mowlana, H. (1994). Shapes of the future: International communication in the 21st century. *The Journal of International Communication, 1*(1), 14–32.

Murphy, P., & Kraidy, M. (2003) *Global media studies: Ethnographic perspectives*. London: Routledge.

Pieterse, N. (2004). *Globalization and culture: Global mélange*. Lanham, MD: Rowman & Littlefield.

Rantanen, T. (2005). *The media and globalization*. London: Sage.

Reeves, G. (1993). *Communications and the third world*. London: Routledge.

Robertson, R. (1992). *Globalization: Social theory and global culture*. London: Sage.

Rodriguez, C., & Murphy, P. (1997). The study of communication and culture in Latin America. *Journal of International Communication, 4*(2), 24–45.

Rosenberg, J. (2000). *The follies of globalization theory*. London: Verso.

Schlesinger, P. (2002). Identities: Traditions and new communities—a response. *Media, Culture and Society, 24*, 643–648.

Shome, R. (2006). Interdisciplinary research and globalization. *The Communication Review, 9*, 1–36.

Shome, R., & Hedge, R. (2002). Culture, communication the challenge of globalization. *Critical Studies in Media Communication, 19*(2), 172–189.

Smith, A. (1998). *Nationalism and modernism*. London: Routledge.

Steger, M. (2004). *Rethinking globalism*. Lanham, MD: Rowman & Littlefield.

Sutz, J. (2002). Globalization: Some reflections from Latin America. *Media, Culture & Society, 24*, 613–619.

Tehranian, M. (1994). Where is the new world order: at the end of history or clash of civilizations? *Journal of International Communication, 1*(2), 71–99.

Thurston-Jackson, M. (2003). Beyond political economy versus cultural studies? The new cultural economy. *Journal of Communication Inquiry, 27*(1), 104–114.

Thussu, D. (2000). *International communication: Continuity and change*. London: Arnold.

Tomlinson, J. (1991). *Cultural Imperialism*. Baltimore: Johns Hopkins University Press.

Tomlinson, J. (1994). A phenomenology of globalization? Giddens on global modernity. *European Journal of Communication, 9*, 149–172.

Tomlinson, J. (1999). *Globalization and culture*. Cambridge, MA: University of Chicago Press.

Waterman, P. (1990). Reconceptualizing the democratization of international communication. *International Social Science Journal, 23*, 77–91.

2

Singing in a (New) Nation: The Early Films of Raj Kapoor

Long years ago we made a tryst with destiny, and now the time comes when we shall redeem our pledge . . . At the stroke of the midnight hour, when the world sleeps, India will awake to life and freedom. A moment comes, which comes rarely in history, when we step out from the old to the new, when an age ends, and when the soul of a nation, long suppressed, finds utterance.

—Jawaharlal Nehru to the Indian Constituent Assembly,
New Delhi, August 14, 1947

Hindi cinema projects the *imagined* nation . . . through contestations that throw into relief its social structures and realignments.

—*The Cinematic ImagiNation*, Jyotika Virdi (my emphasis)

One of my earliest memories of growing up in India was being taken to a movie by a visiting relative. I was so taken up with the plot, that I kept gripping and pinching my aunt's arm (and I am told on occasion even biting her), repeatedly asking (loudly, to her immense embarrassment), *Ab kya hoga*? (What will happen now?) Apparently, I could not handle the pleasures of an unfolding narrative—I had to know at every stage, *exactly* what would happen *next*. Needless, to say, I was banished from the *picture hall* (as it was called then) until a more suitable age when I might acquire both manners and the ability to understand that most common of pleasure's—the suspension of disbelief, an openness to narrative enigmas and a willing participation in *going to the pictures*—an experience common to the lived experience of an (emerging) modernity in India, and other

27

parts of the postcolonial world. In this way was I introduced to that preeminent Indian cultural text, the Bollywood film.

Bollywood, the Hollywood inspired name for Bombay's film industry,
occasionally surfaces in the constantly brewing pot of American popular
culture: an episode of *The Simpson's*, a hip hop video, *Moulin Rouge*, fashion styles inspired by an Indian/Bollywood chic, and stand-alone texts
like the musical *Bombay Dreams*. This is a process that began much earlier
in the United Kingdom with TV shows like *Goodness Gracious Me*, Ivory-
Merchant films, and dance forms like the Bhangra. On a recent visit to
London, I saw larger than life posters of the current film star Shah Rukh
Khan outside Madame Tussad's—inviting people to see the waxwork inside. Warwick Castle, nearby, opened one of its recent exhibitions by inviting Khan to do the honors. This spreading recognition has begun to be reflected in the academy with a stream of scholarly books and essays
engaging with Bollywood as an important site of cultural production.
With the development of a (recent) canon, an argument can be made for
the (emerging) field of "Bollywood studies."[1]

Growing up in India in the 1960s and 1970s, I witnessed the development and maturation of the Indian nation-state, as it moved from the
Nehruvian "tryst with destiny" to the stable but sycophantic political culture of the Indira Gandhi years. My childhood was marked by a persistent background noise—coming from my parents and all their friends—
about the sense of promise and hope that the Indian nation once held, and
which had now all but disappeared. This was usually followed by an extensive critique of the ruling Congress party and its undoing of the "national unity" of the postindependence years. My response to this background noise was to try and ignore it, focusing instead on important
matters like Rajesh Khanna's latest film or Sunil Gavaskar's cricketing
form. But the past intrigued me and I wanted answers to questions like,
"What was this national unity? What led to its demise?" and the most important one—"How did this national unity come about in the first place?"
It is this last question (my research question if you will) that is the subject
of this essay in exploring the role of Bollywood cinema in the early years
of the postindependence Indian nation.

NATIONALISM AND BOLLYWOOD

I want to begin with a simple assertion about the background noise of my
childhood—*to pose the question of national unity is to pose the question of nationalism*—understanding its constitutive role in the *making* of the postcolonial world. It is this "making"—the manufacturing of a national identity that locates my subject, Bollywood cinema center stage. The answer

to the questions of my childhood were in a sense just down the road—on the film posters plastered on the walls, the huge hoardings that had the effete smile of Rajesh Khanna painted on them, the long queues for cinema tickets. I just did not have the language (and yes, attentiveness) to make the connections—and so here decades later, is an exploration in understanding how the (Indian) nation was *imagined into reality*; how Bollywood cinema breathed into life the constitutive subjects of the Indian nation (my parents) and in time their descendents.

Panikker (2002) in an important essay centers the role of culture in the project of Indian nationalism.[2] He argues that "culture is of crucial importance in defining the nation and in the making of national sentiment . . . the relationship between culture and nationalism is complex, implicated in the entire process of *realizing* the nation" (p. 533, my emphasis). Nationalism as a discourse is marked by some common elements: a narrative account of self-identification characterized by a set of symbols (flags, totems, languages), rituals (anthems), and historical circumstances (from the 1940s to the 1960s). Nationalism arises from (and in the process of) the removal of direct colonial control of European powers to a postcolonial era marked by the "birth" of nation-states. Since nationalism emerges out of the same discursive space as colonialism (rather than functioning in some prior indigenous essence) the kinds of cultural practice that it gives birth to reflects the tensions in the process of this political-cultural-social transfer. This transfer is marked fundamentally by a process of cultural (and mediated) reconstruction, or what can be called the *national imagination*. In the oft-quoted words of Benedict Anderson, "communities are to be distinguished, not by their falsity/genuineness, but by the *style* in which they are imagined."[3]

I want to build on the idea of style as seen in the imagined community of Bollywood cinema. Extending Anderson's quote to the specificity of the Indian imagination. I would like to suggest that Bollywood cinema (the most popular and pervasive of all Indian cultural texts) is a key ingredient in the understanding of Indian nationalism. As Mishra puts it "Bombay cinema is self-consciously about representing, in the context of a multicultural and multiethnic India, the various disaggregated strands of the nation-state, the political, social and the cultural" (Mishra, 2002, p. 65). In doing so, "an average normal Bombay film has to be to the extent possible everything to everyone. It has to cut across the myriad ethnicities and lifestyles of India and even of the world that impinges on India. The popular film is lowbrow, modernizing India in all its complexity, sophistry, naiveté, and vulgarity. Studying popular film is studying Indian modernity at its rawest, its crudities lade bare" (Nandy, 1998, p. 6). In sum, a beginning point (and assumption) in the analysis to follow is that "Hindi cinema is a virtual teleprompter for reading the script called the nation" (Virdi, 2003, p. 7).

I will discuss an early "star-text" (Virdi, 2003, p. 61) of Indian cinema, Raj Kapoor, focusing on songs from two of his films, *Aawara* (The Vagabond, 1951) and *Shree 420* (The Cheat, 1955), as they reflect ideas/anxieties about national identity in the immediacy of the postindependence period.

FRAMING BOLLYWOOD

Before beginning this task, an important caveat about Bollywood cinema. Prasad (1998) suggests that one of the key issues is to not see third world cinema as merely regional/local extensions of Hollywood. It is important to not presuppose that "there was some profound, ineluctable kinship between cinema and modern euro-American culture . . . students of Indian cinema confront here a pre-emptive force that defines it in advance as not-yet-cinema, a bastard institution in which the mere ghost of a technology is employed as purposes inimical to its historic essence" (Prasad, 1998, p. 2).

Rather, it is important to center the very specific aesthetic and cultural markers that mark the specificity of Bollywood without descending into the essentialist logic of a nativist nationalism or ethnic/cultural/religious reductionism. In that spirit, perhaps the most common elements of a Bollywood film are those of a hybrid genre—usually termed *Masala*. The term *Masala*, which literally means a blend of different Indian spices, can be interpreted in a number of ways. For a diasporic Indian filmmaker like Mira Nair, who made *Mississippi Masala*, it refers to the "polyglot culture of the Indians" (Mehta, 1996, p. 198). The main character in the film Mina describes herself as a *Masala*, "a bunch of hot spices" (Mehta, 1996, p. 198). Mehta (1996) suggests that terms like *Masala* complicates notions like "identity," "family," "community," and "nation," including in it the idea of inventing something new out of the old (p. 198). In the broadest sense then, a *Masala* film is potpourri of elements—music, romance, action, drama—designed to appeal to the broadest possible public (Ganti, 2004, p. 139). In this sense, the *Masala* film is structurally amorphous drawing inspiration from local, regional, national, and transnational spaces/texts as it works through its two main elements—melodrama and musicals.

Melodrama in the case of Bollywood is predicated around "a narrative form characterized by the sharp delineation of good and evil, the use of co-incidence, an excess of emotion, and the privileging of moral conflicts over psychological ones . . . Hindi films present a moral universe, the disruption of which initiates narrative action" (Ganti, 2004, p. 138). The narrative is framed through the motives, actions and backgrounds of the films "heroes," "heroines," and "villains" (rather than specific occupational or character driven bases for the actors). Gopalan (2002) argues that the Bollywood film has "certain conventions unique to Indian cinema, a *constellation of interruptions* [which] allows us to consider national styles of film-making" (p. 3, original emphasis). The narrative of the story is often temporally interrupted with flashbacks; the film itself is longer than the western standard of 165 minutes, the narrative interrupted with elaborate song (and dances), that have no regard for spatial continuity (in one song, the scene may move between a Bavarian village, the Eiffel Tower in Paris, Times Square in New York, and various locales in India). All films have an "interval" in the middle of the film, where the audience takes a break for tea, *samosas*, and *pakodas* (typical Indian snacks). "The interval is a crucial punctuatory device, producing two opening and closing sequences and structuring narrative expectation, development, and resolution" (Ganti, 2004, p. 139).

The musicals (song and dance number) are an important part of the industry, with their own star system—the playback singers, music directors, composers, lyricists, and recordists (Pendakur, 2003, p. 124). Unlike Hollywood, the music from a film is often released before the film and on the giant cinema hoardings that dominate urban public space in India the music director is often given equal importance to the director of the film (Pendakur, 2003, p. 126).[4] The actors never sing their songs allowing the playback singers to reflect the narrative premise of the moment—usually the expression of emotion. The film song ranges across the emotive spectrum often in tandem with the playback singer—Mukesh, focusing on the ruminative and melancholy; R. D. Burman on the boisterous; with Lata Mangeshkar emphasizing the poetic and philosophical and her sister, Asha Bhosle, the up-tempo and "modern."

Hindi films songs draw on a number of influences—folk, classical, regional, national, and transnational. "Music directors rearrange motifs from across India and elsewhere—1940s swing, African drumming, Algerian Rai, wailing, Latin salsa. Indian traditional instruments such as tabla, dholak, harmonium, tambura, sitar, sarod, and sarangi are employed alongside clarinets, violins, electric guitar, xylophones, and congas" (Pendakur, 2003, p. 126).

Hindi film songs are also crucial in that they speak directly to the role of emotion in the assembling of identity, along a range of "national" emotions. Pendukar suggests that it "may not be an exaggeration to state that the central government failed to establish Hindi as the national link language, but the Bombay film industry succeeded in that effort by popularizing Urdu-Hindi film songs all over the country" (2003, p. 139). Sarrazin (2008) suggest that songs are a critical element of the "message" of a film. As she puts it:

Song lyrics [are a] logical and rich source for cultural and emotional analysis [and] few expressive mediums convey more information than that of sound, where centuries of historical and cultural resonance can be embedded in a single pitch, melody, or rhythmic cycle, and most specifically, vocal and instrumental timbres. Film songs, therefore, are in unique positions to aurally illustrate cultural concepts such as emotion and "heart" to their audiences, relying on pre-composed concepts of emotional sentiment and common codes of musical understanding. (p. 1)

Elements of melodrama and musicals blend together in a distinct way to define the *Masala* film. "Melodrama foregrounds language, *as it makes all feelings exterior*, with the characters verbalizing their feelings and creating discourses on their emotions. One of the key places for an outpouring of feeling is the song lyric, where visuals and language are simultaneously foregrounded. This also applies to the dialogues . . . which are a major pleasure for movie fans who relish their grandiloquent statements frequently by learning chunks by heart" (Dwyer and Patel, 2002, p. 29; my emphasis).

This blend of elements creates what Vasudevan has called "a cinema of attractions" (quoted in Dwyer and Patel, 2002, p. 30), a kind of "exhibitionist cinema which includes the sets and costumes, the song and dance sequences, comedic interludes and action sequences, grand dialogue and special effects—the cumulative effect being akin to a cinema where popular traditions such as the fairground and the carnival meet an avant-garde subversion" (Dwyer and Patel, 2002, p. 30). Gopalan uses the idea of "pleasure" as a key component in her theory of Bollywood as a "cinema of interruptions." She uses the analogy of sexual performance, specifically coitus interruptus, to evoke the experience of watching a Bollywood film, a site where state film policy and the postcolonial audience intersects. She concludes "just as continuity in classical Hollywood narrative offers us both pleasure and anger, in this cinema too, we find pleasures *in* these interruptions and not *despite* them. Indian cinema is marked by *interrupted pleasures*" (Gopalan, 2002, p. 21; original emphasis).

In sum, what Bollywood configures is a specific set of cultural predicates—populism, fantasy, melodrama, and a relentless intertextuality. I now turn to an examination of what Virdi (2003) calls "Hindi cinema's own agenda—imagining a unified India" (1) focusing on one major "hero" in Indian cinema—Raj Kapoor.

RAJ KAPOOR[5]

Time Magazine called Raj Kapoor, "the primal star of Indian cinema . . . to most of the planet, Raj Kapoor was India in all its vitality, humanity, and poignancy" (www.time.com/time/2005/100movies). An actor, director, producer, nicknamed "the showman of Hindi cinema" by film magazines and the celebrity media industry in India "was young and bursting with creative energies at the time when the Indian nation-state was born on 15 August 1947. In some ways the enterprise of Kapoor and the Indian project ran parallel. The first decade of his work, intense and hopeful, culminated in *Jis Desh Me Ganga Behti Hai* (This Country, Where the Ganges Flows). Twenty-five years later, fatigued and jaded, he made another film using the same metaphor and called it *Ram Teri Ganga Maili* (Ram, Your Ganges Is Soiled). During the same period, the new Indian nation had also journeyed from Nehru to Indira Gandhi's assassination and growing political and social violence" (Bakshi, 1998, p. 94).

While Raj Kapoor can be evaluated as a stand-alone director, I want to focus on his early work as an actor, where his identity as a tramp (a reworking of the Charlie Chaplin project[6]) is key to understanding Bollywood's imagination of the early Indian nation. Before discussing the two pivotal texts (the films *Aawara* and *Shree 420*), Raj Kapoor's early work needs to be counterposed with the films of his contemporary, Guru Dutt (Kapoor was born in 1924, Guru Dutt in 1925). Guru Dutt's key films included *Pyaasa* (Thirsty One, 1957) and *Kagaz Ke Phool* (Paper Flowers, 1959) and focused on a sustained social critique of the changing Indian cultural/national order from tradition to modernity through two interrelated themes: the loneliness of the artist and the discursive imprisonment of the artists work within the expectations of the marketplace. Sardar (1998) suggests that in "Guru Dutt's films, modernity is always presented as rampant materialism that drowns the selfless love and innocence that is integral to tradition. No synthesis is possible between the two: The one devours the other [tradition is replaced by] a very specific form of modernity—westernization" (p. 39).

Sardar reads Guru Dutt's films not simply as an anti-Western tract but as a locally grounded narrative about "the idea of justice and unconditional love. All [his films] have a longing and respect for the integrity of tradition. [However] it is not romanticized, traditional utopias that these films seek or promote; rather they argue for a *tradition based on the integrity of its own authentic idealism*. Indeed, in Guru Dutt's films there are only two options—suicide or return to traditional idealism. Guru Dutt's idealism is a rounded all-embracing idealism. It addresses women as well as men, it enables men to express feminine emotions and it seeks change in tradition as well as transformation in modernity" (Sardar, 1998, p. 45; my emphasis). Guru Dutt's own life reflected this irresolvable tension between modernity and tradition, which culminated in his suicide at the age of thirty-nine, and today the film *Kagaz Ke Phool* (a box office flop) is seen as a classic text examining the dilemma facing postcolonial societies as they attempt to imagine their national future after the departure of colonial powers.

AAWARA (THE VAGABOND, 1951)

In contrast to Guru Dutt, the narrative topology of Raj Kapoor's films can be read as a "successful" mediation/meditation of the tradition/modernity dichotomy, through its elaboration of a nationalist aesthetic that was simultaneously western and Indian—his work is marked fundamentally by a reflexivity common to modernity. This is manifest symbolically in the character of the "tramp" intimately tied in western cinema with Charlie Chaplin and in the Indian imagination with Raj Kapoor. A synopsis of the film:

> *Aawara*, the film most identified with Kapoor's tramp/Chaplin persona "opens with "Raju" on trial for the attempted murder of a pillar of society, Judge Raghunath (brilliantly played by Prithviraj Kapoor, Raj Kapoor's real-life father). He is defended by a beautiful young lawyer, Rita (played by Nargis, Kapoor's muse and mistress in real life), an orphan who also happens to be the Judge's ward. Her interrogation of the latter leads to a long flashback that occupies most of the film. Its opening segment evokes the Ramayana, with Judge Raghunath (an epithet of Rama) abandoning his pregnant wife Leela (Leela Chitnis) because he wrongly believes she has been raped during a brief abduction by the robber Jagga (K. N. Singh), and the Judge's conviction that the "seed" of a criminal necessarily seals the fate of his offspring (ironically, we learn that Jagga only became an outlaw after being wrongly convicted of rape by the same Judge). Leela raises her son in the Bombay slums, slaving to send him to school so that he may become a lawyer and judge like his father, but with Jagga always hovering in the background, intent on luring him into a life of crime. As a schoolboy, Raj falls in love with the carefree Rita, despite the class gulf between them, but Judge Raghunath (a friend of Rita's father who takes an instinctive dislike to the "wayward" boy) contrives to separate them. Jagga and the Judge's struggle for Raj's soul—a variation on the nature vs. nurture debate, with resonances of caste ideology—continues when Raj and Rita reconnect after twelve years. (www.uiowa.edu/~incinema/awara.html)

In its thematics, *Aawara* was more than a nature and nurture story. India became independent in 1947, and *Aawara* celebrated/critiqued the enormous hope and ambivalence of the liminality of the postcolonial moment where both the immediacy of self-discovery and the germination of a new national definition was in progress. Salman Rushdie's novel, *Midnight's Children*, often celebrated as a masterly rendition of this collective national moment, is of course a facsimile, a contemporary (and postmodern) rendition of the moment of independence. The films *Aawara* and *Shree 420* on the other hand, made shortly after independence, resonate with the immediacy of the moment. The themes of the film *Aawara* resemble those of a culture-in-transition and a nation-in-formation. *Aawara*, the vagabond is literally, a story about the possibility of reinvention. As

Nagaraj puts it, "Kapoor was an enthusiastic modernist who endorsed the revolt of the young against stifling traditions; for him, the best creative space was in the values created by modernity. He celebrated the arrival of the new and nurtured a profound fear of the old" (2006, p. 91). The narrative vehicle that he chose to make this transition from tradition to modernity was "love"—defined in broad, humanistic terms (but also profoundly restrictive in its overall paternalism). Love is the key to the relationship between Raju and Rita, working against the matrix of family and communal expectations and embracing the idea of a new "free" (another meaning of the word *Aawara*) nation. *Aawara* has a very direct cinematic message about national identity: "The traditionalists, those opposed to love, are washed away in the magical flood of song and dance; it is the vibrant lyricality of the victor. Kapoor had confidence in history, the forces of modernity over other lifestyles" (Nagaraj, 2006, p. 96).

"AAWARA HOON" (I AM A VAGABOND)

At the heart of the film is a song, "Aawara Hoon" (literally, "I am a vagabond" but can be also translated as "I am free"). The song/film became an enormous hit in the Indian subcontinent, the U.S.S.R., Eastern Europe, China (Chairman Mao singled it out as his favorite film/song), the Middle East, and Africa (Ganti, 2004, p. 99). "Aawara Hoon" is that rarest of cultural texts, an early example of a contra-flow, its impact all the more remarkable given a (just born) postcolonial world of dominance by colonial (Western) media and the paucity (or in many nations, the complete lack of) of a media infrastructure. It is not too much of an exaggeration to say that India entered into the consciousness of many parts of the postcolonial world through people watching, singing, and dancing to the songs of Raj Kapoor, the Indian Charlie Chaplin.

"Aawara Hoon" is a complex, multilayered, and rich text held together by simple visual progression, that of Raj Kapoor walking (skipping, running) jauntily through a number of paradigmatic settings—a street scene, riding a truck, and finally a (poor) urban settlement or *basti*. The sequence begins with an (unusually long) musical introduction to the refrain of the song ("Aawara Hoon") setting the mood, which is simultaneously soothing and intoxicating where Kapoor is seen as the merry vagabond, swinging and lightly dancing through the upscale street as he picks the pockets of two establishment figures—an Indian Seth (businessman/moneylender) wearing the diacritical signs of nativism (he is attired in a *topi* and *dhoti*) and a nattily attired Indian gentleman (mimicking the style of the British gentleman). Kapoor himself is dressed in Chaplinesque attire, pants riding high, jacket too tight, cap askew and frequently doffed.

Shot composition and mise-en-scène in the song speak directly to a literal/historical intersection—that of tradition and modernity; autonomy and dependence; a can-do spirit versus an acceptance of fate. I tracked the semantic/visual progression of the song/story line.

Scene 1

The opening shot of the song is a study in subtlety—a close-up of mulling feet, rapidly fading in and out of focus; working through a set of double exposures and then finally settling on the shuffling, jouissance of Kapoor as he moves humming through the upscale neighborhood; he bumps into an old Seth, relieves him of a gold chain (with a large watch attached to it). He swings the watch merrily and sees that an Indian gentlemen in a three-piece suit and bowler hat (quintessentially British) is watching him with a fatuous, foolish expression, clearly enjoying/ admiring the attitude of the vagabond. Kapoor catches his eye and sidles up. Seeing him advance, the gentleman panics and runs away, but not before Kapoor has relieved him of his wallet. The camera cuts to the old Seth, returning to the scene having discovered that his gold watch has disappeared. Kapoor runs away with Chaplinesque urgency. This opening scene is rhetorically direct—the vagabond is marked neither by his vagrancy or his outsider status as by a sense of quiet certainty, a sense of well-being and a persistent mocking of the establishment figures, who are presented through a comedic/critical representation of their status. The long musical introduction and the refrain of the song, "Aawara Hoon" repeatedly sung is an incantation, a key to the mythic role of this film. Additionally, the voice of the singer, Mukesh is intimately tied to the textual presence of Kapoor. Unmatched by any other singer after him, Mukesh's voice is a perfect mix of the pleasurable and the profound, a weighty awareness of the changing world, yet effervescent. It is a voice that speaks intimately to the postcolonial condition—an understanding of a world coming undone, yet containing within it an ability for rebirth. If ever there was a voice that spoke to both certitude and loss; tradition and imagination, it is the voice of Mukesh. The lyrics of the song's refrain (sung in this section of the song) "aware hon, aware hon" (I am a vagabond) followed by "garish mien hon, asman ka Tara hon" (I am out of luck and a star in the sky) reflects this thematic—by being simultaneously without luck *and* a star in the sky. In sum, the opening scene speaks to the condition of the tramps personal fate and that of a nation—struggling in the aftermath of a brutal, violent partition of India (into the nations of India and Pakistan) while engaging with the broad opportunity and promise of a new nation.

Scene 2

Kapoor runs away from the Seth who is chasing him. He runs into a man on a bicycle, grabs the cycle from him and pushes it and runs alongside it, finally jumping onto it. The pacing is a series of fast-forwarded edits. The man runs after him as he cycles away. The street itself is a contrast to the first scene—a middle-class neighborhood without any cars or pedestrians. Kapoor cycles alongside a truck carrying three young women, dressed as casual day laborers (from a rural background), and hangs onto the side of the truck (this is a common practice in India, where speeds are slow and holding onto a passing truck is an easy way to get somewhere without the hard work!). He then proceeds to leap into the truck. The three women alternately flirt and rebuff him while dancing to the tune of the song. Kapoor sings of "having no home, no family life, and no community," continuing with "he has nobody's love but belongs to the unknown." He falls/is pushed off the truck onto the road. He gets up, holding his hurt back, but keeps smiling, bowing, and doffing his hat to the three women as the truck disappears. Reading this scene, there are two immediate referents that speak to the moment's liminality, its gendered and class structure—women made up (and still make up) the bulk of India's construction laborers, carrying heavy loads of rock, sand, and cement, literally building the "temples of new India" (then prime minister Jawaharlal Nehru's expression for modern India's dams and factories). Kapoor hitches a ride on this journey, traveling with these laborers as they (presumably) ride to the next construction site. His falling off/being thrown off this real/rhetorical journey of national reconstruction displays both the ambivalence of this journey for the new urban migrants and a sense of opportunity presented/lost/critiqued by the vagabond. While the scene refers to the role of labor in the enterprise of nationhood, the reference to love at the end of the verse, signals an important direction in Kapoor's vision for the hero (and nation's) journey, the possibility of "love" as an agent of personal/national reconstruction. It is a theme as I have suggested that is at the heart of a broader, humanistic vision in all of Kapoor's early films.

Scene 3

Kapoor walks away from the truck and enters a street scene/urban neighborhood or *basti*. He walks through a jostling crowd of children, vendors and men milling around singing, "I sing songs of happiness even though my heart is full of wounds." He walks up to half a dozen women squatting cleaning plates by a public tap as they smile and nod in assent to the song. This scene is a continuation of the discourses of labor, urban migration and the dramatically (changing) landscape of postindependence India marked by partition, migration, and changing religious/ethic/gender dynamics. This scene is a direct ethnographic statement of this moment of modernity—the pain of leaving the old, and the danger of the new. It is a moment, enumerated throughout all of Kapoor's early films—the weight of cultural disjunction, the idea of exile and reinvention, in an earlier era, marked not by transnational movement but by widespread rural-urban migration as agrarian societies deal with the realities of industrialization and modernity in the postcolonial context.

Scene 4

He picks up a naked (male) child and simultaneously sings the first word of the last verse—"dunia" (or world). The symbolic reference is clearly over determined (child/world/nation) with the nakedness itself a diacritical sign—representing invention (providing clothing) and a critique of the existing social formation (nakedness and the poverty of the nation). He picks up a second, smaller child (also naked and male), and sings of the brutal nakedness of the (collective) national moment. He swings the children joyfully, signaling not the desperation of dislocation but joy in the possibility of creation. The song continues with an extended repetition of "Aawara Hoon" as he puts his hat on the older child, transferring presumably that same jouissance, and sense of pleasure/dislocation to him. The child runs after him, as he walks away skipping lightly and fading into the narrow, empty street. As Mukesh's voice fades out, the music that introduced the song bookends the narrative—opening up a space for Kapoor's personal journey and the migrants/exiles that he represents. An important detail to note is the last scene's mise-en-scène—three separate sets/settings are used here. Behind the wall in front of which Kapoor holds the two boys is an electric line for Bombay's trains, a symbol of the new modernity the nation is entering into; followed by a rundown *basti*; and finally a clean and well-constructed settlement that he walks out of at the end of the song. In his travel through these different settings, a literal journey of renewal is taking place in the nation—from its paternalistic certainties (the male children) to its placement of the working class (women washing plates, vendors selling goods, men going to work) as key elements of nation building.

SHREE 420 (THE CHEAT, 1955)

The discursive journey begun by *Aawara* is extended/completed by the film *Shree 420* with the latter perhaps a more important text in its role as

an agent of how Bollywood constructed the imagined community of India in the immediacy of independence. The premise of *Aawara*—an acute
awareness of cultural dislocation that comes with modernity and the pre-
sumptive power of love is brought to its fulfillment in *Shree 420*. Specifically, the film presents an unabashed vision of Indian modernity—a reassembling of tradition; a repudiation of capitalism; a privileging
of socialism; and a subtly modulated formulation of gender politics—
especially around the key construct of Nargis (the actress) as a model of
Indian femininity and of Kapoor as the common man. Like *Aawara*, the
film is anchored in the history of Indian cinema by its music—in this case
a fabulous trilogy of songs, which have been subsequently reworked in a
number of films. First, a synopsis of the plot focused on the three songs
(on which I will base my analysis):

The title refers to section 420 of the Indian penal code, which deals with
fraud; in everyday speech, to call someone "a 420" is to imply that he is a
cheat; "Sheri" is an honorific prefix. As the film opens, the hapless orphan,
Raju is seen hitchhiking along a rural road. Feigning unconsciousness, he is
picked up by a wealthy capitalist, Seth Sonechand Dharamlal and (which
translates as "wholesale-merchant, gold-silver, delighting in righteousness"),
but is quickly thrown out of the car when it is perceived that he is a fraud;
each man accuses the other of being "a 420!" Back on the road he sings the
song "Mara Jota Hai Japan" (My Shoes Are Japanese). Traveling by every sort
of rural transport, Raj arrives, bewildered, in the great metropolis of Bombay,
where a beggar informs him that the city is a heartless place, where even
Raj's "BA-pass" degree and prize for honesty will not assure employment.
He meets a kindly woman selling bananas who is so amused by his innocence that she gives him several for free. Entering a pawnshop, Raj sees
Vidya ("wisdom," played by Nargis) pawning her bangles and is instantly
attracted to her. He pawns the honesty-medal he received in college and gets
40 rupees, of which he is instantly relieved by a pickpocket.

   Resolving to win Vidya by proving himself a capable wage-earner, Raj gets
a lowly job in the Jai Bharat ("Viva India!") Laundry, but sneaks away from
work with someone else's suit to impress Vidya. Raj woos Vidya at a street
side tea stall and on the moonlit streets of Bombay, where they sing a famous
duet, "Pyaar hua ikraar hua" (Love Arises, a Promise Is Made). They talk of
marriage and a home.

   Delivering clothes from the laundry to a posh flat, Raj meets the voluptuous
Maya ("illusion," played by Nadira) and accidentally reveals his extraordinary skill at cards. Maya dresses him as an urban dandy and brings him to a
nightclub, where he dances with the showgirls, wins a tidy sum for her, and
catches the eye of Seth Sonechand. Soon, Raj is back at work in the laundry,
but Sonechand finds him and offers to make him his "partner." Captivated by
the promise of quick wealth, Raj agrees. On the night of the Hindu festival of
Divali (which honors Lakshmi, goddess of wealth and fertility), Raj returns to

Vidya's house with a stylish sari, and asks permission to escort her to "the temple of Lakshmi." This turns out to be the club, but the materialistic and sensuous (and "Western") atmosphere repulses Vidya, who is insulted by Maya and flees. Raj wavers, but Maya entices him to remain with the song "Mud Mud Ke Na Dekh" (Don't Ever Look Back!) and Sonechand soon has him winning at cards. (www.uiowa.edu/~incinema/shri420.html)

I will analyze the three songs identified in the above synopsis in the order they appear, both to retain their narrative integrity and as key markers of the films interrogation of India's (emerging) modernity.

"Mera joota hai japani," uses the refrain: "My shoes are from Japan, my pants are English, I wear a red Russian cap, but oh! still my heart is Indian!" and is by most accounts one of the most influential lines in all of Bollywood's film music. Reused in a number of films (including a film with the title *Mera Joota Hai Japani*), the song has entered the Hindi language and the collective Indian psyche as a shorthand for a certain lost innocence; a catch phrase for Indian essentialism; and in recent years—in the wake of market liberalization and the rise of Hindu fundamentalism (as seen in the decade long rule of the BJP) for a regressive nationalism. The song is in this sense, a master text (akin perhaps to songs from the *Wizard of Oz*, with their rendering of agrarian essentialism and American identity) working through the contradictions of the postcolonial moment, articulated in *Aawara*.

"MERA JOOTA HAI JAPANI"

The song has three main scenes, focused on Raju, the main character.

Scene 1

After Raju is revealed as a "420" and left on the road, he looks down at his shoes and speaks to it, saying "Chal re Japani" (Lets Go Japanese) and starts to walk down a winding, deserted road, as the song's lilting musical introduction starts, segueing into the refrain, "Mera Joota Hai Japani." Raju plays a flute as he struts Chaplin style, his (English) pants hitched up, his Russian cap askew and his Indian heart unabashedly singing with joy. As he turns around, he sees that a snake has followed him, entranced with his flute playing. He is startled, runs away, the camera recording his zip-zagging across the empty road in high-speed, a direct reenactment of Charlie Chaplin's numerous mad dashes. Coincidentally, running away from the snake is a direct repudiation of an Orientalist trope about identity—snakes and snake charmers. Raj slows down, and four young rural women carrying loads on their heads, smile, and pout as they pass him singing the opening refrain of the song, a number of times. The repeated rendition of the song's refrain, a mantra if you will, is the defining statement of the song. It is a statement filled with the pleasure of a quietly stated essentialism—the song can (in the language of postmodernism) be read as a celebration of hybridity; of the value of reflexivity, but I would suggest that this does not do the song justice. It is certainly hybrid, but it is primarily a song about the *process of cultural assembling along lines of the newly imagined nation-state*. It draws on the specificities of the historical moment. Japan, an ally of the revolutionary end of the Indian independence movement, literally moves Kapoor (by his wearing Japanese shoes) along the road of his (national) destiny; his pants draw sustenance from the colonial context in which they are manufactured in both a economic sense (the textile mills of Birmingham using the cotton of India) and a political sense (especially the role of clothes/cotton in Gandhi's *Swadeshi* movement, where he encouraged people to wear only local clothes and not imported ones); his cap references Russia, both by its unproblematic rendering of socialism (red) and its reference to national direction—the socialism of the prime minister of the time, Jawaharlal Nehru. It is in this last task that the emphatic, joyous ending of the refrain does the most important work of cultural assembling—Raju touches his heart, throws his arms out, and skips with a gay abandon that is so self-consciously theatrical, that it can be read as a statement about a emotive certainty in the future of the Indian nation-state. By being Indian in the heart, the song evokes/configures what is to follow (in the next song)—the central, constitutive element of national identity—love. The rest of the song, while important in its development of other themes (which I detail below) pale in comparison with this first and primordial rendering of self—Indian at heart; the rest is fluff, mere accoutrements of history and politics.

Scene 2

Raju comes across a caravan of travelers, tracking across the desert, their camels, undulating across the landscape. He joins them perched high on a camel, next to an old man, with luxuriant mustaches and turban. The scene (presumably shot in the desert state of Rajasthan) evokes a nomadic aesthetic, where the idea of traveling and community commingle. He sings of "leaving for the open road, with a destination known only to God. I just know I have to travel, like a storm, without knowing . . . just with my hat on my head." It is possible to see this scene as continuous with the first scene, the hero mingling the foreign (his hat, pants, etc.) with the local (the nomads) but I would like to suggest that something more critical is taking place. The nomads track a scene of not just separation but of being rootless and exiled—they are presented without the joyous accompaniment that one might expect of a happy band of nomads. Instead their expressions are blank, almost grim, but more than anything else, determined. It is a landscape, I suggest of the Indian Partition—scenes like these were not the stuff of history when this film was released, but of immediate memory—it is impossible not to read into this scene, a reworking of the partition as it begins to take its searing place in this stillborn (no pun intended) nation. Kapoor's evoking of God and the final destination in the lyrics of the song suggests such a reading. The partition is not just a master text in the construct of Indian national identity, it is at the heart of the postcolonial enterprise that makes up the Indian nation. Much like the Civil War in the United States, it is continually revisited; a veritable litmus test for the assertion of national identity reworked in the decades to come through fiction, journalism, and later, television. But in this primordial moment, it is film that works to create the first reflexive account of this bloody birth of the Indian nation.[7]

Scene 3

In this final scene, the song is marked by two crucial edits—the first is of a elephant carrying a king through a city (most likely a coronation procession) which is followed by Raju astride an elephant, being escorted by two sadhus (saints) and the second is at the end of the song where images of Raju on a elephant are superimposed on those of a crowded Bombay street. These scenes are underscored by the song where Raju sings of "Life's ups and downs. Life flows like a stream. Don't ask about the nation, while standing on the shore. Moving [movement] is the purpose of life. Standing still is death." These two edits and the lyrics offer a reflexive account of tradition and feudalism, simultaneously empowering and distancing and a visual cross-stitch of a recurrent motif in early Kapoor films—the pastoral/urban disjunction, with the hero traveling from the rural to the urban; from tradition to modernity. In the first scene, the elephant functions as the diacritical sign of feudal authority—once again, the specificities of the historical moment are critical in reading this text. The birth of the Indian nation-state was coterminous with the removal of Indian aristocracy—the legal and political structure of centuries of feudal authority, divinely ordained. This was restructuring of an entire social and political order, very real power taken away by the stroke of the secular pen. References in the song's lyrics about being part of the current of national life can be read along with the obvious countercurrent that still animated public life (and personal identity) in India—allegiance to king, god, and religion.[8] It is Raju, the orphan-penniless-rural-drifter who sits astride the elephant, replacing (literally and visually since the edits follow each other) the king with the commoner. This continuity in narrative movement signals ambivalence about this transfer—an ambivalence reiterated in the escorts of Raju's elephant, sadhus, standard-bearers of Hindu essentialism that march with/escort him (presumably) into that preeminent space of modernity, the urban cityscape. Watching this scene today, there is considerable discomfort in this vision of the nation—religion and masculinity; power and theology mixing unproblematically—prefiguring the rise of the BJP many decades later with its ideology of Hindutva and a revivalist Hindu nationalism.

"PYAAR HUA HAI" (LOVE ARISES)

The second song in *Shree 420* came to define an entire genre of romance songs in Bollywood films—the song "Pyaar Hua Hai" is a peerless performance—simultaneously theatrical and understated, its erotic charge is undiminished by the passage of time. It still remains arguably the greatest romantic song in the history of Bollywood. The song tells the story of an encounter between Raju and Vidya and the declaration of their love for each other. Within the narrative of the film (and nationalist modernity), the song functions with one clear, unambiguous message—the centrality of love, as a force for both identity formation in the new nation-state and as a matrix for thinking through issues of gender politics. The song's lyric's question the "promise" evoked in the song's title (love arises, a promise is made) by asking "Why does the heart fear love?" and then answering, "the heart says the road is hard and the destination unknown." The verses that follow, reiterate the endpoint of love, the collapse of personal boundaries of self ("if our love breaks, we, together, break"); the raising of children ("One day I will not be alive, nor will you. But our signatures/children will"); but more than anything else, the love spoken of here (through repeated enumeration of the songs refrain) is self-referential. Love is seen as fundamentally elemental in nature (marked in one of the song's lines this: "the night will speak/spread word of our love everywhere"), suffused with a paradox—its evanescence.

For Kapoor, the construct of love is central to his construct of the nation, where narrow concerns of individuals and communities are to be replaced by a broader, humanistic sense of collective identity. Love in a sense has its own agency that pushes the performance by the lovers into the realm beyond the romantic to the social. Kapoor defined it thus:

> There is nothing in this world except love. The more you spread it or give it, the more it expands. The more you accept love, the stronger it becomes. The more you bring out love, the better and greater you become. There are many forms of love. If you make it narrow, then it becomes selfish. Selfish love can benefit a person but he loses his significance. (www.imdb.com/name/nm0004292/bio)

The performance by Kapoor and Nargis in this song are for a lack of a better word, postmodern. They are acutely aware of their own referentiality, and of the role they are playing as agents of a new kind of national identity. This identity is shot through with the idea of representation; of visuality—a very specific kind of modernist practice that is given a name by/through this song. Shot entirely on sets, with lightening, rain, and wisps of clouds ranging around the singing lovers, the song overlays visual intimacy (Nargis's famous kiss-me look) with longing (close-ups of faces; long shots of the couple walking) and disengagement (the repeated separation and coming together of the lovers). There is a sense of agency and control in the bodies of both the actors—they move in small, deliberate steps, each motion representing an entire universe of emotion. It is in some primordial sense, *love making*.[9]

"MUD MUD KE NA DEKH" (DON'T KEEP LOOKING BACK)

The last song, that I want to examine is "Mud Mud Ke Na Dekh" (Don't Keep Looking Back) which is perhaps the paradigmatic text in this film (and arguably in all of Kapoor's early films), and one that completes the narrative premise begun by "Mera Joota Hai Japani," offers a modulated critique of the humanistic topos of "Pyaar Hua, Ikrar Kiya" and firmly centers the concerns of the nation—around a negotiation/indigenization of capitalist modernity. The issues the song takes (apart) are weighty but the tone it takes is light—this is a beautiful, lilting, sweeping serenade of a song it grasps the listener, it pulls at her feet to get up and dance, it is a song about participation, about creating the new world—a song inevitably about citizenship.

The refrain of the song, "don't look back," is repeated over and over again, the chanting speeding up as the song progresses and is dizzying in its rendition at the end. This repetition is not tautological, but seeks to address what I believe is at the heart of this song—a shared willingness to move/dance the nation into the heady promise of modernity without looking back. The song does not need a more contextual reading—this is Kapoor's unabashed hope in the possibilities of the postcolonial moment.

Scene 1

The song (see synopsis above) begins with an important break in the film's story line. Vidya is upset, disoriented with the nightclub that Raju has brought her to. In the frame immediately preceding the song, she walks out of the club, a close-up shows her wiping away a tear, wrapping the *pallu* (the top half) of her sari closely around her shoulders—this is a key diacritical sign for the Indian audience, indicating a closing up of tradition, a tight covering of the (female) body, functioning as a stand-in for the fencing in of culture, of the maintenance of a traditional femininity re-moving itself from the site of what is about to happen—a brazen assertion of sexuality, the presentation of a Western/colonial identity politics, pre-suming a new kind of communication between the nation and tradition.

Maya (which translates as "illusion" played by the sumptuous Nadira) begins the song center stage, a long shot, framed by a circle of ballet dancers. The music begins and the ballet dancers proceed to create a series of circles, around Maya; the editing is a careful mix of slow motion, close-ups, and (what became) a common motif of the cinematography of Kapoor's films—shots of the sexualized female body, focused on the waist, the feet, the bosom, the close-up of the tilted face, the rapid cut away, signaling the near-ness of male desire, the ability of feminine power to resist it (just yet). Raju is dressed impeccably in a bowtie and suit, his face cast in shadows, aloof and distraught with Vidya's departure. Maya first gesture is shot from above, Raju's eye view. She reaches out and takes his hand—the song begins. Her message is achingly clear—"don't look back, don't think of the past." This is not a plaintive call or a beseeching message; rather it is an assertion and an invitation. It is not merely sexual, focused on the mobilization of fem-inine charms, but something else—something that can be approximated by a new kind of intimacy—a call to (her) arms and an invitation to the imagi-nation of what Raju (and the nation) might become should they both go down this path (to modernity). Maya makes it clear that this is a journey they will take together ("I will be your companion, you will not be alone in life's journey"), a journey marked by the pleasure of the moment and the certainty of the destination ("our destination is clearly before us, the clouds are like waves rolling past us. The caravan of life never stops"). The camera lingers lavishly on Maya during this entire scene, especially a critical track-ing shot, where the ballet dancers move behind her, presented in half-focus, creating a sense of visual disorientation and vertigo; all the time, her hand is outstretched, reaching out to Raju, willing him to join the dance. The use of the ballet dancers, referencing a classical Western modernity does not just bring a Western aesthetic to this song, it brings an entire vocabulary around the mobilization of sexuality and identity politics—a vocabulary engaged with by Raju in the next scene.

Scene 2

The scene begins with a key transition. Raju is first amused, interested, engaged with Maya, but still distant. As the first verse of the song ends, a long musical break starts and the camera focuses on Raju, who smiles, ab-sently at first, then in full recognition of the decision he is about to make.

He nods his head, squares his shoulders, and his transformation begins. The screen/night club goes black for a second, the blinking neon lights are the only thing breaking the silence, and a trumpet medley starts as the lights come on, the camera focusing on the players. Raju stands up (presumably from the floor) and plays a trumpet solo, signaling his acceptance of Maya's invitation. The dancers have changed from ballet to Spanish folk dancers, their long skirts swirling as Raju walks between them. His trumpet has disappeared but he sings the second stanza of the song, "smile with each passing season, the world belongs to the one who looks ahead, let us keep our eyes, out and on each other." The lyrics signal the rhetorical force of Raju's answer to Maya. He collapses the personal with the sociological, the sexual with the political, and the camera does the rest of the talking—cutting rapidly between Raju, Maya, and the dancers, it speeds up the narrative of progression/progress in the repeated rendition of the song, "don't look back, don't look back."

Scene 3

The last scene in the song is an extension of the second, but with one important progression—the song is sung with the gradual incorporation of Seth Sonachand (the businessman who represents capitalism) and his business cronies being steadily incorporated into the dance, and by the end of the song, the entire night club is on its feet, dancing in a mad swirl of celebration of looking ahead, of building the (national) future. The lyrics are stunning declarations of a new sensibility—"the world belongs to the person who adapts; the world belongs to the person who fits the mould; the world belongs to the person who forges ahead." Seth Sonachand stands out for his visual intensity in this scene (and in cutaways in the other scenes)—he is not the deceptively meek moneylender of rural lore, the tradition-bound exploiter of caste rules, but a fully developed man of modernity—corpulent, bug-eyed, with a luxurious moustache, he is fully clothed in the manner of a western businessman. He joins in the song, at the invitation of Raju, who extends his hand out to him to pull him into the crowd, and as the song enters its last dizzying stage, is seen dancing with control and nuance with Raju and Maya, the trio making an unabashed statement about what constitutes success in the new imagined nation. Later in the film's narrative, Raju offers a critique of capitalism and through his final coupling with Vidya rather than Maya, an embrace of socialist humanism, but within the space of this song, what is made abundantly clear is the importance of understanding the *range of national possibilities* in this, India's postcolonial moment.

CONCLUSIONS AND DIRECTIONS:
NATIONALISM, SONGS, AND BOLLYWOOD

I want to address the question of national unity and nationalism that I began with (how did national unity come about? or more formally, how is
nationalism as a discourse constituted?) with some theoretical specula-
tions around the role of songs/music and Bollywood cinema in the project of Indian nationalism.

To begin with a non-Bollywood example, Will Smith in the film *I Am
Legend* speaks about the music of Bob Marley (his deceased daughter in
the film is named "Marley") and says that the singer believed that the
power of song and music was so strong that it could inject into people the
ideas and beliefs that it sang about—in the case of Bob Marley, ideas about
love, peace, and community. I am not suggesting such a "hypodermic
needle" effect for the songs in the early films of Kapoor, injecting "national unity" into the bodies of the Indian (national) subject. *I am however,
arguing that the texts of Bollywood cinema are active agents in the cultural formation that came to be known as the Indian nation.* Asthana (2003) in an
analysis of songs/music in the project of Indian patriotism argues that

> After Indian independence in 1947, patriotism also meant participating in the
> tasks of nation-building, development, and modernization, the three rhetorics
> of the post-colonial nation-state. The articulation of patriotism during the
> 1950s–1960s [is] a period marked by the *nationalization of the private* . . . this
> modernist developmental aesthetic was the lens through which patriotism
> got refracted. The portrayal in media and cultural production . . . (particularly
> film songs and national songs) . . . drew on a wide variety of symbols depict-
> ing patriotic acts, feeling and sentiments. (pp. 339–340, original emphasis)

In the above analysis I have suggested how songs in the early films of
Raj Kapoor take their shape, narrative, and cultural agency in the immediacy of the postcolonial period suggesting that these songs are important
for their willing participation in the act of national imagination and their
inextricable relationship to the project of Indian modernity. In sum, I am
suggesting not only that these early songs articulate both change and continuity in the unfolding of Indian history but create an emotive space
within which the manufacturing of an Indian "national" identity takes
place. By capturing the range, complexity, and form of Indian feelings
around/about the new nation-state, it creates a readily constituted engagement with the contemporary moment of national self-realization. It is
the memory of this moment, reflexively constituted in the songs and films
of Raj Kapoor that my parents and their friends remember. It is, I realize,
a very postmodern claim about the emergence of modernity, but a claim

sustained by both the textual agency of the songs; the intertextual construct of Raj Kapoor and Nargis in that historical moment and perhaps most critically, the historical weight that these texts have accrued in the decades to come—lending substance and credibility to a state of "national unity" in texts that were aimed at creating a nation. To put it another way *these songs are simultaneously acts of creation and creative acts*—or what Panikker calls "instruments of nationalist mobilization" (2002, p. 533).

A concluding thought: While I have attempted to show in the textual analysis, the specificities of the emotive and discursive imprint that texts, like film music and songs powerfully deploy in doing the work of "national unity," this "production of the national" is needless to add, complex and contradictory (attempting as it does to bring together the disaggregates that make up a nation) and *almost always incomplete*. It is that sense of incompleteness, of a desire expressed but not (yet) fulfilled that points to the other question that I began this essay with—what happened to India's "national unity"?

The question of "what happened" is not the focus of this essay. I have left unexamined the key issue of the *discursive mutability* of the national/modernist construct in the songs of Kapoor's early films over time—in other words, the *temporal* rather than the discursive question. I can, however, offer some initial thoughts on this important question. Kapoor's vision of the nation as I have suggested is focused on the construct of "love," simultaneously personal and sociological. How is this relationship articulated over time as the discursive construct of the nation reaches outside the frame of the modern into the postmodern and outside the national to the global? In other words, the *emotive* imprint of cinema needs to be examined in *tracking* the national.

In the case of Raj Kapoor, his film *Mera Naam Joker* (I Am a Joker, 1970) provides some insight into the nature of this (changing) relationship. The film, a box office failure when it was first released (but now characterized as a misunderstood "classic") is a long, reflexive, often maudlin narrative about a clown and the many women that he has loved and lost and who are connected to him by virtue of this fact. The clown and his persona are central to a reading of the question of nationalism and emotion as seen in Kapoor's later work. Chakravartry (1993) suggests that,

> Appearing in a clown's make up and his baggy clothes, Raj Kapoor would seem to be trying to deglamorize his image, to play the anti-hero. However, the clown also suggests continuum of the Raj Kapoor brand of screen hero, since from the persona of the tramp to the clown is but a short step. Kapoor takes back his screen name, Raju to slip back to his habitual role of inhabiting the margins of mainstream society. The dynamics of inner and outer, surface and depth, inclusion and exclusion is played off with the iconicity of the

clown's smiling face hiding his sorrowing heart. But the sorrow is as much for a failed vision of masculinity as for the lack of appreciation of a fickle public. The film opens with the aged clown Raju having sent invitations to the women he loved to witness his last performance in the circus. These women are Mary, his schoolteacher, Marina, a Russian trapeze artist, and Meena, a film star. (Chakravarty, 1993, p. 226)

In contrast to this humanistic, collective (i.e., national) understanding of "love" in *Aawara* and *Shree 420, Mera Naam Joker* is grandiloquent in its narcissism of Raju (the individual) admitting to the failures of Raju (the nation), and to the needs of the hour: a reliance on the obsession with the self, displayed in the placement of the failures of the nation in the audience (the three women who represent love unrequited) and Raju himself, center stage, displaying an early sign of contemporary (corporate) celebrity culture—the willing disposition to present personal life as public commodity. I am not suggesting that this is only "work" that the text performs—there are other alignments of the national/personal/emotional at work: Mary, the teacher, represents colonial nostalgia; Marina, the love for a nonaligned and socialist humanism; Meena, the love of celebrity, but in each case, the film returns to the figure of Raju, at center stage, clowning, crying for attention. By using this singular narrative frame (that structures the entire film) *Mera Naam Joker*, while a box office failure, is eerily accurate in its orientation to the moment of globalization that came with satellite television across the postcolonial world in the early 1980s. This direction is clearly evident in his later films *Bobby* (1973), *Satyam, Shivam, Sundaram* (Truth, God, Beauty, 1978), and *Prem Rog* (Afflicted by Love, 1982) where Kapoor turns away from concerns of the nation (and unconditional love) to the sexualization of the female subject and the problematics of love fettered by bonds of caste, class, and religion become recurrent themes.

And so an answer to "What happened?" is simply: globalization (in two stages). The first stage is built into the premise of the song "Mera Jhoota Hai Japani" which refers to a specific historical period and a specific global orientation—the Nehruvian ideal of nonalignment. An ideal deployed to deal with the realities of the Cold War that shaped the economic ties, political affiliations and cultural bonds for most parts of the newly independent postcolonial world. It would signal the development of a relationship *within the nation* that was bound with a system of political-cultural practices *outside the nation* (different in its institutional arrangement from the colonial era). This discursive reach is almost always seen in ideological terms (communist/capitalist) but it does not have to be, as seen in the popularity of Kapoor's songs in the Soviet and postcolonial world. It does, however, signal a complex accounting of the national formation that begs comparison with other societies (and more crucially, nations) and sets in place the mode of comparison that the paradigm of development assumes (England is more developed than Japan; Japan is more developed than India and so forth) and which makes up the basis for the background noise of my childhood. This first stage of "globalization" (with a small *g*) along lines articulated by the Cold War, then gets shifted and moved into increasingly more corporate centered narratives (across news, entertainment, and film) as the second stage—"Globalization" (with a big *G*) takes center stage in the economic-political and cultural realms of media production. This second stage has little explanatory value for the background noise of my childhood, but certainly is the key to the background noise of my children's lives—who have to endure the noise of Bollywood cinema in our home!

And so to end on a personal note, the films of Raj Kapoor (and other early Indian film makers) resonate with audiences in the Indian diaspora (such as the one I belong to). I have watched how discussion around Indian cinema (in the Indian community of Athens, Georgia) is centered equally on the latest Bollywood hit and the "golden oldies." There is considerable emotional investment in taking ownership of "classic" Bollywood films as both a (comforting) visual aesthetic, anchoring notions about personal identity and perhaps more crucially, as an account of Indian authenticity (as startling as that sounds). Sardar, writing autobiographically about his childhood in Fiji says, "to us Indian cinema was just that: Indian in a true multicultural sense. There were no divisions between Muslims, Hindus, Sikhs, or Pakistanis and Indians—all of us identified with the characters and found meaning in the narratives. The films testified to the fact that we were culturally and socially one" (Sardar, 1998, p. 21). Pratibha Parmar notes, "As diasporic Asians, we hunger for images which in some ways reflect our dreams and our desires and our realities. Media representations are a critical component of our identities, particularly for those of us who are on the margins of the mainstream, the male stream, and the white stream" (1991, p. 18).

A range of questions that future essays might address include: how is "classic" cinema, reworked in the space of diasporic cultures? (especially in the ambit of youth dance and performativity). Specific to the project at hand, how does Raj Kapoor as a construct become part of the conversation of media globalization through contemporary technology—his early songs, frequently watched on YouTube; the songs, remixed in new versions, and his "inheritance" displayed through different generations of his family that act and star in "shows" across the scattered Indian Diaspora? These are all useful points of departure for understanding the legacy of Kapoor and early Bollywood in the continuing project of Indian nationalism.

NOTES

All translations were done by the author.

1. Kavoori and Punathambekar (2008) bring together some of the best known (and new) scholars in "Bollywood studies" examining Bollywood as a global culture; a prism through which to see national and diasporic identity politics and the role of contemporary media technologies in the circulation of Bollywood. Literature engaged with for this essay can be organized around three broad categories: overviews of Bollywood, textual histories and analysis, and those specifically focused on Bollywood and nationalism. The key texts were:

- *Overviews of Bollywood*: Pendakur (2003) and Ganti (2004) are the most "introductory" texts for locating Bollywood. Pendakur examines Bollywood in an even handed way as both a media industry and a cultural practice while Ganti is a compact "guidebook" detailing key periods, stars, films, and auteur in Bollywood history. Books that provide "theoretical overviews" of Bollywood include Dwyer and Patel (2002), Nandy (1998), Prasad (1998),Vasudevan (2000), Dwyer and Pinney (2001), Lal and Nandy (2006). Dwyer and Patel (2002) provide an overview of style, art, and aesthetics of Bollywood's "visual culture" (and has a superlative collection of old Bollywood posters reproduced in full color!) outlining a theory of public culture in India focused on "the complex and fluid interactions that exist between high/elite and low/mass culture" (p. 9). In a similar vein, the essays in Dwyer and Pinney (2001) focus on the history, politics and consumption of public culture in India examining a range of texts including films, fan clubs, public theatre, magazines, and audiences. Nandy (1998), Prasad (1998), and Vasudevan (2000) are pioneering works in the theorization of Bollywood (I outline Prasad and Vasudevan below). The essays collected in Nandy (1998) are anchored by a class centered psychological analytic offered by Nandy in the introduction, which is developed by essays examining both individual stars (Raj Kapoor, Amitab Bachchan), state policy, and genre. I was especially drawn to the auto-ethnographic style of Ziauddin Sardar's extended essay, *Dilip Kumar Made Me Do It* (1998, pp. 19–91) and influenced the writing of this essay in important ways.
- *Textual histories and analysis*: Gopalan (2002), *Cinema of Interruptions* is a critical text in thinking about the constitutive experience of watching a Bollywood film—she argues for a process of in-built coitus interruptus in how such films are constructed and viewed. Prasad (1998), *Ideology of the Hindi Film: A Historical Construction* is a landmark analysis focusing on what he calls the absolutist gaze of Bollywood and its aesthetics of mobilization. The essays in Vasudevan's (2000) influential *Making Meaning in Indian Cinema* outline a range of perspectives through which Bollywood can be examined including those of institutional structures, film form, and links between Bollywood and democracy.
- *Bollywood and nationalism*: In addition to Gopalan (2002), three influential books on the subject are Virdi's (2003) *The Cinematic ImagiNation: Indian Popular Films as Social History*, which is informed by postcolonial studies and emphasis (in favor of a linear narrative) a critical reading of gender, violence, romance/sex in

a range of foundational texts; Chakravarty (1993) *National Identity in Indian Popular Cinema, 1947–1987*, which frames ideas about national identity through the prism of gender politics and indigenes cultural dynamics. The essays in Dwyer and Pinney's (2001) *Pleasure and the Nation: The History, Politics and Consumption of Public Culture in India* examine ideas about cinema and nationalism across multiple sites—regional theatre, Bollywood film, fan clubs/magazines, and ethnographic encounters.

2. My engagement with the literature of Indian national history and nationalism has been selective—relating to the topic of culture and cultural production in the work of nationalism. Two general accounts of India's postindependence history that I have relied on are Guha (2008) and Sen (2005). Guha's eminently readable book, *India after Gandhi*, succinctly details the myriad problems faced by the Indian nation after independence (a heterogeneous population divided by religion, caste, language, region; a largely illiterate and poor population) and the vast odds against which Indian national identity and a workable democracy came about. Amartya Sen's *The Argumentative Indian* (2005) outlines the cultural traditions that underlie much of Indian nationalism focusing on the role of Tagore, Gandhi, and Nehru as key mobilizers of an indigenious political philosophy. See especially his section on "tryst with destiny" (pp. 193–203) and "Inequality, instability and voice" (pp. 34–44). Jawaharlal Nehru's classic *The Discovery of India* (first published in 1946) is a text I revisited both for the pleasure of its writing and his insights into the task of national imagination that he saw ahead (from his prison cell in the Ahmadnagar Fort Prison).

For more scholarly accounts of early Indian nationalism see the essays in Dube (2004) especially the essay on "Disciplining Difference" by Gyanendra Pandey (pp. 159–176). The essays in Karlekar (1998) are wide ranging and the focus of the book is welcome as it focuses on the first fifty years after Indian independence—especially an account of how democracy fits within the discourse of Indian national identity (with key essays by Romila Thapar and Ravinder Kumar). For an account of Indian nationalism from a critical/Marxist lens see the essays in honor of Irfan Habib (Panikkar, Byres, and Patnaik, 2002), especially the chapters by Javeed Alam (pp. 405–439), Aijaz Ahmed (pp. 440–477), and Panikkar (pp. 533–549).

For overviews of modern Indian history (among several candidates), I relied on Stein (1998, especially pp. 284–358), where he articulates the attempt of Indian politicians to "recover the nation from the British" (p. 284). For the immediate context of the partition, my favorite remains the journalistic account by Collins and Lapierre (1975), *Freedom at Midnight*.

3. See www9.Georgetown.edu/faculty/sources/Anderson/extract.

4. The most well-known music directors and their key films include S. D. Burman (*Baazi*, 1951; *Pyaasa*, 1957; *Chalti Ka Naam Gadi*, 1958; *Guide*, 1965; *Aradhana*, 1969; and *Abhimaan*, 1973), Naushad (*Andaz*, 1949; *Mother India*, 1957; *Pakeezah*, 1971), Shankar-Jaikishen (*Aawara*, 1951; *Shree 420*, 1955; *Sangam*, 1964; and *Mera Naam Joker*, 1970), R. D. Burman (*Teesri Manzil*, 1966; *Kati Patang*, 1970; *Amar Prem*, 1971; *Yadon ki barat*, 1973; and *A Love Story*, 1994) and A. R. Rehman (*Roja*, 1992; *Taal*, 1999; and *Lagaan*, 2001).

5. For studies of Raj Kapoor's life and work see, Dissanayake and Sahai's (1987) *Raj Kapoor's Films: Harmony of Discourses* and Reuben's (1988) *Raj Kapoor, The Fabulous Showman: An Intimate Biography*.

6. See Sahai (1987).

7. Some of the richest narratives about India's partition are in Urdu, Hindi, Punjabi, and Bengali—outside the scope of this essay to detail. The key novels include *A Bend in the Ganges, Kindgom's End, Train to Pakistan, Cracking India*, and *Tamas* (also made into a TV series). Important films include *Komal Gandhar* (1961), *Garam Hawa* (1975), *Earth* (1998), and *Gadar* (2001). The well-known novels *A Fine Balance* (Rohinton Mistry) and *Sacred Games* (Vikram Chandra) have themes focused on the partition.

8. For a succinct account of difficulties mediating the issue of royalty in the making of postindependence India see Guha (2007).

9. Nagaraj (2006) offers a critical analysis here: "Lovers, for Raj Kapoor, have a surreal intensity about them" (p. 97). "The narrative viewpoint of Raj Kapoor's films was a product of the director's identification with the young male lover, which could also accommodate the heroine who is created by the adoring gaze of the male public. Raj Kapoor sought to create a magical world of love with enchanting songs and dances. Indeed efforts have been made by Raj Kapoor's biographers to bring in an element of personal authenticity by creating an almost one-to-one relationship between the love stories in his films and the women in his private life" (p. 91).

REFERENCES

Anderson, B. (1991). *Imagined communities: Reflections on the origin and spread of nationalism.* Rev. ed. Excerpts from the introduction accessed at www9.George town.edu/faculty/irvinem/cc7510/sources/Anderson_extract.html.

Appadurai, A. (1997). *Modernity at large.* Minneapolis: University of Minnesota Press.

Asthana, S. (2003). Patriotism and its avatars: Tracking the national-global dialectic in Indian music videos. *Journal of Communication Inquiry, 27*(4).

Bakshi, R. (1998). Raj Kapoor: From Jis Desh Mein Ganga Behti Hai to Ram Teri Ganga Maili. In Ashish Nandy (Ed.), *The secret politics of our desire: Innocence, culpability and Indian popular cinema* (pp. 92–133). New Delhi: Oxford University Press.

Chakravarty, S. (1993). *National identity in Indian popular cinema.* Austin: University of Texas Press.

Collins, L., & Lapierre, D. (1975). *Freedom at midnight.* New York: Simon and Schuster.

Dube, S. (2004). *Postcolonial passages: Contemporary history writing in India.* New Delhi: Oxford University Press.

Dwyer, R., & Patel, D. (2002). *Cinema India.* New Brunswick, NJ: Rutgers University Press.

Dwyer, R., & Pinney, C. (2001). *Pleasure and the nation: The history, politics and consumption of popular culture in India.* New Delhi: Oxford University Press.

Ganti, T. (2004). *Bollywood: A guidebook to popular Indian cinema.* London: Routledge.

Gopalan (2002). *Cinema of Interruptions: Action genres in contemporary Indian cinema.* London: BFI publishing.

Guha, R. (2007). *India after Gandhi.* London: Macmillan.

Karlekar, H. (1998). *Independent India: The first fifty years*. New Delhi: Oxford University Press.

Kavoori, A., & Punathambekar, A. (2008). *Global Bollywood*. New York: New York University Press.

Kohli, A. (2001). *The success of India's democracy*. Cambridge: Cambridge University Press.

Lal, V., & Nandy, A. (2006). *Fingerprinting popular culture: The mythic and the iconic in Indian cinema*. New Delhi: Oxford University Press.

Mehta, B. (1996). Emigrants twice displaced: Race, color and identity in Mira Nair's *Mississippi Masala*. In Deepika Bahri & Mary Vasudeva (Eds.), *Between the lines: South Asians and postcoloniality* (pp. 185–203). Philadelphia: Temple University Press.

Mishra, V. (2002). *Bollywood cinema: Temples of desire*. New York: Routledge.

Nagaraj, D. (2006). The comic collapse of authority: an essay on the fears of the public spectator. In Vinay Lal and Ashish Nandy (Eds.), *Fingerprinting popular culture: The mythic and the iconic in Indian cinema* (pp. 87–121). New Delhi: Oxford University Press.

Nandy, A. (1998). Indian popular culture as a slum's eye view on politics. In Ashish Nandy (Ed). *The secret politics of our desire: Innocence, culpability and Indian popular cinema* (pp. 1–18). New Delhi: Oxford University Press.

Nehru, J. (2004). *The discovery of India*. New Delhi: Penguin.

Panikkar, K. (2002). Culture, nationalism and communal politics. In K. Panikkar, T. Byres and U. Patnaik (Eds.), *The making of history: Essays presented to Irfan Habib* (pp. 533–549). London: Anthem.

Panikkar, K., Byres, T., & Patnaik, U. (2002). *The making of history: Essays presented to Irfan Habib*. London: Anthem.

Parmar, P. (1991). Column in *Rungh: A South Asian Quarterly of Culture, Comment and Criticism*, 1(1), 17–18.

Pendakur, M. (2003). *Indian popular cinema: Industry, ideology and consciousness*. New Jersey: Hampton Press.

Prasad, M. (1998). *The ideology of the Hindi film: A historical construction*. Delhi: Oxford University Press.

Sahai, M. (December 1987). Raj Kapoor and the Indianization of Charlie Chaplin. *East-West Film Journal*, 2(1).

Sardar, Z. (1998). Dilip Kumar made me do it. In Ashish Nandy (Ed.), *The secret politics of our desire: Innocence, culpability and Indian popular cinema* (pp. 19–91). New Delhi: Oxford University Press.

Sarrazin, N. (2008). Songs from the heart: Musical coding in India's popular film music. In A. Kavoori & A. Punathambekar (Eds.), *Global Bollywood*. New York: New York University Press.

Sen, A. (2005). *The argumentative Indian: Writings on Indian history, culture and identity*. New York: Farrar, Strauss and Giroux.

Stein, B. (1998). *A history of India*. Oxford: Blackwell.

Vasudevan, R. (2000). *Making meaning in Indian cinema*. Delhi: Oxford University Press.

Virdi, J. (2003). *The cinematic imagination: Indian popular films as social history*. New Brunswick, NJ: Rutgers University Press.

3

Time to Kill:
Gaming and Terrorism

The time spent playing games trains the gamer to be close to the machine, to be quick and responsive, to understand interfaces, to be familiar with simulated worlds.

—Alexander Galloway

The valley was deathly quiet. I couldn't stop shivering, and then I felt afraid . . . there is something about heavy artillery that is inhuman and terribly frightening. You never know whether you are running away from it or into it. It is like the finger of god.

—Walter Bernstein, "Search for a Battle,"
The New Yorker, September 23, 1944

Everything is digital and yet the digital is nothing. No human can touch it, smell it, and taste it. It just beeps and blinks and reports itself in glowering alphanumerics.

—McKenzie Wark

Shortly after the invasion of Afghanistan, the *New York Times* carried a front page picture that caught my attention—shot from overhead, it showed three young boys, their heads craned together, hunched over a Game Boy that one of them had been given by a U.S. soldier. It was a scene that was eerily similar to the one happening in my (then) eight-year-old son's bedroom each time he had two of his best friends over—I would find them all sitting on the floor, their heads crammed together, watching a virtual duel or battle.

It is easy to read too much into the similarity in these scenes—perhaps this is what boys always do—cluster around the favorite pastime of their generation, whether it is playing marbles or Game Boys. Theoretically, too, one can easily read the two scenes as the collusion of first world practices (of consumption) reworked in the space of the third world, following the dictates of American foreign policy, the "winning the hearts and minds" agenda that follows victory in the battlefield.

Whatever casual (or over determined) reading I made taking in these scenes—they set off the research questions that shape this chapter: What is gaming? (A necessary starting point—since, like most middle-aged adults, I had no clue about what gaming was.) What kind of games deal with terrorism? And most crucially, what kind of story about terrorism are these children learning through gaming?

I will suggest in this chapter that gaming is a key ingredient in thinking about terrorism—constituted as both reality and discourse. While gaming is central to youth culture, it is a mass medium in its own right, rivaling the financial clout and investment of film and television and gaining widespread use in the adult population—structuring the lives of bored office workers (where a window to online fun is always open), and through the emergence of the Internet and cell phones as nodes of perpetual contact and pleasure (wondering why those cell phones come with games?).

I will undertake a broad theoretical accounting[1] of the intersection between the discourse/reality of terrorism and gaming in four subsequent sections: (a) "framing gaming" where I outline how gaming can be understood as a cultural artifact with specific rules of narrative and visual grammar; (b) "framing media and terrorism," which outlines important themes in the coverage of terrorism on film and television as an entry point to examining similar issues in gaming; (c) a detailed auto-ethnographic reading of the game *Counter-Strike* where I write about the experience of playing the game, followed by an account of "lessons learned" from that experience; and (d) a "conclusions and directions" section where I provide a critical overview of other games that deal with terrorism.

FRAMING GAMING

Two interrelated concerns—those of (a) gaming and culture and (b) the textual/narrative universe of games will be addressed in this section.

Gaming and Culture

Galloway (2006) offers a beginning point: "A video game is a cultural object, bound by history and materiality, consisting of an electronic computational device and a game simulated in software. The electronic computational—the machine, for short, may come in a variety of forms. It may be a personal computer, an arcade machine, a home console, a portable device, or any number of other electronic machines" (p. 1). McAllister (2004) expands this understanding and suggests that computer games can be conceived more broadly as a confluence of different kinds of "work": "They require work to create; they require players to work to engage with them; they themselves are works of art and industrial works; and finally they *do* work, particularly rhetorical and cultural work" (McAllister, 2004, p. vii). The idea of doing, of *action* is what separates video games from other media that preceded them. As Galloway (2006) puts it, "if photographs are images, and films are moving images, then video games are actions. *Let this be one word for video game theory*. Without action, games remain only in the pages of an abstract rulebook. Without the active participation of players and machines, video games exist only as static computer code. Video games come into being when the machine is powered up and the software is executed; they exist when enacted" (p. 2, my emphasis).

What also separates video games from other media is that these actions or enactments are undertaken across multiple actors—creators, developers, gamers (in the case of online games often with a cast of thousands). This creates some unique problems for analysis: "Computer games are extraordinarily difficult to study because they are so socially complex; recollections of how they were inspired and of the myriad collective and negotiated decisions that gave them their final form, as well as explanations of how and in what contexts they are eventually to be experienced, are difficult to identify and reconstruct" (McAllister, 2004, p. viii).

Part of the problem lies not only in that computer games do not offer an easy accounting of "authorship" but that they do not—as a cultural technology—offer any one message or cultural/ideological stance: "Computer games can work to maintain the status quo, celebrate liberation, tolerate enslavement, and conjure feelings of hope and despair, assent and dissent, clarity and confusion. They can play equally well on emotion and rationality, pervade radical discourse and common sense alike, and exists comfortably at all points on a semiotic continuum that spans the idiosyncratic to the universal" (McAllister, 2004, p. ix).

The idea of gaming as an open-ended, polysemic media technology devoid of specific discursive orientations or media effects is of course countered in popular media and journalistic accounts of gaming. Computer games "continue to be denigrated by critics and commentators of many persuasions. They are frequently condemned as a vehicle for sexism and mindless violence, as antisocial and antieducational, or alternatively as just a pointless waste of time" (Carr, Buckingham, Burn, and Schott, 2006, pp. 2–3). Robinett (2003) writes with directness and humor: "It is hard to say what ranks lower on the artistic food chain than video games. Comic books? TV sitcoms? X-rated films? These rat-like vermin at the bottom scurry to avoid the thunderous footfalls of the towering behemoths of the art world" (2003, pp. v–vi). McAllister (2004) offers a middle-of-the-road approach that suggests that the "fact" of computer games having particular psycho-physiological effects (usually seen as creating more violent youth) is clearly a matter of some dispute, but the fact that they exert *some* influence on people in *some* way (and that the discourse surrounding these claims exerts a powerful influence on the gaming industry and on cultural understandings about gaming) is beyond question (McAllister, 2004, p. 17).

I would like to locate an understanding of gaming away from the restrictive coding of gaming in popular journalistic accounts (violent or non-violent; passive or active; educational or entertainment). In other words, an account of gaming away from the model of direct "hypodermic effects" and toward a contextual frame that locates gaming within wider social, cultural and global forces. McAllister (2004) provides a theoretical justification for such a perspective: "In general, analysis of cultural artifacts like computer games are doomed to remain little more than interesting hermeneutic exercises if they are not somehow connected to an understanding of the dialectic. By describing how an artifact (for example, an arcade game emulator) affects discursive systems that exist seemingly beyond the artifacts (for example, U.S.-China trade relations), the computer game scholar addresses the 'so what' question that otherwise render irrelevant an astute analysis. A way to establish a connection between a rhetorical analysis and the dialectic is to explain how in-game struggles (miners versus company thugs, for example, in *Red Faction*) are a representation of real-world struggles. An analysis of this sort will point the scholar toward at least two important sites of inquiry. First, what are the components of a given struggle? For example, who is involved in the struggle, and what interests are they serving? What ideologies are in contention? What factors historically—including fictional in-game histories—have contributed to the current state of the struggle? What do participants in the struggle say are their objectives? Does the struggle seem to be more antagonistic or non-antagonistic?" (p. 33).

What McAllister is suggesting most centrally (for the purpose at hand here—gaming and terrorism) is that gaming needs to be understood less as a media technology but as a *political vocabulary* that has a significant impact in modern societies, which relies on the central role of those media technologies in organizing its sociopolitical life. To conclude with two quotes:

> Those societies in which computer games have become popular are also
> transforming . . . virtually every aspect of life is being touched by the influ-

ence of computer games, from art to business, and from education and entertainment . . . as these forces are manipulated, concentrations of power shift, advancing some sociopolitical agendas, while others lose ground and altering both personal and collective understanding of what constitutes "play." These shifts are one way that computers do *real work in the world*. (McAllister, 2004, p. 67; my emphasis)

In short, a good deal of the work of computer games is that they are always making and managing meanings, sometimes by demonstration and sometimes through interpretation. Such work is always simultaneously, then, the *work of power negotiation*. (McAllister, 2004, p. ix; my emphasis)

The Textual/Narrative Universe of Gaming

While the field of game studies is relatively new, there are a number of theoretical positions that scholars have brought to the understanding of the texts of games/gaming. While a survey of all these positions is outside the scope of this chapter, three (interrelated) frameworks that I will draw on can be briefly reviewed—these are gaming as drama, gaming as grammar, and, finally, gaming as narrative.

The "gaming as drama" approach centers the player—or performer—at the heart of understanding gaming. As Whitlock (2005) puts it, "to play the game is to perform it due to its interactive nature. The video game player of today is a performer. He or she is actively engaged in an interactive state that is both physical and mental, playing a character. Narrative, however simplistic, houses this performance in a virtual world, a performance space made up of pixels that can allow an unlimited creative freedom" (p. 189).

When the player becomes a performer, the question arises as to what is the stage and props he or she is using? The stage is the game of course, and the props the actual equipment used to perform: "the Sony Play station and PS2's dual-shock controller, the various throbs and vibrations of which attempt to make us not just see and hear the phenomena of the game but literally 'feel' them. The comparable physical dimension in a stage context is the use of props. A mixture of psychological and physical apparatus makes possible the processes of 'becoming,' with the consequences that the dialectics of internal and external are indeed blurred" (Hand, 2005, p. 213).

In taking such an approach, the analyst can evaluate the dramaturgical ability of the player/actor as a key element in assessing the working of the game. Since the player/performer in the game is usually a digitally constructed "avatar" (derived from Hindu mythology, the etymology of the word means "incarnation" but is usually used as synonymous with online "identity"), the goal is to see the complex of relations, actions, and "performances" of the player/actor. Hand (2005) suggests "it is possible for the actor and the player to become the avatar/character. This is psychologically facilitated at one extreme by the Stanislavsky ethos of naturalist acting which finds an equivalent in the player 'getting seriously into' a game . . . In order to 'become' the game avatar or stage character, to find an appeal and thrill in the experience or, to put it simply, to care about the game or performance . . . Brenda Laurel explores the relevance of Samuel Taylor Coleridge's famous expression of the 'willing suspension of disbelief' in relation to this. As Laurel says, 'pretending that the action is real affords us the thrill of fear; knowing that the action is pretend saves us from the pain of fear'" (pp. 213, 215).

Besides focusing on the role of the player/actor, the "gaming as drama" approach can also focus on the nature of the play (game) itself. What kind of production is it? Does it draw on other texts (like films and novels)? Since most video games are centered in grand action narratives, Hand (2005) suggests that games as plays are marked by "sensation and spectacle": "The 'Sensation and spectacle' of the video game is what lies at the heart of its pleasure as a theatrical performance. 'Sensation' is a central component in the experience of the actor and the endeavor to convey it to the audience is a fundamental challenge. 'Spectacle' in many ways defines the nature of the totality of theatrical performance" (Hand, 2005, p. 211).

In sum, the "gaming as drama" approach centers the player as actor, structures the game as an interactive play and attempts to find parallels "between theatrical performance and video games. Both realms create 'virtual' worlds through the creation of 'illusory' spaces governed by integrity if not complete verisimilitude" (Hand, 2005, p. 211).

The "gaming as grammar" is outlined by McAllister (2004) who draws on Kenneth Burke's concept of "grammar," and a Marxist understanding of dialectic and "proposes that one way to make meaning out of an artifact like a computer game is to see how it 'works' in five integral areas of power: agents (who have the power to catalyze transformative effects); functions (the purported and actual purposes of those effects); influences (the external forces that impinge upon agents and inevitably change the transformative effects of historically situated artifacts); manifestations (the ways in which transformative efforts are realized in particular contexts); and transformative locales (the spatiotemporal instances in which ideologies—individual, communal, or societal—have *specific* transformative effects). This grammar affords computer game scholars a flexible framework by which they may arrange their examination of particular struggles they see playing out in computer games and in the electronic entertainment industry (pp. 1–2).

McAllister (2004) suggests that "visual metonymy"—the simplification of complex information—is a common element in the grammar of gaming.

Such metonymies "result in immersive and interactive mass media, a form of communication that teaches players a host of behaviors, attitudes and concepts quickly, albeit grossly. Such realistic or at least sensorialy rich simulations suggest to players that they really understand phenomena like battle, city planning, and detective work when in fact they understand one version, one very reductive model of the phenomena. This model, designed with principles in mind that includes engaging players quickly and keeping their attention for long periods of time, is necessarily selective" (p. 14).

The result of this selectivity suggests McAllister is that gaming shares some of the same grammar as television and other mass media—their reductiveness of complex sociological facts into easily absorbed storylines. In doing so he stakes a clear position as to the effects of using such a grammar and puts it trenchantly: "to observe, then, that computer games operate with the force of mass media, is also to observe that computer games operate with the force of propaganda. Scholars who recognize how computer games are both influenced by other mass media and how they exert their own mass media force on broader social antagonisms will be able to ask after the ways that computer games metonymize complex issues for a broad demographic" (McAllister, 2004, p. 14).

The "gaming as narrative" approach has broad appeal for a number of theorists. Jenkins's (2004) outlines a theory of "spatial storytelling," through which games can be "read" as narratives (created by both designers and players). Jenkins suggests that games create four types of narrative experiences: evoking associations with external narratives, enabling (or prescribing) players' enactment of a game's scripted narrative, revealing a game's "embedded" narrative through players' activation of certain spaces or artifacts, and finally allowing players to craft "emergent" narratives (cited in Castell, Taylor, and Jensen, 2005, pp. 133–134).

Wolf (2003) looks at issues of narrative by focusing on the video game as "video" or as a medium of visual imagery: "Since the substance of video games is simultaneously imagery and events, their elements can be abstract in both appearance and behavior. Among the first tasks that a player encounters while learning to play a game is the identification of the different elements seen onscreen and understanding how they function and behave. Elements occurring in video games can be divided into four general categories: those indicating the players presence in the game (the player-character); those indicating the computers presence in the game (computer controlled characters); objects that can be manipulated or used by game characters; and the background environment that generally serves as the setting and is not manipulated or altered by any of the characters during the game" (Wolf, 2003, pp. 49–50).

The relationship of narrative to reality is also the focus of Galloway (2006) who suggests that a key element in discussing gaming narratives is

to see relationship between the gaming world and the real world. He outlines the terms of this (old) question for the world of gaming narratives:

> In previous theories of visual culture, this is generally referred to as the prob-
> lematics of representation. But in gaming the concept of representation does
> not account for the full spectrum of issues at play. Representation refers to
> the creation of meaning about the world through images. So far, debates
> about representation have focused on whether images (or language) are a
> faithful, mimetic mirror of reality thereby offering some unmediated truth
> about the world, or conversely whether images are a separate constructed
> medium thereby standing apart from the world in a separate semantic zone.
> Games inherit this same debate. But because games are not merely watched
> but played, they supplement the debate with the phenomenon of action. It is
> no longer sufficient to talk about the visual or textual representation of mean-
> ing. Instead the game theorist must talk about actions, and the physical or
> game worlds in which they transpire. One might call this the problem of
> "correspondences" rather than just "representation." (pp. 70–71)

Finally, McMahan (2003) suggests a method for analyzing gaming narratives by examining the kinds of participation they create. She does this
by drawing on the concepts of "immersion," "engagement," and "presence." The concept of "immersion" suggests that the experience of playing
a game has specific cognitive effects: "Our brains are programmed to tune
into stories with an intensity that can obliterate the world around us . . . the
experience of being transported to an elaborately simulated place is pleasurable in itself, regardless of the fantasy content. We refer to this experience as immersion. Immersion is a metaphorical term derived from the
physical experience of being submerged in water . . . in a participatory
medium immersion implies . . . to do things that the new environment
makes possible" (p. 68).

The concept of "engagement" is based on the idea that "many users appreciate games at a non-diegetic level—at the level of gaining points, de-
vising a winning strategy, and showing off their prowess to other players
during the game and afterward, during replay. To be so engaged with a
game is sometimes referred to as deep play. Geertz used this term to refer
to the kind of substantial emotional investment humans make in violent
rituals such as Balinese cock fighting. The term deep play when referring
to video games, then, is a measure of a player's level of engagement"
(McMahan, 2003, p. 69).

The concept of "presence," refers to "the artificial sense that a user has
in a virtual environment that the environment is unmediated. An increased sense of presence can result from a combination of all or some of
the following factors: quality of social interaction, realism in the environment (graphics, sound), from the effect of 'transportation' from the degree

of immersiveness generated by the interface, from the user's ability to ac-
complish significant actions within the environment and the social impact
of what occurs in the environment and from users responding to the computer itself as an intelligent social action" (McMahan, 2003, p. 3).

Each of these different approaches offer important analytical tools to
engage with the complex, interactive worlds of gaming and will inform
my discussion of *Counter-Strike*.

FRAMING MEDIA AND TERRORISM

The events of 9/11 were a liminal moment not just for American foreign
policy—with the ensuing "war on terrorism" in Afghanistan and Iraq—
but for the work of media as well. A process that began with live coverage of the first Gulf War, when the world became compressed into the life-
space of the CNN crew in Baghdad, had now become commonplace, with
a global news environment, a twenty-four-hour news cycle, the growth of
sectarian broadcast media, a deeply polarized political leadership, and
the emergence of new technologies of information and dissent. As is often
remarked, September 11 was a global media event that could only happen
in a globally networked society.

How has terrorism been narrativized in the years after 9/11? While
space does not allow for a detailed consideration of all the films and television programming devoted to the subject, there appears to be a broad
thematic that has informed narratives about terrorism: In both films and
television, after an initial period of nationalist enthusiasm and patriotic
fervor there has emerged a more critical, and reflexive accounting of global
terrorism. In Hollywood, films such as the political allegory, *V for Vendetta*,
an action-thriller follows the mysterious V, a freedom fighter against a to-
talitarian state. Based on a graphic novel by Alan Moore, the film is, in the
words of its director,

> Very prescient to how the political climate is at the moment. It really showed
> what can happen when society is ruled by government rather than the gov-
> ernment being run as a voice of the people. I don't think it's such a big leap
> to say that things like that can happen when leaders stop listening to people.
> (vforvendetta.warnerbros.com)

Similarly, other Hollywood films such as *Casino Royale* and *Déjà vu*
make ample reference to the war on terrorism as a backdrop to storylines.
Independent cinema has covered an impressive range of narrative possibilities, from the faux documentary *D.O.A.P. (Death of a President)*, which
imagines Bush being assassinated in 2007, to *The Prisoner or: How I Planned*

to Kill Tony Blair, which tells the story of a journalist who was wrongly imprisoned and tortured by U.S. authorities for nine months. International films have reflected on a range of national, cultural, and ethnic anxieties around terrorism. Some examples that stand out are films about the psychological/sociological background of terrorists, such as *Paradise Now* (Palestinian suicide bombers), *My Life as a Terrorist* (a German revolutionary in the 1970s), *Babel* (a Moroccan boy's gunplay triggers fear of a terrorist attack), *Catch a Fire* (the true story of a member of the African National Congress), and *The Lives of Others* (a Berlin playwright's life before the fall of communism). In sum, filmic narratives are beginning to do what films do best: explore the complex intersections between the personal and political, as seen in one of the defining conditions of contemporary modernity—terrorism.

Television's coverage of the subject has been dominated by news rather than entertainment (with some exceptions—shows like *24*, *Sleeper Cell*, *The Wire*) and there has been a gradual but firm narrative trajectory mirroring that of film—from unproblematic acceptance of American foreign policy imperatives to a more critical treatment of the situation in Iraq and Afghanistan. At the heart of such an (ongoing) understanding has been the deconstruction of "terrorism" and "war" as politically contingent terms. As Murdock (2004) puts it,

> Terrorism is a term that cannot be given a stable definition; to do so forestalls any attempt to examine the major feature of its relation to television in the contemporary world. As the central public arena for organizing ways of picturing and talking about social and political life, TV plays a pivotal role in the contest between competing definitions, accounts, and explanations of terrorism. (p. 2305)

While American news media may (arguably) be presenting competing definitions of the war in Iraq, it has a long way to go to overturn what Thussu (2006), in a critical analysis of news narratives outlines what he calls "the myths" of television coverage of terrorism. He uses "myths" as a conceptual term to refer not to falsehood but to socially constructed myths, he identifies the "myths" of Islamic terrorism (arguing that Islamic terrorism has to be seen as rooted in global relations of access, power, and economics): the myth of madness (arguing that continued coverage of religious fervor coalesces with historical discourses about Orientalism), the myth of nuclear threat (focusing on the patently false claims about weapons of mass destruction), and the myth of morality (critiquing American foreign policy in Central America and the Middle East based on the central value of "freedom"). He suggests these myths "help consumers of mass media to construct a worldview [that plays] a crucial ideological role, promoting the values of dominant groups" (p. 4).

Where does gaming lie in this equation? It is a question that remains largely unexamined. What follows in the rest of this chapter is an attempt to begin to answer this question. The next section is based on a participatory observation exercise playing one of the most popular first person shooter game focused on terrorism *Counter-Strike*. In addition to playing *Counter-Strike*, I sat in on numerous sessions when one (or both) of my two sons played a number of first person shooter games, including *Counter-Strike*, *Ghost Recon* (based in Mexico and focused on fighting militias), and the blockbuster hit *Halo 3* (which, while focused on battling a variety of alien life forms, can be seen as an allegory about terrorism). Following the auto-ethnographic narrative I outline some of the generalizations that can be made about terrorism as a gaming construct. The concluding section "zooms out" from this detailed analysis to provide a panoramic view of a range of other games that deal with the terrorism. In sum, by conducting both a detailed reading of one game and an overview of other games some of the conceptual issues at the heart of the question of gaming and terrorism are engaged with. Needless to add, the exercise remains partial and incomplete, but nevertheless an important starting point.

READING AND EXPERIENCING THE GAME *COUNTER-STRIKE*: AN AUTO-ETHNOGRAPHIC EXPLORATION

I am not a gamer. My two sons (twelve and seventeen) on the other hand are avid gamers. They talk incessantly and passionately about the virtues of the latest game (the months before the release of *Halo 3* was especially heated). Family walks always means having to listen to nuanced arguments about the values, attributes, and features of different games (I have tried unsuccessfully to ban all gaming conversation). This last Christmas, they both saved up money over the year to buy themselves an Xbox. I was powerless to stop them—and had only one request—that they keep the sound down. I told them I did not want any "noise pollution" in the living room—machine gun fire, I felt, was not the best ambient sound for a home. The first days after the Xbox arrived can be characterized as a long uninterrupted bout of teenage hyperbole—loud proclamations of victory, crowing, one-upmanship, and in general making a complete nuisance of themselves.

As is evident, I had a bad attitude—an attitude marked by common parental assumptions ("if they think its good, it's got to be bad for them") and a set of normative expectations about gaming narrative—a genre that I "knew" was dominated by a singularly reductive formula: kill and then kill some more. As is also evident, I had left my scholarly apparatus—as a student of communication—firmly behind in the office.

But I knew that I was missing out on something. Something big. My students at work, my kids at home, were all being swept in the world of gaming. It was time for me to join up as well—if for no other reason than to stay relevant. I began with a simple assumption: "Computers subtly model our way of thinking about the world. Through computers, new cultural phenomena and abstract ideas are presented to the public in a simple and accessible way" (Filiciak, 2003, p. 87).

I began the mission. I called the local Game Stop in Athens, Georgia, and I was lucky, they had a used copy of *Counter-Strike*—it was just $6.99. For the first time, I drove to Game Stop on my own. It was in the middle of a workday afternoon and I found the place strangely empty—on week-ends, it is packed with teenagers and preteens, packed into aisles, hag-gling with their exhausted parents, while the two obese clerks patiently deal with each customer's detailed requests and questions about trade value and playability of the game they were buying. The normal conver-sations in the store were frequent renditions of the words, "cool" and "sucks" interspersed with the specific vocabulary of gaming: levels, cut scenes, graphics, and so on.

I tried to get over my bias toward the clerks who confirmed my stereo-type about the links between obesity and game culture, and asked some preliminary questions about gaming and terrorism. Their response over-whelmed me. It was generous in its intellectual scope, talking about ter-rorism broadly; locating terrorism within a wider set of gaming perfor-mativity—rattling off a number of games focused on wars (real and imagined), militias, drug runners, and, most commonly, aliens. They had an animated discussion about the different kinds of violence in gaming, suggesting that while this was a central aesthetic in all games—car chases, animal antics, and digital board games—there was a need to examine the context of violence, rather than just its occurrence. I asked a specific ques-tion: which games feature Muslim or Middle Eastern terrorists? The an-swer was stunning: none. The clerks vaguely remembered a game in early 2000 that featured some Islamic terrorists but it was quickly pulled off the shelves. I had hit the first theoretical stumble—I had assumed that terror-ism would, as it does on television news, be centrally coded with largely regressive discourse about Arabs, Islam, and the Middle East. It looked like I had my conceptual work cut out for me—but the immediate task was more experiential. I had to learn to be a gamer—luckily, in my sons, I had two good teachers.

Or so I thought—when I held the Xbox remote (which I learned was called a controller) in my hand, I had no idea what the buttons meant, which toggles to push, which of the triggers to press at what point. Look-ing at the screen, I had little idea about what to do with the figure on the screen, brandishing a nasty looking weapon. I did not have a clue about "moving" my character (myself?) in the virtual landscape, no idea even how to "look" at things. I ran higgledy-piggledy into walls, zoomed mindlessly into the sky, got shot repeatedly, and had to watch the game as a dead observer (now that's a contradiction, I thought). My seventeen-year-old repeatedly yelled at me, his frustration boiling over at my sheer incompetence (and in his view complete stupidity) at understanding the basic rules and practices of the game. He stomped off in disbelief. I had hit not just a pedagogical wall (not knowing how to play) but an epistemological wall as well (I did not even know the paradigmatic context that playing assume). Reading the scholarly literature on gaming had helped little. Gaming was not like TV, knowing how to use a remote did not help much. It was time to understand this much like a child learns—through small, deliberate, and repetitive actions. In other words, I had to rely on the graces of my more pliable younger son—and approach the exercise, one very small (textual) step at a time. Here is what I learned.

First, understand the narrative premise. The game *Counter-Strike* is based on a conflict between two fictitious groups of "terrorists" and "counterterrorists." It is a first person shooter game that is played through a console or online (in both first person and third person) and is widely considered as an important text in the history of gaming. The game involves participation in teams of antiterrorists and terrorist using a range of "real" weapons and scenarios, played out over a range of locations. The antiterrorist teams are "real" as well—including American Seals, Germany's GSG, England's SAS, and France's GIGN. The terrorists are based on fictitious terrorist cells but with identifiable real-life counterparts in the Middle East, South America, and the former Soviet Union. Both groups are unproblematically gendered—supremely muscled men. The terrorists wear large goggles, a hood, sport swarthy moustaches, and on close examination have thick, callused skins. They wear tight fitting black pants and a loose red jacket around which are strapped rounds of ammunition and a backpack filled (presumably) with tools of their trade. Their ethnicity is ambiguous—the only diacritical sign are their cone-like white caps (vaguely resembling those worn by priests of the Greek Orthodox Church) nestling under the hoods. A close-up of the design on the cap shows a floral pattern, vaguely Middle Eastern. Race is unclear, though the skin color appears to be olive or off-white. Their boots complete the picture: black, high strapped, chunky, and resilient. The counterterrorists, on the other hand, need little deconstruction—they are generic army—camouflage jackets, pants, high boots, and straps for ammunition and bags for holding supplies. They are all white.

Second, figure out the mise-en-scène. The game is played between these two groups in a variety of settings over several rounds. The settings seem arbitrary, ranging from the titles that evoke the natural environment (dust, tides), the built environment (airstrip, fast line, stadium, cobble), national/cultural contexts (Italy, Aztec, Havana, Miami, Vastok, and Chateau), moral states (corruption, truth). I looked at the visual iconography and the constructed environment in each of these settings trying to find contexts in which issues of Middle Eastern/Islamic terrorism might be reflexively engaged with. I settle on the game "dust" for its sparse but readily accessible evocation of an Islamic city—minarets, domes, and alleyways of an old city (in one place with laundry strung across two walls!). The name "dust" can also, I surmised, be read as a signified for the desert, a trope that extends back (at least) to *Lawrence of Arabia*. I am ready to play.

Third, choose your props. Once I have chosen "dust," I have to make a bewildering range of decisions—weapons, equipment, missions, and levels. Each decision has consequences for what is to follow. Money plays a central role. I have $6,000 to spend to fully prepare myself. There are four types of weapons—pistols, heavy weapons, rifles, smg's (semiautomatic machine guns). Under each type of weapons there are at least four choices available: pistols (nighthawk, knm45, 57, 228, 9/19 mm, 40dual), heavy weapons (12 gauge, auto shotgun, swat shield and pistol, esm249), rifles (magnum, defender, d3/au1, the craig552, cv47, and the Schmidt), and smgs (mac10, esc90, k&mump45, k&msmg). Decisions about choice of weapon need to be made keeping in account the mission (dust has two types of missions—demolition of a planted bomb and rescuing hostages). Close range fighting lends itself to smgs and pistols, long distance lends itself to rifles. Where large numbers of enemies need to be dispatched, heavy weapons come in handy. Help in decision making comes in the shape of a chart, which lists the values of each weapon along with four categories (firepower, fire rate, accuracy, reload rate) and their cost. One example (pistols) illustrates the complexity of the decision making required: the Nighthawk has the most firepower and costs $650; the Knm45 has the best fire rate and costs $500; the 57 has the most accuracy and costs $750; the 9/19 has the best reload rate and costs $400. A player can choose two weapons—a primary and a secondary weapon, going through the same calculations for each weapon. Ammunition and equipment are next. Ammunition rounds can be purchased before the game starts and during the game (but at the cost of time—the player has to return to the beginning point of the game to get ammunition). Equipment is all-important— the game recommends (in clear declarative language) that getting Kevlar armor (and ballistic helmet) is the most important piece of equipment to buy. The other decisions about equipment are mission sensitive and include, a smoke grenade (to create conditions for camouflage), a flash bang grenade (to temporarily blind the enemy), a high explosive grenade (to kill large numbers), and a bomb defuse kit.

Fourth, become the narrative. This involves first and foremost, coming to terms with the controller. Coached by my younger son, I learn that the right trigger is for shooting and the left thumb stick moves my character around. The right thumb stick is to look around and direct where you are looking. The A button is to make selections, X is reload, Y is change weapons, B is zoom. There are others that come later on (making a jump, changing views of the same situation, etc.). I am reminded that while I may have spent my money wisely, I need to shoot only when necessary and that if I get enemy kills, I will get more money and can get added ammunition. I have to choose the level of game I want to play (beginner, standard, professional, and expert). The setting stays the same (dust) but the enemies are more crafty, their actions more realistic and its harder to survive. There are a number of numbers blinking at the bottom of the screen—from left to right they signify my health (0–100), armor (0–100), time left in the game, amount of ammunition (rounds) left, and amount of money (gained/lost). It's pretty nerve wracking having to keep track of all this information. I choose (naturally) to be a counterterrorist. I click the start button and start down the wall, moving with geriatric nimbleness.

I get shot. Repeatedly. The game is very unforgiving. Over the next two days, after the boys leave for school, I settle down in front of the Xbox, thumbs on buttons, fingers on triggers. There are things that I learn quickly—how to weave through the walls of the medieval city. I learn there are about half a dozen alleyways. I learn to identity them—"this is where the two barrels of explosives are kept," "this is where the street with the clotheslines appear," "this is where the long underground passage with the marbled walls appear," and so forth. My learning curve is affected by my need for textual analysis—I keep stopping to examine/admire the motifs on the walls—leaves, flowers, and a mosaic that appears inspired by Mughal architecture—the floor in the inside halls are marbled as are parts of the wall. Lamps, wall hangings, and architectural oddities take my attention from the game—and I am promptly killed, the blood splattering in front of my eyes, as the inevitable message pops us: "you are dead and watching another player." In time, I learn to ignore the architecture and focus on what's important—which walls to hide behind, where the enemy appears to be clustered and to figure out parts of the game that matter—the visual markers on the right top corner of the screen, that indicate which AI (artificial intelligence) character on my team is fighting which of the enemy; signs on the walls that tell me where the bomb is located. I learn that the rules of the real world apply: listen for the sound of the gunfire and then run in that direction; anticipate what may happen next—on three separate occasions, I ran through a half open door and find that a gun battle is happening just beyond, and I am shot before I can react. I am getting pretty worked up about getting killed each time, and heartily sick of the faintly mocking tone in the narrator's voice as he (once again) says, "terrorists win."

I decide to get serious about this—deconstructing television was much easier, you could watch the text over and over again, it lay there supine, waiting to be dissected into its semantic referents. The game was a different proposition altogether—it spoke back, and in my case, scorned all my efforts at understanding it—by killing me and then rubbing it in by telling me that I was dead and watching another character (as you can see this hit a raw nerve). I began to replicate the same mission (demolition) and weapons/equipment (Smgs, Kevlar, pistol, demolition kit) over and over again. When the message popped up "bomb has been planted," I ran pell-mell through the streets until the sign showed up that I was near the bomb. If any terrorists showed up, I was less interested in killing them as in dodging them and getting to the bomb location. I had learned that while getting a few kills gave me more money, I lost time and that inevitably the bomb would go off (the controller in my hands would vibrate in silent declaration of the terrorist's victory) and the game would be over. Once I found the bomb, I activated the demolition kit and found to my immense satisfaction that it worked and finally, finally, I had proof of my coming-of-gaming-age. The voice intoned: "counterterrorists win."

Fifth, use the force. Once I had won my first game, I had a curious setback—I lost interest. I had a sense that this was it—winning was textual closure, the analysis was complete, its representational universe mastered through my actions. I was wrong. Watching my son play the game later that evening and then watching it being played online with players from other places in the virtual universe, it became apparent that I had only reached mastery at one level of one game—and that too, the *wrong way*. I had approached it much like I would approach the world of representation—figure out the rules, learn the scenarios, plot your analysis, reach the conclusions— in most cases already predetermined. It was in retrospect, a very modernist journey—which is all I knew and all I had learned in my years as a student of communication. What matters, as I saw my son and his friends play *Counter-Strike* (and *Ghost Recon*, *Halo*) was the operationalization of *play as an organizing principle*. It mattered little to them that they did not know all the commands, the scenarios that were unfolding in front of them. They did not even particularly care about being killed or hurt, nor even it seemed about winning the game. What mattered most it seemed was the pleasure of discovery, of a muttered conversation with the self (the most common expression was "holy crap, where did he come from?") or with each other as they played a dual player mode, laughing and ribbing each other's efforts at virtual maneuvering and decision making. It was I realized with numbing clarity, not the game that mattered, but the commensality that came with it. Fights over the remote had morphed into fights over characters, actions, sequences, scenarios, and consequences. But even more than this sociological insight into the working of postmodern sociability was the *nature of the play itself*. Shinkle (2005) discusses the "feel it, don't think" motto on Sega's *Rez* website and suggests that the best way to understand gaming is "for players to get caught up in it, to dance with it, to lose themselves in it . . . in the case of *Rez*, players are not simply playing the game, *they are in the game—they are the game*—and this implies a different kind of alliance with the technology, one that lies outside the conventional dynamic of 'tool' and 'user.' Playing *Rez*, in other words, is not a matter of controlling a technology but of allowing it to merge with the self. In effect, a players body becomes the controller, the player moves their body in real space in order to make things happen onscreen" (Shinkle, 2005, p. 27, my emphasis). I realized that I had not done any of this—I had merely mastered a few tools to achieve a set goal (defusing the bomb, winning the game). Since I could not get "in the game," I had "no game." With some irritation, and more relief, I decided to hang up my controller—after a short, brutal and mediocre career—and figure out the lessons I had learned.

LESSONS LEARNED

However, incomplete my exploration may have been, it became evident to me that there were some crucial ways in which the game *Counter-Strike* constructed a specific discursive frame for terrorism:

1. The "text" of terrorism in *Counter-Strike* is unarguably _performative_. Centered on the "player" or "actor" the game does indeed assume acting a role with the choice of role (terrorist or counterterrorist) coming with its props (bombs, kits, weapons) and ability to play the role well or not (needless to add, my performance was not remotely Stanislavsky). Comparing my performance with that of my son's was illuminating as well—they were immediately at ease with the game, made fun of its poor graphics even as they marveled at the range of weapons available. They unabashedly weaved, bobbed, ducked, and cringed with the playing of the game—something that I did with reluctance. What kind of a play is "terrorism" in _Counter-Strike_? It readily falls into Hand's (2005) "sensation and spectacle" classification, working through a central idea: terrorism needs to be *acted upon*, not reflected or critiqued or discussed. In this central sense, terrorism is refashioned through the prism of action (rather than political debate or cultural insight)—narrowly defined as detonating or defusing a bomb; killing or being killed. Simply put, if terrorism is a drama, it is a very bloody drama—with clear consequences for all the "actors" involved.

2. The "text" of terrorism in *Counter-Strike* lacks narrative complexity. The game can be easily plotted along the relatively simple models of understanding gaming narratives, such as Wolf (2003) distinctions between player-character (the terrorist or counterterrorist role in *Counter-Strike*), the computer-controlled characters (the AI characters in the game who take over the game once you are dead and whose actions are not determined by the players actions), the objects in the game (bomb, weapons, and equipment in *Counter-Strike*).

When more complex modes of accountability such as McMahan's categories (immersion, engagement, presence) are applied, *Counter-Strike* falls short. There is little in the game that creates an immersive experience or even approximates the idea of presence, where the player forgets the mediated nature of the experience. I discussed these concepts with my two sons and they were emphatic in their criticism of the game *Counter-Strike* as not being "realistic" enough or sophisticated enough in its graphics and storytelling to warrant the kinds of engagement that the categories of immersion and presence calls for. They both pointed to *Halo 3* as the only game currently on the market that approximates some of this sensation. My younger son, who is a Harry Potter fan (fanatic is a better word), kept bringing in the book as an example of how immersion works for him (he gets so lost in reading, that we have to repeatedly call out for him to "return to earth"). I asked him—in speculative fashion—whether he had ever had a dream that he was playing a video game. He said "no" but was pleased to tell me that he had frequent dreams of being a character or participant in the Harry Potter books.

The only category (in McMahan's formulation) that was relevant to the *Counter-Strike* experience was that of "engagement"—where elements of gamesmanship showcased the non-digetic level of the game. Some phrases that were often used by my two sons were "I pwned you" (which I learned means "owned," with the *p* in front of it and the *o* removed—no rationale for adding the *p* and removing the *o* was given, except that somebody in the online gaming community had used it and it had caught on) and "you are a noob" (which means that the player is a novice and not good at the game).

The overall judgment about *Counter-Strike* was, as I have suggested, that this was a game with poor graphics (my older son would repeatedly zoom in on details of characters or weapons and say "these graphics suck") and where the narrative "lagged" (i.e., was slow in visual movement and sometimes froze) and did not really qualify as a complex gaming experience.

3. The "text" of terrorism on *Counter-Strike* is determined by the "discourse of modulated action" as compared to the news, which is

focused on the "discourse of annihilation." By "discourse of annihilation," I mean the stable representational universe of journalism, which presents terrorism within the ambit of violent acts by terrorists—especially those of attacks on buildings and institutions, suicide bombings, kidnappings, and random killings. The discursive focus is on *the results* of terrorist activity—annihilation, which is usually attributed to the terrorist's cultural, religious, or ideological worldview.

Gaming on the other hand presents what can be called a "discourse of modulated action" where the work of rational militarism rather than religious ideology is the dominant mode through which actions/narratives are deployed. Concerns central to McAllister's categories of the working of power (the five grammars) in gaming are made manifest *through* the game's rational/technical social order. *In other words, this is a utilitarian world, stripped of a complex power structure.* It involves the spending of finite amounts of money to buy weapons and achieve objectives. In sum, it is a world where the laws of plausibility, rational accountability, and realism rule rather than religion or fundamentalism.

Since gaming is an "action" genre, how is the "discourse of modulated action" experienced? Or to put it differently, what is its phenomenology? Based on my playing/watching *Counter-Strike*, some elements can be outlined. The first is how the body of the player/viewer/performer of terrorism is located. Gaming action is predicated on

> The release of the subject from the limitations of the human form, dismissing the body as little more than a container for the self—an imperfect and ultimately temporary habitation that could be left behind as a technology replaced it with something more durable. Though the postmodern fantasy of the downloaded mind may have lost a measure of currency, the decorporealized subject—the "floating eyeball" is still alive and well in today's technocultural world, and remains a touch stone for the visual, spatial and temporal structure of most digital games. (Garrelts, 2005, p. 23)

The idea of the "floating eyeball" is the first person shooter perspective that is often suggested is the same as the "first-person subjective camera angle" (Galloway, 2006, p. 40). This angle "is not just about seeing, but rather primarily about motion through space . . . Events unfold in real-time, in a single take, from a single point of view. These sequences are tactile or haptic, more than they are visual. The subjective camera doesn't just look at a scene. It moves actively through space. It gets jostled, it stops and starts, it pans and tilts, it lurches forward and back. It follows the rhythms of the whole body, not just that of the eyes. This is a pre-subjective, affective and not cognitive, regime of vision" (Galloway, 2006, p. 62–63).

Counter-Strike, like all other first person shooter game shares and creates such a "vision" for thinking/acting/playing terrorism (and by extension, "the war on terrorism.")

The second feature that illustrates the "discourse of modulated action" is the *normative values* associated with the floating eyeball or first person subjective camera angle vision. It reproduces what is referred to as the "automation of sight . . . where the camera adopts a machinic gaze" (Galloway, 2006, pp. 39–40). The machinic gaze is now present across media— in news through video of a "smart bomb" hitting a target or "in the film *Terminator*, to underscore the computerized artificiality of the cyborg's visual cortex. James Cameron (the director) includes four shots where the Terminator's eyes and the camera lens merge . . . computer readouts, diagrams, graphics, flashing cursors, and scrolling texts are all used to give the Terminator's image a computer-like patina" (Galloway, 2006, p. 53). Overall, "in film, the subjective perspective is marginalized and used primarily to effect a sense of alienation, detachment, fear, or violence, while in games the subjective perspective is quite common and used to achieve an intuitive sense of motion and action in game-play" (Galloway, 2006, p. 40). Galloway suggests that the "computerized visuality" of the first person shooter vision replaces the traditional cinematic point-of-view shot and becomes "so omnipresent and so central to the grammar of the entire game that it essentially becomes coterminous with it" (2006, p. 63).

4. The "text" of terrorism in *Counter-Strike* is over determined in its "visual metonymy" (McAllister, 2004) leading to a "closed" rather than an "open" one. In the literature of television and film analysis, such categories are usually described with terms like "polysemic" (where a text has many meanings) or "polyvalent" (where the meanings of a text are many but not infinite) and so forth. These categories do not do justice to the "correspondences," (Galloway, 2006) the complex scenarios, settings, actors, motives, and sequencing of play that I have seen in evidence at "play" (pun intended) in *Counter-Strike*. I would like to extend the scope of the idea of "open" texts (and the concept of "correspondence") in the case of gaming by suggesting that there are two separate processes that are at work in the world of gaming. These processes are those of "laboring" and "modding."

The idea of "laboring" extends the idea of "interactivity" and "polysemy." McAllister (2004) provides some initial frames for the discussion of "labor":

Whereas Chris Crawford defines a computer game as a computer based, semi-realistic scenario in which a player safely interacts with conflicts of the designer's making and learns things in the process. Brian Reynolds, another prominent game designer, operates from a simpler definition. "A game," he says, "is a series of interesting choices" (Saltzman, p. 42). By this Reynolds means that a computer game, a good one, at least, allows players to "interact with a story rather than simply sit passively and receive it" (p. 42). Similarly journalist Steven Poole argues that computer game designers should be guided by an "aesthetic of wonder" and observes that "modern video games—dynamic and interactive fusions of colorful graphic representations, sound effects, music, speed and movement—are unquestionably a fabulously sensual form" (p. 12). Pool emphasizes that what makes this new artwork so compelling is that "you *play* it." (McAllister, 2004, p. 33)

In his discussion of gaming he suggests that an understanding of any game should not be limited to the console or the software but the entire universe of players and their relationships to the game—this is fundamentally a process of rethinking polysemy or interactivity beyond single or multiple player but in the hundreds or thousands in the case of online games (including *Counter-Strike*). Discussing the game *Splinter Cell*, McAllister suggests that it "required the work and labor of hundreds—perhaps even thousands—of people, and in an important way changed the computer game industry by advancing the art of skillfully crafted language around plot twists, scene descriptions, and dialogue" (McAllister, 2004, p. vii).

Similarly, Galloway (2006) argues "one should resist equating gamic action with a theory of interactivity or the active audience theory of media. Active audience theory claims that audiences always bring their own interpretations and receptions of the work. Instead . . . an active medium is one whose very materiality moves and restructures itself" (p. 3) through the labor of the games creators, producers, and developers.

Finally the idea of "laboring" exists in the work that players put into it. Ideally the player in an interactive game collaborates with the designer in producing a tale that bears the players stamp, that is actualized and to some degree coauthored by her or him—which brings up the practice of "modding." In gaming, the narrative elements in a game are not coded by a designer and then set in stone but rather open to the process of making "mods" or modifications to the game by players. These "mods" extend the narrative life of a game which otherwise dies once "you defeat the game" (hence "trade-ins" are an integral part of the gaming culture). The "mod effect" as Matthews (2007) calls it is the process of making changes to the original game. Such changes, he argues,

> has led to an empowerment of the gamer. The empowered gamer is no longer at the mercy of the game's developers. The new gamer can change textures, characters, clothing, storylines, and can even create new games altogether. The empowered gamer can freely distribute his/her creation to the

world through one of the many websites dedicated to the dissemination of mods. The best mods may gain world-wide recognition, allow the modder entrance into game development teams, or even become saleable games. (Matthews, 2007, pp. 1–2)

A little detour is needed at this stage to more fully understand the implications of "the mod effect" for gaming narratives. The game *Counter-Strike* is a "mod" that originated through changes (mods) made to a game called *Half-Life*. The game *Half-Life* was designed by the company (*Valve* software) in a way that it encourages users to modify the game, create bots (AI forms), add-ons that enhance the game. This was done through "the level design program the development team used to create the game's levels, and a software development kit to encourage mod use of the game" (Matthews, 2007, p. 5). The result was that modders "were responsible for extending the shelf-life of *Half-Life* beyond what it would normally have been" (Hyman, 2004, cited in Matthews, 2007, p. 5). Because of this, *Valve* created the *Half-Life* Mod Expo, which awarded modders monetary compensation for their products and one such mod, *Counter-Strike*, created in 2000 by a team of modders became the most widely played online shooter game in the world. By 2002, there were over 30,000 *Counter-Strike* servers on the Internet. Statistics by *Game Spy* showed over 85,000 players simultaneously playing and according to *Valve* by February 2007, players collectively contributed to nearly seven billion minutes of playing time each month (Au, 2002, cited in Matthews, 2007, p. 5). Thus the narrative of *Counter-Strike* is often seen as a landmark in user generated content as it relates to gaming, especially online gaming. *Counter-Strike* has developed its own community of scriptwriters and modders. Some add bots, while others remove features of the game, which some players found annoying, while yet others create different modes of play and new kinds of weapons. Each of these work in a complex, interactive narrative that presumes no starting point—there is no (modernist) prior text, outside of the original construct of *Half-Life*. Rather it's the very picture of a postmodern sensibility around the production, distribution, and consumption of (gaming) narrative around the topic of terrorism.

5. Finally, the "text" of terrorism in *Counter-Strike* works contextually— across other media texts and news events in the real world raising key issues about media effects, power, and ideology. Some initial formulations on this subject follow.

First, is the question of how gaming "remediates" older media narratives about terrorism and in turn contributes to them. Here *Counter-Strike* has achieved an iconic status. *Counter-Strike* resonates in a range of institutional, cultural, and discursive contexts illustrating how gaming is mainstreaming into a mass medium. This is reflected in the game's technical complexity (its use of maps, graphics, and numerous design features), which it shares with (and influences) sports and news programming, the emergence of a language around the game. For example, the use of prefixes in the game are now in the hundreds, with examples like "AWP," which stands for Arena Maps; "surfing," the use of certain keys to surf certain ramps in the game; "XC" which stands for extreme climb. It has created a prescribed set of behaviors characterized by people in the game, usually referred to as "professionals" and "cheaters." Perhaps the best evidence of *Counter-Strike's* arrival is its popularity within the realms of popular culture with phrases like "boom," "headshot," the web-comic *Concerned*, the TV show *Mythbusters*, the singer Jan Hegenberg.[2]

Second, games like *Counter-Strike*, center the debate about terrorism in the realm of "play"—and through that experience "playing off" on a number of political, cultural, and ideological themes that impinge on an understanding of terrorism. As McAllister (2004) puts it "the computer gaming complex is a network that draws on human beings' innate desire to play, and it intermingles that desire with *a host of ideologies that reproduce themselves through the medium of the game* (McAllister, 2004, p. 69, my emphasis). What are these ideologies? And how do they impact on the discursive construct of terrorism? There are at least three emergent issues that can be briefly outlined. These are play and consequences, the act-on narrative, and reality matters.

Play and Consequences

A simple assertion: gaming functions as a discourse without "real" consequences. Since it is "play" it doesn't count as having discursive energy. I saw this repeatedly in how my sons played the game without a thought about the killing sprees they were unleashing. This is fundamentally different from the relationship that viewers enter into when viewing television or film where specific political, national, and gendered positions structure the reception of a text. Gaming action on the other hand occurs "within a separate semiautonomous space that is removed from normal life . . . games are accompanied by a special awareness of a second reality or of a free unreality, as against real-life" (Galloway, 2006, p. 6).

Paradoxically, while distancing itself from "reality" gaming simultaneously encourages a specific immersive relationship *to* the world of gaming. I saw as I spent increasing amounts of time playing *Counter-Strike* and in marathon sessions that my sons play their different games, a willing insertion into the "reality" of the game—this discursive step, makes the "terrorism" in a game all the more problematic, because it *subsumes the real into the virtual*. This is not a new formulation. In *Neuromancer*, William Gibson, did not have the Internet in mind when he coined the term cyberspace. Instead, he found an inspiration for it in video games:

> in arcades, I could see in the physical intensity of their postures how rapt these kids were. It was like one of those closed systems out of a Pynchon novel: you had this feedback loop, with photons coming off the screen into the kid's eyes, the neurons moving through their bodies, electrons moving through the computer. And these kids clearly believed in the spaces these games projected. Everyone who works with computers seems to develop an intuitive faith that there's some kind of actual space behind the screen. (cited in Lahti, 2003, p. 157)

The implications for thinking about terrorism in the world of gaming are significant. Gaming presents an intertwined set of discursive possibilities around "play"—games are simultaneously unreal and real—the virtual and the physical become forces for the mobilization of self, which can take actions without consequences, killings without agency. I saw this especially evident in the one task that I had the most (modernist) reluctance to take on—the role of a terrorist. My sons (and numerous others online), however, had no such problem—the taking on and off of discursive masks may just be an element of gaming's postmodern readiness but also signals a delinking of personal agency from action—from which one can surmise a slippery slope to political apathy and a complete submission to the pleasure of play.

The Act-On Narrative

Atkins (2003) provides an entry point:

> It should always be remembered that however much the computer game might be "more than a game," it is still a fictional form. As a form of mass entertainment, like punk, rock and roll, and the novel before it, the computer game has been seen as offering some sort of threat to society, particularly by providing a space in which otherwise taboo or outlawed behavior is given free range. This is fiction, and should be treated, and subject to rigorous examination, just as other forms of fiction are. Its fictionality does not remove the need for the development of its understanding of how it works. (p. 22)

And the ways the narrative works, I want to suggest is very simply through something analogous to the TV "sound bite"—a category that can be termed "act-on." In television news, a sound bite is a short, segmented narrative that collapses the complexity of any social/political situation into a narrowly constructed set of narrative possibilities. Much like television news reporters, who listen and conduct interviews with an ear out for the "right" sound bite, the game player watches, listens, and acts with just one goal in mind—to maximize his or her life/goal and taking away the life/goal of others—through *narrowly constructed decisions* (pressing a button, choosing a weapon, making a turn, killing or saving people) that require action, or need to be acted on—hence the term "act-on." This narrative calculus is not just about the reification of the self, but fundamentally about using "act-on"—in its multiple realms—shooting, hiding, detonating, rescuing, and the like. Shorn of its multiple contexts of "play scenarios," "levels," and "online play," gaming is a call to "act-on"—that is almost always direct in its *visual consequences* (shots to the body, watching blood splatter on the wall and ground) and *normative valuation* (the taking of lives preferred to the rescuing of lives). In this fundamental reductive sense gaming narratives foreclose any complex understanding of terrorism.

Reality Matters

The final extended point that I want to make is that while gaming offers a vastly more complex mode of use and interactivity, we still in the end have to ask the "so what" question that is asked of all media—does it matter? Does the experience of gaming bring about a more complex, understanding of the roots and contexts of terrorism? In the preceding section I suggested that both journalism and films have been marked in the American context by a move from foreign policy machismo to more complex narratives. Is there a similar trajectory for gaming? In some ways the very strengths of gaming (its open ended, interactivity, etc.—the points made in the bulk of the narrative above) may be its weakness. Discussing gaming's interactivity, McAllister (2004) points out is important but it does not change the structures that the game works within:

> The gaming experience may well change the player, but it does not change the game, and thus cannot be described as truly interactive. Critics note that the "free" choices a player seems to make in any game are circumscribed by choices the designer has already made, and even games that provide alternate endings according to a players decisions can only offer something that has already been written. Aarseth, in fact, goes so far as to say that "interactive fiction is best understood as a fiction: the fiction of interactivity." (p. 51)

Does gaming's virtuality take away from the "real" realms in which terrorism actually operates—in marketplaces, homes, and streets in countries where the "war on terrorism" is being waged? It is worth pointing out that while the rest of the country and the world saw 9/11 as a media event—effectively as voyeurs—the citizens of New York saw it in real, bloody terms. A similar experience is currently happening in the various fronts of the war on terrorism—where suicide bombings, kidnappings,

torture, and killing of innocents are the facts of daily life for those who
"live" through terrorism rather than watching or performing it "live."
It is worth considering whether games about terrorism remove that sense
of connection to the actuality of global terrorism. Wark (2007) offers a
trenchant critique of how such "simulations" might affect social and political order:

> Once games required an actual place to play them, whether on the chess-
> board or the tennis court. Even wars had battle*fields*. Now global positioning
> satellites grid the whole earth and put all of space and time into play. War-
> fare, they say now looks like a video game. Well don't kid yourself. War is a
> video game—for the military entertainment complex. To them it doesn't mat-
> ter what happens on the ground. The ground, the old fashioned battlefield—
> is just a necessary externality to the game. Even the soldier whose inadequate
> armor failed him, shot dead in an alley by a sniper, has his death, like his life,
> managed by a computer in a blip of logistics. (Wark, 2007, p. 10)

Wark, thus, locates gaming within a wider conceptual grid where "the
digital emerges as military, but achieves acceptance as entertainment . . .
the military versions of digital telesthesia makes the world over as a military space . . . the coming together of the digital and the entertainment
commodity inscribes the digital not just in space and time but in cultural
perceptions of space and time" (Wark, 2007, p. 95).

In the above auto-ethnographically informed reading of *Counter-Strike*, I
have outlined some of the discursive elements in the construct of gaming,
suggesting important ways in which gaming needs to be engaged with
that are substantially different from the world of terrorism on television
and gaming. The question(s) left unaddressed are that of *discursive range*—
what are the other ways in which gaming intersects with terrorism—and
discursive agency—what are the ways in which these games resonate with
the ongoing war on terrorism. In the (next) concluding section, I will
broadly address these issues by presenting an overview of other games
that deal with terrorism, and provide a brief assessment of their import.
Such a survey will of necessity be incomplete but should provide a template for future studies of the links between gaming and terrorism.

CONCLUSIONS AND DIRECTIONS:
A CRITICAL SURVEY OF GAMES ON TERRORISM

Since violence is a key (and perhaps defining) element in most video
games—and violence against institutional interests (states, armies, civi-

lizations, cultures) a recurring leitmotif, it begs the question, How is it possible to limit issues of "terrorism" in gaming? For the purpose at hand, I use the products own definition of the game. Hence games like *Halo* are not included. The following games were chosen for their direct referencing of terrorism. In the first section, games originating in United States like *Deus-Ex*, Tom Clancy games (*GhostRecon, Splinter Cell, Rainbow Six*), *America's Army*, and *Kuma/War* are discussed and in the second section, games originating in the Middle East like *Special Forces* and *Under Ash* are discussed. In each case I will sketch the key elements of each game (drawing on websites of the shows), offer a brief critical engagement with the game and then a collective consideration at the end of each of the two sections.

American Games

Deus Ex

Deus Ex is an award winning first person shooter/role-playing game, acclaimed as "best game of all time" in a poll by the gaming magazine *PC Zone*. Set in a dystopian world during the 2050s, the plot focuses on JC Denton, a rookie agent for the UNATCO (United Nations Anti-Terrorist Coalition) as he sets out to combat terrorism in a world that is slipping into chaos. Later versions of *Deus Ex* included *Deus Ex: Invisible War* and *Deus X 3. Deus X* features twenty-four weapons ranging from crowbars, electroshock, weapons, and riot baton to laser guided antitank rockets and assault weapons. Game play is focused on role-playing, which includes stealth, sniping, front assault, dialogue, or engineering/computer hacking. The main character is a nanotech augmented (i.e., his human basis can be modified with nontechnology so that he can perform superhuman feats). Cybernetic devices can be used by players to augment different body parts in different skills—these choices affect game play and plot of the player. Nonplayer interaction is an important element of the game, since meetings and interaction with persons in the game help construct JC's performance in the game. The term "JC" it is suggested may stand for "Jesus Christ" with the assumption that JC is a descendent of Christ, or has a distant family connection. A combination of choices made by the player—relating to skills, role playing, augmentations, interactions affect how objectives within the game are achieved, leading to levels of freedom and performance of the player as JC goes about focusing on the central narrative function of the game—saving the world from the chaos of terrorism. The back-story revolves around the effects of a lethal pandemic known as "grey death" the effects of which can be nullified through a vaccine called Ambrosia, which is in short supply. The terrorists—especially the NSF (national secessionist force) of the United States and Silhouette, a French group—try to steal, fight for the vaccine against the UNATCO which is headquartered in New York City in a bunker under Liberty Island, placed there after a terrorist strike on the Statue of Liberty.[3]

Deus Ex can be easily critiqued as another "shoot 'em up" focusing on violence but as the thumbnail sketch above indicates, there is much more going on. There are also numerous subplots focusing on JC's family, the insider politics of the NSF and the UNATCO and mediation on class relations between those who have ambrosia and the underprivileged who do not. It is an environment in short that speaks to contemporary concerns around the effects of global capitalism and global terrorism. Reading *Deus Ex* as a text around terrorism also appears unproblematic—it is a text anchored in relatively unproblematized ideas about national identity, using the construct of "liberty" as a centering rubric for structuring the world around the untied states as the center of gravity, and a global order that it is holding in place. The echo of such discourses with the ongoing war on terrorism, the ethnocentric nationalism of the Bush presidency, its sense of global entitlement and positioning lend a reading of *Deus Ex* as unproblematically hegemonic. A similar reading can be centered on the name "JC" centering a Judeo-Christian vocabulary for the presentation of identity in an apocalyptic future. While acknowledging the overdetermined nature of these constructs, I would suggest some caution in assuming such an unproblematically critical position—*Deus Ex* is fundamentally a postmodern text, with multiple intertextual connections to both the world of fiction and film. The game features a text-reading system, which allows the player to read terminals and notes, which includes excerpts from newspapers, books, and novels. These comments from works like *The Man Who Was Thursday* by G. K. Chesterton, Sun Tzu's *The Art of War*, Shakespeare's *Richard III*, with the influences of other writers like William Gibson, Asimov, Neal Stephson work as a kind of reflexive bookend to the consequences of action—lending a kind of personal positioning that most critiques of gaming do not address, something that can be summed up in an aphorism—"pause and decide." As a commentary on real-life terrorism also *Deus Ex* incorporates the missing twin towers by including it in the storyline of the game where terrorists had destroyed the twin towers earlier in the game. The game also lends itself to modding, which includes not just the usual features of changing the graphics and levels of difficulty but completely altering the storyline of the game—in sum, providing a process of alterity to the discourse of terrorism. Finally, as a global text, *Deus Ex* provides both historical embedding, through fictional organizations like the Hong Kong triads who JC encounters through his travels—in each case, a combination of both cultural knowledge and tactical engagement mediates these interactions.

Tom Clancy Games

The American author Tom Clancy's video game company, *Red Storm Entertainment*, has established a market for games that draw narrative sustenance from his novels and include three popular series—*Ghost Recon*, *Splinter Cell*, and *Rainbow Six*. *Ghost Recon* is a series of military tactical shooter video games where the player is in charge of a fictive squad of the U.S. Army's Special Forces, referred to as "the ghosts." Their mission changes in the different versions of the game. In the original, the ghosts deal with ultra-nationalists in Russia, who want to rebuild the old Soviet Union, with support from rebel factions in Georgia and the Baltic states. In *Desert Siege*, they intervene in the resurgence of the conflict between Eritrea and Ethiopia. A rogue Ethiopian army general undertakes an illegal arms trade with the Russian ultra-nationalists (of the original game) and tries to reclaim Eritrea. In *Island Thunder*, Cuba is about to break free of communist rule, with its first free elections. Different factions in the body politic are using violence to change the equation and it is up to the ghosts to both monitor and make sure that they are not seen as controlling the election process. In *Jungle Storm*, a drug cartel in Bogotá, Colombia, has aided and financed one of the political factions in Cuba and are now initiating terrorist's attacks against the Colombia government who are allies of the United States. The ghosts are sent in to restore order and take out the cartel. Finally, in *Ghost Recon 2*, North Korea in the middle of a famine accord with Russia and blames China for the famine, put- usands of lives, a possible nuclear war, and the deaths of e ghost's mission is to cripple the North Korean threat and ders.[4]

creators of the game calls it "a tribute to military profes- where" (www.ghostrecon.com/introduction) but there is tical work going on through the game, which has an active chat rooms, and an international community of users (with s for French and German users on the product's website). e interconnected issues that are emergent from the game's hey relate to the logic of terrorism, all counterintuitive to an unproblematic critique of gaming, One, there is a *differentiated* use of force (and its legitimation) around *a range* of sites (Russia, Korea, Ethiopia) allowing for a discursive range outside the limits of television news's coverage of terrorism, focused around the Middle East and the traditional ambit of "coups and assassinations." Two, there is an interplay between the process of realpolitik and the use of military force that reveals the duplicity of geopolitics, an issue found only on the margins of traditional journalistic discourse, which remains reliant on the voices of institutional authority, that speak at the level of geopolitics rather than realpolitik. Here too, gaming provides an intervention of sorts, showing "their legs," revealing what happens behind the curtain. Third, the connections between these games also reveals a process of understanding globalization that is outside the range of traditional journalistic accounts—involving drug use, money laundering, arms supply, investments in the official infrastructure of politics by those in the criminal/terrorist underground. This narrative focus is found in the occasional documentary (that is brave enough to take on these subjects) but appears to be a central element in games like *Recon*.

Tom Clancy's two other series, *Splinter Cell* and *Rainbow Six* complement the thematics of *ReCon* but also extend it in some interesting ways. *Rainbow Six* (a tactical first-person shooter game) revolves around a fictional character, John Clark, who is director of the counterterrorism unit *Rainbow Six*. It defined the tactical shooter genre forcing players to focus more time and effort on stealth, teamwork, and tactics rather than on firepower. It also broke new ground in having "local" versions of the game, especially its *Mission Korea*, which had South Korean operatives rather than American ones. *Splinter Cell*, also based on a novel (written under the pseudonym David Michaels), has as its chief protagonist Sam Fisher, a highly trained Black-Ops antiterrorist organization. To reduce redundancy, I will focus on *Splinter Cell*. Well known for Fisher's trifocal lenses (distance, thermal, and night vision), the game has versions with two-on-two multiplayer modes and cooperative modes involving teams. The storylines in the games vary with different versions (and will not be detailed here) but include planned attacks by terrorists using weapons of mass destruction, cyber war and insurgency.[5]

Two elements that deepen the narrative of *Splinter Cell* are those of identity (the main character is a double agent) and interactivity (the multiple player mode has a range of skills, problem solving, dilemmas, and expectations) that frame the playing of the game. Both are relevant for examining the mobilization of terrorism as a discourse through gaming— the development of multiple role playing is significant for obvious reasons—a movement away from the discourse of the individual male subject affecting change (a leitmotif of most mainstream films and television that focus on terrorism, including Jack Bauer in the show *24*) and equally in the decentering of the white European subject that speaks as much to the necessities of regional marketing as to developments in narrative form. The use of a double agent is perhaps the more innovative of the two developments, engaging as it does a topic almost absent in mainstream American cinema and television—the perspective of the terrorist. Here, the game goes into dilemmas like having to assassinate a person you are supposed to defend in order to get access to the terrorist inner circle—a dilemma that results in a version of the game (*Splinter Cell: Conviction*) where Fisher is a wanted man becoming a terrorist.

In all these games (*ReCon, Rainbow Six, Splinter Cell*) it is possible to find ways, opportunities for a range of action and motivation that are polysemic, open to discursive possibilities around issues of terrorism. Having said that, I want to reiterate the inherent limitations of these narratives— they are as the genre suggests "shooter" engagements that must in the end fulfill the objectives of the game—to shoot. They are also fundamentally masculinist, eschewing any rendering of ambiguity about identity. It is a narrative grounded in an account of the state—where the nation-*state* (with an emphasis on the work of the state rather than the nation) emerges, continually as the center of the stated objective (no pun intended)—the preservation of certain national order—one overwhelmingly white, masculine, and majoritarian. It is also easy to read too much into its localization in different regional markets (the Korean in this case)—what is being mobilized is a set of narratives where the action is reenacted (by a different set of majoritarian national subjects) rather than a restocking of the narrative question around terrorism in each location. In sum, if terrorism can be said to be disappearing (in the moment of its appearance), what appears in its wake (or along with) is a kind of nationalism—not necessarily violent, but branded with the kind of equanimity of the rational modern subject—making the taking of lives a balance of opportunities and risk—a process common to the working of capitalism as well.

Kuma/War *and* America's Army

Two highly successful games that work through the logic of nationalism in their representation of terrorism are *Kuma/War* and *America's Army*. *Counter-Strike* was instrumental as a model for the development of both games (especially *America's Army*) as was Tom Clancy's *Rainbow Six* series. Both are tied in terms of funding, narrative, and intent to the U.S. Army, the Department of Defense, the U.S. Navy, and the Pentagon. I shall outline *Kuma/War* followed by *America's Army*.

Kuma/War is a free tactical first and third person shooter game developed in an episode format that recreates real-world conflicts using information from news accounts, military experts, Department of Defense accounts, and original research. First released in 2004, episodes include a playable mission, extensive background text, and often include interviews with military experts, soldiers, and actual soldiers involved in the real events described. Most episodes are drawn from the war in Iraq but *Kuma* has also recreated events in Afghanistan, Iran, South Korea, Sierra Leone, and Mexico. Many of its battles are just days or weeks old. The first mission in the game was called "Uday and Qusay's Last Stand" and depicts the battle in which the two sons of Saddam Hussein were killed. In 2006, *Kuma/War 2* was released with the first episode recreating the killing of Abu Musab al-Zarqawi. Each episode is introduced by television footage and a cable news-style anchor. It places a great importance on accuracy in military strategy and realism including satellite photos and a multimedia library (Turse, 2003, p. 1; kumawar.com; kumagames .com; en.wikepedia.org/wiki/Kuma_War).

Kuma/War is conceptually interesting for at least three reasons. One, it extends the terms of the information/entertainment debate. Taking apart the construct of news as a stable discourse about the real (or "information") and entertainment as the "fictional," the game begins with a different starting point: Pure "infotainment." It presents the real as fiction, a narrative strategy adopted in literary journalism and creative nonfiction in the world of print but with an important difference—it invokes the personal through participation—by placing the narrative within the hands of the "reader" rather than through the act of verisimilitude. The key ingredients that make this possible are the games reliance on the discourse of the rational and the real—the use of anchors, experts, and soldiers to encourage authority and the use of maps, photos, and data to locate authenticity. There is something taking place here that is more than just the merging of the genres of news and gaming—there is an act of imagination, that marries the citizen to the solider, the journalist to the citizen, and then a collapse of all three categories—soldier, citizen, journalist, creating a mode of voyeurship/participation where the track of the real is crossed over again and again, reliving the pleasure of ethnographic immersion, without leaving the comfort of your gaming station.

Two, it presents a vocabulary for identity politics centered on nationalism. This is self-evident but needs to be emphasized. In an age of hypernationalism in the United States (fascism in the eyes of some critics), the use of technologies in the manufacturing of specific identity forms is relevant—and in the case of *Kuma/War* it is unproblematically gendered—the cast of characters in the game are overwhelmingly male (and armed) constructing an image of national character and content that is militaristic, armed, and willed to action. While *Kuma/War* is not a tool for recruitment for the U.S. Army, it does something as important—it puts into play a mode of citizenship that is focused on a regressive nationalism that is oriented toward a unproblematic rendering of identity politics and reflexively engaged through its rendition of the real and its centering of the white, male subject.

America's Army is a team based on an online tactical shooter game with the player depicted as a solider in the U.S. Army—used actively as a recruitment tool through free distribution of CDs and online. Owned by the U.S. government, and first made available in 2002, it is the first computer game to make recruitment an explicit goal. Leading American players to the army recruitment website has been a goal of the game and approximately 30 percent of players click through the recruitment site from the game site. No data is available for its direct influence in recruitment but its success as a game in itself is clear. It has nearly nine million registered accounts and ranks among the top ten first person shooter games played online. It has been described a training and combat video game, praised for its realism (especially weapons, scenarios, and team work) and for its use of high-end graphical and artistic elements. Created with the help of the gaming industry, including Epic Games and the THX division of Lucas Films, it is heavily focused on the technology of war, especially the use of weapons and military hardware (Turse, 2003; Galloway, 2004; www .americasarmy.com; en.wikipedia.org/wiki/America's_Army).

Negotiating *America's Army* presents an unproblematic set of connections—a direct referencing of militarism as an ideology of nationalism; an active orientation to the promise of American expansionism and the creation of a community of gamers/soldiers that can "move" (be recruited) from one mode of activity to another. Like *Kuma/War* it presumes similar modes of identity politics and nationalist storytelling but the centering of the state/military apparatus forces a different set of questions about nationalism, as it engages with terrorism. There are at least two overarching questions—both dealing with "effect" that may be asked.

One, is the question of participation—*America's Army* is centrally focused on the use and mobilization of technology—a key ingredient in the "show and awe" military campaign of the real war. American soldiers in Iraq also play war games on their downtime, once again raising questions about the very (postmodern) orientation of participation in the Iraq war. Naturally questions of emotional trauma, cross-cultural negotiation and the unpredictability of war are not part of how this simulation of the war is constructed. If violence is decentered in video war, it returns in the gaming war, but again decentered by its rendition as a force of technology rather than human intent. Galloway (2004) argues that "what is interesting about *America's Army* is not the debate over whether it is thinly veiled propaganda or a legitimate recruitment tool, for it is unabashedly and decisively both, but rather that the central conceit of the game is one of mimetic realism."

Two, what are the implications of such a game for issues of public culture and political process? Turse (2003) examines the collaboration between the gaming industry and the U.S. Army and offers an indictment:

> With no public outcry over the militarization of popular culture, the future of such collaboration seems assured. Can the day be far off when the Department of Defense gets a producer credit for a Paramount film and Reality games is granted office space in the Pentagon? Before that happens, we need to start analyzing the effects of blurring the lines between war and entertainment. With

more and more toys that double as combat teaching tools, we are subjecting youth to new and power forms of propaganda. This is less a matter of simple military indoctrination than near immersion in a virtual world of war where armed conflict is not the last, but the first, and indeed only resort. The new military-entertainment complex's games may help to produce great battlefield decision makers but they strike from the debate the most crucial decisions young people can in regard to the morality of war—choosing whether to fight or not to fight and for what cause. (pp. 2–3)

I want to end with a brief discussion about all the American games and their import for the "war on terrorism." Several critical works (Kumar 2004; Zhan Li, 2001; Nieborg, 2004; Graaf and Nieborg, 2003) offer some insights (and directions for future research).

Graaf and Nieborg (2003) draw on the concept of "the military entertainment complex" to suggest that "realism" is reworked to fit into the narrative expectations of war—with the use of real time and place visual effects, training on weapons, learning maps, understanding strategies, and a complete immersion in the vocabulary of war so that what results is something akin to submersing the individual (and individual judgment) into what they call "community branding" and "aesthetic totalitarianism." This may result in understanding the war on terrorism in terms of gaming (rather than the other way) with the war seen as a ludological construct, where action needs to be taken within a rule-based system, with its clearly articulated set of practices, expectations, and motives (Nieborg, 2004).

Games, when seen as part of the military entertainment complex, serve a number of functions—"being a recruiting tool, a propgame, a edugame and a test bed and tool for the Army" (Nieborg, 2004, p. 3). In other words, the "reality" of terrorism is lost in the maze of entertainment functions that games about terrorism provide—they are simultaneously propaganda, education, training, and recruitment as gamers come to understand terrorism from a specific vantage point—that of the military. Paradoxically, while such games prepare gamers for a specific political reading of the war on terrorism, it may simultaneously distance him (since most gamers are male) from the reality of the war itself. Zhan Li (2004) spent hours on *America's Army* missions online, talking to players, as the second Gulf War began and found that "there was little discussion of the outbreak of the war. It was more common for the players to express a reluctance or even annoyance about the idea of discussing the unfolding events in the Gulf. The players who were active in the missions were there for escapism and entertainment. For most, the idea of discussing real war seemed to threaten their sense of carefree pleasure and represented the encroachment of the serious into the liminal space of gameplay" (p. 5).

Finally, Kumar (2004) addresses the role of videogames in making possible the war on terrorism in direct, referential terms. He suggests that "war is made possible within a field of representation and video games, as products as well as producers of representation, are implicated in the construction of that possibility" (pp. 1–2). He argues that video games "contribute to making war imaginable by elevating it to common sense. This is not to say that video games are the only generators of a discourse of war or even that there is a temporal dimension that can be traced in terms of cause and effect (the discourse being treated as an event prior to the effect). Rather war and security are intertextual. They are materialized through the interplay of signifiers that populate the political imaginary. Video games along with other forms of popular culture can be implicated in the production of war and security precisely because these concepts cannot be understood outside of discourse" (2004, p. 2).

Middle East Games

How do concerns of terrorism play out in games produced in the Middle East? While there is a history of the study of Arab representations in traditional media, little work has been done in the context of gaming. A project on "Digital Islam" by Vit Sisler maps some of the ground that is needed to be covered. Sisler (2006) suggests that "game representations of Arabs and Muslims do not circulate in a vacuum, but are tied into a wider matrix of media constructions. He suggests that there are four key themes—most followers of Islam are seen as a threat; Islam is most likely linked with terrorism; The representation of ordinary Muslims is marginalized and a conflictual framework dominates" (p. 2). Similar constructions exist in games like *Delta Force, War in the Gulf, Splinter Cell, America's Army, Desert Storm, Full Spectrum, Back to Baghdad, Conflict: Global Terror, Battle in Sadr City,* and *Kuma/War.* Two episodes of *Kuma/War* can be mentioned specifically, *Spring Break Fallujah,* which was released immediately after the battle over Fallujah—a battle that saw heavy civilian deaths, and is often seen as the turning point for the radicalization of many parts of the Iraqi population Another episode of *Kuma/War* deal with real events, one called *Assault on Iran* dealt with a future scenario and reinforced ideas about fundamentalism and terrorism (Sisler, 2006, p. 4).

While gaming is different from other media in that it allows role playing of different groups, there are discursive limits:

Generally speaking, the player controls American or coalition forces against terrorists, while insurgents or enemy regime's units are controlled by the computer. The enemy is depicted by a set of schematized attributes, which often refer to Arabs or Muslims, head cover, loose clothes, dark skin color. In many cases the in-game narrative thereafter links these signifiers to international terrorism and/or Islamist extremism. (In America's Army) the concern has been raised that the Arab and Afghani enemies are predominant and the American soldiers are only of Caucasian or African-American origin. (Sisler, 2006, p. 5)

The response in the Middle East has been to produce games that construct an American and Israeli "Other." Two examples of this trend are the games *Under Ash/Under Seige* (produced by a Syrian company) and *Special Forces* (produced by the Central Internet Bureau of the Lebanese Hezbollah movement). The game *Under Ash* (and its sequel *Under Seige*) both focus on the Palestinian territories. It allows the player to play the role of a young Palestinian facing Israeli occupation during the first *Intifada*. The story line is focused on Ahmad caught up in a demonstration, throwing stones at Israeli soldiers who shoot, maiming the protestors. The task of the player is to get out of the demonstration alive and to the get to the Al-Aqsa Mosque. The player has to help wounded friends and fight off attacking soldiers. The story line progresses with him joining the *Intifada* against the Israelis. The game shows real events, demolitions of Palestinian houses, and conditions of Israeli jails. The website outlines the rationale for the game: "The Palestinian nation is disposed: their homes are being torn down, the land is taken, trees fallen, property confiscated, cities besieged. They are put into jail, tortured, killed. The world ignores them; no one hears their cries. No one cares for their rights" (Sisler, 2006, p. 26). The game does not include suicide missions and if you kill a civilian the game ends. In *Under Seige*, the player is Ahmed again and is set during Ramadan 1994 when Baruch Goldstein shot twenty-nine praying Muslims in the Mosque of Abraham in Hebron. The player has to survive the first minutes of the shooting hidden between pillars and try to disarm him. Later missions involve sabotaging the Israeli army, pursuits, and the kidnapping on an Israeli general. Crucial (to both games) is the construction and genesis of the main hero, Ahmad, who is narrativized as a fearful person who refuses violence but is exposed to an attack and is forced to defend himself. The game attempts to be real—if Ahmad gets shot, he dies. There is no miracle cure and there is also no ultimate victory against the Israeli. According to one of the producers of the game "it is about history. So in our modern history there is no solution for the conflicts and the game is some kind of a mirror" (Sisler, 2006, pp. 25–27).

The rationale for *Special Forces*, its website outlines is to address "the problem behind electronic games, especially designed for computers, is that most of them are foreign made, especially American. Therefore they bear enormous false understandings and habituate teenagers to violence, hatred, and grudges. In addition, some enfold humiliation to many of our Islamic and Arab countries, where battles are running in these Arab countries; the dead are Arab soldiers, whereas the hero who kills them is—the player himself—an American" (cited in Sisler, 2006, p. 4). While the English is poorly formulated the underlying rationale is clear—the game is explicitly located within a larger discursive strategy—to oppose the restrictive coding that American games focused on terrorism construct. The website goes on to focus on the game's role in the power struggles of the Middle East, suggesting that it is part of the "struggling decision to fight the usurping Zionists" (Sisler, 2006, p. 5). The actual text of the game is focused on Lebanon and Israel. It outlines the goals of the game as follows: "Lebanon was invaded by Israel in 1978 and 1982 and was forced to withdraw in 2000. We decided to produce a game that will be educational for our future generations and for all freedom lovers of this world of ours. In the game you will find pictures of all the martyrs that died during their struggle to liberate their land so that our children may live in freedom" (Sisler, 2006, p. 5).

The title of the game *Special Forces* is interesting as well—it may or may not be accidental that it parallels *America's Army: Special Forces* released the same year. The game itself involves similar rhetorical devices— training, missions, and operations:

> Players train at a Lebanese war college, firing guns and lobbing grenades at images of former prime minister Ariel Sharon and other Israeli politicians and are awarded medals by real-life Hezbollah Secretary, Hassan Nassrallah. When battling Israeli forces in Southern Lebanon, players can honor photos of actual "martyrs" at spots of their real-life deaths. Israeli soldiers shout, "You killed me," in Hebrew before they die. The game has detailed renditions of military posts attacked and events. A March 23 Reuters item reported that Hezbollah promoted *Special Forces* with advertisements on Lebanese television. One Internet café operator promoted its release by decorating his business with plastic rifles and sand bags because "guys like that stuff" (a tactic not too far removed from the guns-n-camo militaristic displays decorating American game boutiques around the same time). "The goal is to create an alternative to similar western games where Arabs and Muslims are portrayed as terrorists," Hezbollah spokesman Bilal as-Zein told the reporter, while an eight-year-old interviewee said he liked *Special Forces* "because it kills Israelis . . . I can be a resistance fighter, even though in real life I don't want to do that." (Halter, 2006, p. 40)

The game *Special Forces*, then can be seen as part of a discursive strategy that is part of what can be termed the "double reflection"—each side mirroring the cultural and ideological biases of the other—where the logic of terrorism is created by a set of (mass mediated) binaries (us/them; Israeli/Arab; American/Arab; Christian/Muslim; Muslim/Jew) working on each side of the divide—working, I would suggest in the *same space* of discursive/ideological formation.

One of the few studies that have tried to examine the "double reflection" question (American, Middle Eastern) is Machin and Sulemain's (2006) paper on Arab and American computer games. They conduct a comparative analysis of the discursive constructs of the American game *Delta Force* and Arab game *Special Forces* and find that in the American game, the "forces are linguistically functionalized, understood in terms of what they do, but visually categorized, both biologically, through their body type, and culturally, as a mixture of collective identity (uniforms). In the Arab game, on the other hand, they are classified in terms of what they believe, through Islamic references, and visually through connotations that express their reliance on the will to fight, rather than on technology" (p. 13).

What are the implications for the war on terrorism as games in America and the Middle East work through the specificities of their national and cultural prisms? Stahl's (2006) important essay, "Have You Played the War on Terror?" offers a theorization (while focused on American games) that can be applied to both sides. He sees a graduate erosion of the categories of "citizen" and "soldier" morphing into what he calls "virtual citizen-soldier." He also introduces the idea of "gametime," referring to a discourse of action over reflection and historical understanding. I want to end with two (extended) quotations from his essay that explore the implications of these ideas:

> The virtual citizen-soldier is produced by the changing configurations of electronic media, social institutions and world events. The new figure is distinct from the citizen in important ways. The very efficacy of the citizen in participatory democracy resides in a critical space that allows for public deliberation about important political matters. . . . the figure of the virtual-citizen-soldier forecloses this critical space (and) represents a depoliticization of the public sphere. (p. 125)
>
> Game time overcomes the temporal space of ethical reflection . . . the hegemony of game time collapses the temporal space between real-world events and the ability to play them fostering a news environment that approaches real-time interactivity . . . Embedded reporters in the field (at the start of the second Gulf War) went to lengths to prove they were in the now. A decade of earlier scholars such as George Gerbner referred to the manufacture of "instant history" by way of televised media spectacles in Operation Desert Storm. The interactive mode of 2003's Operation Iraqi Freedom (with countdown clocks on the 24 hour networks), in contrast, was less about manufacturing history as annihilating it. In this way, the sedative of the spectacle is transformed into the stimulant of gametime. (p. 119)

The last word on gaming and terrorism must necessarily be this: evolution. Gaming is in its narrative infancy, and the jury is very much out as to its efficacy as a storytelling form that allows for a complex, understanding of global terrorism. It remains chained to a limited set of "correspondences" (Galloway, 2006) that are focused on inflicting violence. While the graphical and visual language of gaming changes at a rapid rate—and this is very much part of the gaming's appeal—where players like my sons constantly evaluate how "real" or "cool" are the game's graphics, the same cannot be said of the growth of storylines. Even *Halo*, which is often seen as the best of the current story driven games, compares poorly with any film or television show when assessed around plot, character, agency, and emotion. Once gaming begins to incorporate the emotive and cognitive elements common in older media, it may indeed have the discursive agency, that its hold on the marketplace currently assumes.

NOTES

1. Two key texts that I have relied on are Ken McAllister's *Game Work: Language, Power and Computer Game Culture* (2004) and Alexander Galloway's *Gaming: Essays on Algorithmic Culture* (2006). Both these texts related directly to the subject matter at hand—understanding the narrative, textual experience of gaming and were eclectic in their theoretical underpinnings—drawing on the literature of critical and cultural studies, textual analysis and language studies. I especially admired their ability at *imagining* how gaming studies needs to be theorized on its own terms, rather than merely the application of older textual methods to the study of gaming.

My reading of the gaming literature—while partial and incomplete—suggests three broad categories of scholarship: overviews of the field, textual studies, and play and media use studies.

Overviews. Carr, Buckingham, Burn, and Schott's edited book, *Computer Games: Text, Narrative and Play* (2006), is easily the most accessible introduction to the field of gaming studies. The first half of the book examines how gaming reworks issues of narrative and genre while the second half examines issues of play and use. Less accessible, but more nuanced is Wolf and Perron's edited book, *The Video Game Theory reader* (2003), which has essays on a range of concepts (embodiment, role playing, abstraction, simulation) that can be usefully applied to topical areas (such as the one attempted in this chapter). The most intriguing book I read was Wark's *Gamer Theory* (2007), which has an stream-of-consciousness style, that offers meditations around emotion (with chapters on agony, allegory, boredom), subject (America, battle), and text (each chapter is based on a specific video game—*Sims, Cave, Rez,* etc.). Finally, Myers's *The Nature of Computer Games: Play as Semiosis* (2003), while largely focused on the nature of play in gaming, has an accessible theorization (pp. 1–57) of gaming as continuous with older forms of symbolic and narrative communication.

Textual Studies. In addition to McAllister (2004) and Galloway (2006), Atkins's book, *More Than a Game: The Computer Game as Fictional Form* (2003) frames gaming narratives through issues of modernist/postmodernist notions of "real" and "fiction" before going on to provide a template for the analysis of gaming narratives through "readings" of *Tomb Raider, Half-Life, Close Combat,* and *SimCity.* Jesper Juul's *Half-Real: Video Games between Real Rules and Fictional Worlds* (2005), while not exclusively focused on narrative, provides a theoretical framework for what constitutes games. Using concepts of storytelling, chance, simulations, role playing, play, and fiction, he outlines what he calls "rules" of games. Extensively illustrated with images of games and representational devices, the book is in a sense, game-like in its narrative organization—something quite unique in the literature I read. Rounding off the book's on the subject is Andrew Darley's *Visual Digital Culture: Surface Play and Spectacle in New Media Genres* (2000), which addresses a topic that most of the other literature addresses only tangentially—the links between gaming narratives and the older media. He theorizes gaming as continuous (and different) with cinema, media spectacles, and television offering a sophisticated rendering of how issues of effects, style, simulation, and experience are reworked in the space of digital culture.

The online journal *Game Studies* is an important forum for students/scholars of gaming. The journal goals are to develop a theoretical/methodological model for the field of gaming studies, rather than just seeing gaming as an extension or modification of other media forms. Three essays in the journal (Ryan, 2001; Simons, 2007; Consalvo, 2006) are explicitly focused on issues of gaming texts and narrative. Ryan provides a detailed theorization of gaming as narrative developing a formula that looks at the intersection between what she calls "internal-external interactivity" and "exploratory/ontological" modes of use. Simons provides (through a discussion of characters, players, representation, simulation, role playing, etc.) how an account of gaming as a narrative can be constructed while Consalvo provides a "methodological toolkit" for studying gaming, which includes the key issues of defining gaming objects, interfaces, maps, interactions, worlds.

Industry journals such as *Games for Windows* and *Computer Gaming World* provide an ongoing conversation about storytelling and narrative around the latest game. A recent issue of *Games for Windows* had a telling set of interviews with leading writers in the gaming business. Entitled "Why Do Video Game Stories Suck?" it addressed issues of what function narrative provides in a game, the links between graphics, writing and playability, and most interestingly the relationship between game designers and writers (vol. 3, February 2007, pp. 26–29). Commentaries on the content of different games appear occasionally on websites like Slate.Com, Salon.Com, ZNet.com, and in the mainstream media.

Play and Media Use Studies. Since playing is central to gaming as a media form, it appears as a central, even constitutive element in all the literature on gaming I looked at. Two essays in the journal *Game Studies* (Walther, 2003; Squire, 2002) stand out for their theoretical overview of the subject. Walther (2003) methodically outlines the differences between "playing" and "gaming" suggesting that there are historical similarities between games and gaming but also differences. He suggests that "moving from playing to gaming is all about transgressing boundaries and assuming demarcations" (2003, p. 4) and outlines (with the use of graphs) differences between the different "orders" of complexity and transgression in playing and gaming. Squire (2002) outlines pedagogy for understanding and teaching gaming. Play appears as a key element in how game playing can be taught as a social practice and what he terms "activity theory."

The bulk of the literature on play focuses on the implications of online lives (since most games can be played in a multiplayer mode in an online setting). Two books that provide a theoretical vision of the meaning of such lives are Consalvo (2007) and Castronova (2005). Consalvo studies "cheating" as a sociological category, suggesting a method for understanding ethics and identity in an online setting while Castronova provides an accessible first person narrative of what it is like to enter and live in what he calls "the synthetic world" showing both the limits of such constructions and the possibilities of an identity that emerges from such an immersion. Kelly (2004) provides an overview of the social dynamics of online gaming in one MMORPG (massively multiplayer online role-playing games) while Kolo and Baur (2004) examine another game (*Ultima Online*) and suggest a threefold category for understanding online play (tenacious, moderate, and heavy playing).

Finally, two edited books were especially noteworthy but did not fit the above categories: Selfe and Hawisher's *Gaming Lives in the Twenty-first Century* (2007) and Garrelts's *Digital GamePlay* (2005). The former examines issues of gaming and literacy, a key issue for teachers and students of gaming and the latter, a broad range of case studies of games examining issues of identity politics, violence, digital aesthetics and form.

2. See www.ivirtualforums.com/real-life-counter-strike-parodies-videos and wn .wikipedia.org/wiki/Counter_Strike.

3. See deusex3.com, deusexgaming.com, and en.wikipedia.org/wiki/Deus_Ex.

4. See www.ghostrecon.com and en.wikipedia.org/wiki/Ghost_Recon.

5. See www.rainbowsixgame.com, www.splintercell.com, en.wikipedia.org/ wiki/splinter_cell, and en.wikipedia.org/wiki/Rainbow_Six.

REFERENCES

Atkins, B. (2003). *More than a game: Computer games as fictional form*. Manchester, UK: Manchester University Press.

Carr, D., Buckingham, D., Burn, A., & Schott G. (2006). *Computer games: Text, narrative and play*. Cambridge, MA: Polity Press.

Castell, S., Taylor, N., & Jenson, J. (2005). Pimps, players and foes: Playing Diablo II outside the box. In N. Garrelts (Ed.), *Digitial gameplay* (pp. 130–145). London: McFarland and Company.

Castronova, E. (2005). *Synthetic worlds: The business and culture of on-line games*. Chicago: University of Chicago Press.

Consalvo, M. (2006). Game analysis: Developing a methodological toolkit for the qualitative study of games. *Game Studies, 6*(1), 1–17.

Consalvo, M. (2007). *Cheating: Gaining advantage in videogames*. Cambridge, MA: MIT Press.

Counter-Strike. (1999). Sierra Entertainment.

Darley, A. (2000). *Visual digital culture: Surface play and spectacle in new media genres*. London: Routledge.

Filiciak, M. (2003). Hyperidentities: Postmodern identity patterns in MMORPG's. In M. Wolf & B. Perron (Eds.), *The video game theory reader* (pp. 87–102). London: Routledge.

Galloway, A. (2006). *Gaming: Essays on algorithmic culture*. Minneapolis: University of Minnesota Press.

Garrelts, N. (2005). *Digitial gameplay: Essays on the nexus of game and gamer*. London: McFarland and Company.

Graaf, S., & Nieborg, D. (2003). Together we brand: America's army. In M. Copier & J. Raessens (Eds.), *Level up: Digital games research conference* (pp. 324–328). Utrecht, Holland: Universiteit Utrecht.

Halter, E. (2006). Islamogaming: Looking for videogames in the Muslim world. *Gaming World, 277*. Retrieved September 7, 2007, from www.1up.com/features/35332.

Hand, R. (2005). Theatres of interactivity: Video games in the drama studio. In N. Garrelts, (Ed.), *Digitial gameplay* (pp. 208–220). London: McFarland and Company.

Jenkins, H. (2006). *Convergence culture: Where old and new media collide*. New York: New York University Press.

Juul, J. (2005). *Half-real: Video games between real rules and fictional worlds*. Cambridge, MA: MIT Press.

Kelly, R. (2004). *Massively multiplayer online role playing games*. London: McFarland and Company.

Kolo, C., & Baur, T. (2004). Living a virtual life: Social dynamics of online gaming. *Game Studies, 4*(1), 1–31.

Kumar, A. (2004). America's Army and the production of war. YCISS Working Paper Number 27, Department of Political Science, York University.

Li, Zhan. (2003). The potential of America's Army the video game as civilian-military-political public sphere. Master's thesis, Comparative Media Studies, MIT.

Matthews, N. (2007). The mod effect. Paper presented at *Culture Club Symposium*, April 24, 2007.

McAllister, K. (2004). *Game work: Language, power and computer game culture*. Tuscaloosa: University of Alabama Press.

McMahan, A. (2003). Immersion, engagement, and presence: A method for analyzing 3-D video games. In M. Wolf & B. Perron (Eds.), *The video game theory reader*. New York: New York University Press.

Murdock, G. (2004). Terrorism. In H. Newcomb (Ed.), *Encyclopedia of television*. New York: Fitzroy Dearborn.

Myers, D. (2003). *The nature of computer games: Play as semiosis*. New York: Peter Lang.

Neiborg, D. (2004). America's Army: More than a game? Munich: SAGSAGA. CD-ROM.

Ryan, M. (2001). Beyond myth and metaphor: The case of narrative in digital media. *Game Studies, 1*(1), 1–17.

Selfe, C., & Hawisher, G. (2007). *Gaming lives in the twenty-first century: Literate connections*. Basingstoke, UK: McMillan.

Shinkle, E. (2005). Corporealis ergo sum: Affective response in digital games. In N. Garrelts (Ed.), *Digitial Gameplay* (pp. 1–20). London: McFarland and Company.

Simons, J. (2007). Narrative, games, theory. *Game Studies*, 7(1), 1–21.

Sisler, V. (2006). Representation and self-representation: Arabs and Muslims in digital games. In M. Santorineos & N. Dimitriadi (Eds.), *Gaming realities: A challenge for digital culture* (pp. 85–92). Athens, GA: Fournos.

Squire, K. (2002). Cultural framing of computer/video games. *Game Studies*, 2(2), 1–16.

Stahl, R. (2006). Have you played the war on terror? *Critical Studies in Media Communication*, 23(2), 112–130.

Thussu, D. (2006). *International communication: Continuity and change*. London: Hodder Arnold.

Turse, N. (2003). The pentagon invades your Xbox. Retrieved on September 7, 2007, from www.Dissidentvoices.org/articles/turse_pentagon-video-games.html.

Walther, B. (2003). Playing and gaming: Reflections and classifications. *Game Studies*, 3(1), 1–12.

Wark, M. (2007). *Gamer theory*. Cambridge, MA: Harvard University Press.

Whitlock, K. (2005). Beyond linear narrative. In N. Garrelts (Ed.), *Digitial gameplay* (pp. 189–207). London: McFarland and Company.

Wolf, M., & Perron, B. (2003). *The video game theory reader*. London: Routledge.

4

Tracking the "Authentic": World Music and the Global Postmodern

Music treated as culture is essentially music treated as meaning.

—Andy Nercassian

World music is not simply a matter of the circulation of capital and culture. It is that, certainly, but as scholars we cannot afford to stop at the question of appropriation and hybridity—we need to develop new theoretical paradigms.

—Anahid Kassabian

I learned about the label "World Music" much after I had been moved by its sound. It began with Cesaria Evora. I had a small grant to get course materials for my international communication class and since I wanted to introduce some international music to my students, I perused the "Global Music" section at a local store ("No Bollywood songs," I told myself—I did not want to be trapped playing native in class) and picked up a CD by a singer I had never heard of—Cesaria Evora. The name itself was appealing. If you say her last name—Evora—enough times, it take a syncopathic rhythm all its own. Like a chant, "Evora" becomes an evocation. Beyond the name, the woman on the cover spoke in an unusual emotional register—she was large and brown. A complete lack of artificiality seemed to surround her. She leaned laughing against a piano, a cigarette cradled between fingers, her eyes looking at the camera but seemingly at a point beyond it—willing you it seemed to see what she was looking at. It was a point somewhere that you felt was not in the future but in the past, a sense of remembrance but also a sense of loss—and a willfulness of the spirit that you knew would resonate in song and music. I bought the CD and with it an introduction to a singer that I have come to identity as the voice of the global postmodern. The *sound* of Cesaria Evora defines the cultural work she is undertaking—a work that does not need the weight of language and autobiography to sustain it—it is this sound that spoke to me and still speaks to me (I am playing an album by her as I write this). Numerous critics have honed in on the sound of Cesaria Evora calling it "drippingly sensuous with a hint of melancholy" (Bobey, 2001, p. 66), "delicate swing" (Plougastel, 2004, p. 1), "hope and suffering (Graham, 2003, p. 1). Trebay (1996) writing in *The Village Voice* said, "few voices in contemporary music are as liquid as Evora's, fewer still less cynical and more spare" (p. 41). These are all part of the equation, but there is something else that is significant about her voice that these accolades do not address—and the best way I can describe it is by recounting/recalling the aesthetics of first *listening* to her—before I proceed, in subsequent sections—to bring the language of analysis to understand the sonic imprint of musicians like Evora who are filed under the label "World Music."

The opening song from that first album I bought is called *Flor Di Nha* (The Dream of My Hopes), which has a lilting long opening on strings, guitars, and an instrument that I cannot for the life of me identify—it has the roundness of a guitar but also the harsh clarity of a *santoor* but without any of the latter's diminutive elegance. This instrument has a louder, more redemptive presence. The opening chords play on for an interminable duration—it is almost as if the singer is an afterthought, the measured, unhurried start finding a space in the listener's imagination. When Evora sings, there is smoothness to the delivery, a definitive sense of control, a nuanced rendition of the message, whatever it might be. I don't know the language—I am familiar with the sounds of many languages but not this one—it has a series of soft flats at the ends of each sentence, a slurred start at the beginnings. The sound of this language is pleasurable, like the rolling in of the ocean on a sandy beach. The second song is called "Vaquinha Mansa" (Little Cow) and the instruments are the same except for the strings, where the pace picks up as compared to the first song, but never shows any indication of being in a hurry. Evora's voice plays suitor to the instruments, rather than dominating them—the punctuation between each verse and the music speaks to a quiet certainty—a sense of speaking from a certain place. Now I realize, that part of what I like about what I am hearing is the pleasure of being in the presence of a grounded person—a person who embodies *authenticity*.

The third song is called "Amor di Mundo" (Love of the World) and there is a new element added in—a flute section, playing with the guitar and the unknown instrument. The pace is much like the first song—the short excursion (in the second song) into a semblance of exertion seems to have spent itself. Evora's voice stitches together a mood—marked certainly by languid expectation—but even more by profound ambivalence. Reflexively considered, this first exposure to Evora, is clearly about one thing: Her voice is the voice of liminality, of transition, of uncertainty. It is also something else—it is a common sound—the sound that one expects to hear in second-rate bars, by second-rate singers. A part of me when hearing her sing for the first time, gets ready to turn it off, shrugging it off as just another "lounge" singer, but I keep listening. And listening. And listening—until I am hooked and the organized engagement with celebrity that is fandom takes over.

In this chapter, I engage with the complex set of sonic connections that goes by the label "World Music." The next section on "Framing World Music/the Global Postmodern/Authenticity" outlines some key elements in how World Music can be theoretically framed—as a specific kind of text, anchored in conditions of global postmodernity and characterized by a defining discourse—that of "authenticity." This is followed by a biographical/textual accounting of four major World Music stars—Cesaria Evora, Ibrahim Ferrer, Ali Farka Toure, and Nusrat Fateh Ali Khan—with a focus on examining how their biographical/textual imprint illustrates the different ways in which the discourse of "authenticity" is mobilized in World Music/the global postmodern. Finally, the concluding section on "Conclusions and Directions" addresses conceptual issues not discussed in the bulk of the essay.

FRAMING THE GLOBAL POSTMODERN, WORLD MUSIC,[1] AND AUTHENTICITY

Aubert (2007) offers a beginning point for understanding music as something central to meaning making in a culture, rather than mere "fluff"—light entertainment for the illiterate and the bored: "If music has its own place in all reflections on culture, it does so by the stakes it represents. Music is indeed never insignificant. It is simultaneously a strong and unifying means of communication and a revealer of identity within the abundance of models that characterize society. We identify ourselves with music we like because it corresponds to our sensibility and vision of the world; we draw apart from other music when it is our foreign to our affinities and fails to 'speak' to us. Through its content music is always a bearer of meanings" (Aubert, 2007, p. 1).

He adds that "if Plato could write that 'the music and literature of a country cannot be altered without major political and social changes' that is because the music he was referring to was at the same time the echo and model of something other than itself" (Aubert, 2007, p. 1). What is that something else that music refers to? I would like to suggest that the "something else" that one kind of music—World Music—refers to is a sociological condition that goes by the name of "global postmodernity."

The Global Postmodern

There are two primary ways in which World Music reflects the idea of the global postmodern—the first is the idea of music as a *structuration of global space* into the constitutive elements that go by terms such as local, national, regional, local, and so forth. World music, like all music "does not then simply provide a marker in prestructured social space, but the means by which this space can be transformed . . . music is socially meaningful not entirely but largely because it provides means by which people recognize identities and places, and the boundaries which separate them" (Stokes, 1994, pp. 4–5). Secondly, World Music acts as a *marker of identity* in the global structuration of space. Identity and its imbrication in power relations is a defining element of postmodernism—and is usually referred to by putting the two ideas together in the term "identity politics" (where one's identity is more a product of social circumstance than individual will). Music, like other media forms, is a key element in how identity politics is mobilized in a culture. Discussing identity politics and gender, Stokes (1994) suggests that music is a key element in how boundaries which separate male and female are naturalized: "It is as natural that men will make better trumpeters than women as it is natural that women make better harpists. Musical performance is often the principal means by which appropriate gender behavior is taught and socialized" (p. 22).

Combing the two elements (global structuration of space and identity politics), Erlmann (1996) suggests, "World Music is a new aesthetic form of the global imagination, an emergent way of capturing the present historical moment and the total reconfiguration of space and cultural identity characterizing societies around the globe" (p. 468). Taking up Erlmann's (1996) proposal that "an aesthetic theory of music in the global age . . . should examine the ways in which world music constructs the experience of global communication . . . through symbolic means" (p. 481) and Jensen's (2002) idea of music criticism "as a form of cultural and social criticism . . . where talking and thinking about music, is a way of talking and thinking about [global] modernity" (p. 195), I would like to offer the following (working) definition of global postmodernism as a guiding principle in the discussion of global music to follow:

Simply put, *global postmodernism is the discursive centering—and movement—of identity politics on a global scale.* This centering/movement/ force can be *observed* across a range of institutional practices, forms and resistances (of which mass media is one—albeit critical—institutional site and global music one set of media practices); *interrogated* at different points in social/spatial organization (for example, local, regional, national, and transnational); made *manifest* around common forms of identity mobilization (race, class, gender, nation, sexuality, ethnicity, religion, and language) and *articulated* through a relatively stable set of mass-mediated binaries such as traditional/modern, authentic/mass-marketed, exotic/familiar, non-Western/Western, tribal/urban, folk/cosmopolitan.

Drawn with such broad strokes, the global postmodern can be used as an analytical category to examine a range of media forms and practices (not just World Music). It is outside the scope of this essay to fully develop the theoretical implications of this definition (across all its constitutive elements) or even its full application on World Music. Rather, the goals here are very limited—to provide *a descriptive account* of "authenticity" which I will suggest is the defining discourse of World Music. I will map out how "authenticity" is mobilized across these different performers in four *specific* contexts—those of gender, age, ethnicity, and religion.

World Music

What is "World Music?" Some like Bohlman (2002) argue that there is "ample justification to call just about anything World Music" (p. xi). Minimally, it can be argued that World Music is a category generated in the industrialized music markets of the developed world. In the introduction to *World Music: The Rough Guide* the editors outline that "the name was dreamed up in 1987 by the heads of a number of small London-based record labels who found their releases from African, Latin Americans and other international stars were not finding rack space because record stores had no obvious place to put them. And so the World Music tag was hit upon, initially as a month-long marketing campaign to impress on the music shops, the critics and the buyers that there were sounds worth listening to. The name stuck, however, and was swiftly adopted at record stores and festivals, in magazines and books, on both sides of the Atlantic" (p. i).

There are some key issues that emerge for international musicians when working under the label "World Music." Their music must be seen as "exotic, different, fresh . . . and (they are) categorized by their ethnicity rather than music" (Taylor, 1977, p. 17). Discursively, too it can be argued that the music reiterates "old sensibilities about Others and their cultures. Several common strands emerge: rejuvenation, novelty, authenticity, originality, the 'real' and the spiritual" (Taylor, 1977, p. 19).

Authenticity

Taylor (1977) suggests that "authenticity" in World Music usually refers to two things: a "cultural-ethnographic accuracy" (where the music speaks from a specific cultural/local/national space) and his or her identity

politics—what he calls the singer's "positionality" as a racialized, ethni-
cized, subaltern, and premodern subject. Both these elements are combined with a psychosocial vision of personal performance where "sincerity or fidelity to a true self" and "credibility, sincerity, and a commitment
to one's art are fused" (p. 21).

He goes on to add that such a model of authenticity is shot through with
issues of unequal discursive power and intent: "These authenticities have at
bottom an assumption about an essentialized, real, actual essence. The West,
while it views its citizens as occupying many different subject positions, allows 'natives' only one, and its whatever the West wants at any particular
moment. So constructions of natives by music fans at the metropoles constantly demand that these natives be premodern, untainted, and thus musically the same as they ever were" (p. 21) Listeners of World Music, he concludes "consume some discernable connection to the timeless, the ancient,
the primal, the pure, the chthonic; that is what they want to buy; since their
own world is open, seen as ephemeral, new, artificial, and corrupt" (p. 26).

Is the authenticity in World Music then merely a market tactic, a product of finding shelf space in Western music stores? In this chapter, I suggest that an understanding of authenticity in World Music must engage
with the specific narrative trajectories that individual artists bring into
play as they deploy ideas about the authentic—even as they intersect with
the needs of western audiences. My goals are primarily descriptive—to
track the authentic as a *beginning* point in a theory of World Music focused
on issues of subalternity rather than appropriation or cultural hybridity
(the focus of much of World Music research).

My choice of artists was driven by several reasons. They are famous
World Music artists—in other words important texts, illustrative of a
wider problematic about global postmodernism. On a personal note, they
are also artists that I am partial to and have a ready familiarity with. They
are all examples of how issues of identity politics and social/spatial structuration are reworked through the prism of World Music. But most centrally, I examine these artists because they allow through their life/work
a close reading of how the discourse of "authenticity" is mobilized in a
range of contexts—those of gender, age, ethnicity and religion. I will suggest that in each case these concerns are played out through the realms of
performance, representation, and reception.

FOUR TRAJECTORIES[2] OF THE "AUTHENTIC" IN WORLD MUSIC AND THE GLOBAL POSTMODERN

Cesaria Evora: Locality, Gender, and Authenticity

Cesaria Evora is from the island of Cape Verde, a former Portuguese
colony, off the coast of Senegal, a place that has lived at the crossroads of

history. During the slave trade between the fourteenth and sixteenth century, it was a stopping point for the transport of thousands of African slaves to the Americas and Europe. Portugal was an indifferent, abusive ruler—allowing the deaths of thousands as the Islands suffered from a series of famines and droughts. Life in the islands was always difficult and hardscrabble—and its citizens left in droves—to diasporic communities in Europe, South America, and the United States. The Cape Verdean experience is often summarized as that of "Sodade." As the liner notes from a Putumayo album on Cape Verde puts it

> Isolated from the rest of the world, from their compatriots overseas, and even isolated by stretches of sea from their own countrymen on other islands, Cape Verdeans have developed a sense of pensive longing that permeates their cultural expressions. There is even a word that has come to describe this emotional state, one that has been immortalized in literature and song and has come to define the Cape Verdean character: *Sodade* (so-DAHJ). A sentiment of nostalgia, yearning and missing of home and beloved, *Sodade* describes a bittersweet feeling that has no direct English translation.

It is this history that speaks through the songs of Cesaria Evora songs—she sings in *kriolu*, a creole that blends old style Portuguese with West African languages. The instrument that defines much of her music—and that I could not identify—is the *cavaquinho*. "The *cavaquinho* is very much like a ukulele, with four strings, steel or gut, that are tuned like the top four strings of a guitar" (Broughton et al., 1999, p. 276). She sings a soulful genre, called the *morna* often compared to the blues but seen as quintessentially local—coming from the specificity of the Cape Verdean experience—an experience it seems mirrored in the personal story of Evora herself.

Cesaria Evora was born in 1941, on the Cape Verde island of Sao Vincente. Her father who died when she was seven years old was a *cavaquinho* player. One of five children, she was raised by her mother in abject poverty. Cesaria's early career was spent singing for her dinner—and fighting off depression. Occasional appearances on Radio Mindelo and in the numerous bars that dotted the port city of Mindelo allowed her to become well known in the neighboring islands as well. Never without her cigarettes, she sang *mornas* for aid workers, lawyers, traders, adventurers, chicken merchants, civil servants, until eventually she was recorded by a local retail businessman who sent the tape to Portugal to be made into a single. Soon after a local producer made another record—both records were complete failures. In 1975, Cape Verde became independent after a long struggle and the country, devastated by repeated droughts and no economic trade sank into a depression—a condition reflected in Evora's life as well. She withdrew from singing for ten years, profoundly depressed and an alcoholic. Local accounts spoke of her wandering naked and wild through the streets of Mindelo in the grip of a "fetico" (evil spell). At the start of the 1980s, an old friend found a place for her on a delegation of Cape Verdean singers for a tour of Lisbon. Singing in a restaurant, she met Jose da Silva who was to become her mentor and producer. He suggested a recording in Paris with leading Cape Verdean musicians—it was now 1987 and Cesaria Evora was forty-seven years old. Her first album, *La diva aux pieds nus* (The Barefoot Diva) met with limited success. A performance in Paris was reported on by the *Le Monde* paper that said, "Cesaria Evora, a lively fifty year old, sings morna with mischievous devotion . . . [she] belongs to the world nobility of bar singers." In 1992, a new album, *Miss Perfumado* was released and went on to sell more than 300,000 copies and was nominated for a Grammy in 1999 (after its American release). In 1997, she won the prestigious South African Kora Music award. In 2004, she won a Grammy for her album, *Voz d'Amor*. She has continued to perform and record ever since, with her tenth album, *Rogomar* (Prayer for the Sea) being released in 2007 (Graham, 2003; Coetzer, 1997; NPR, 2007; Plougastel, 2004).

I want to suggest that the sonic construct (music, songs, presence) of Evora draws on a specific discourse of authenticity—*one located in a gendered account of African locality* (the Cape Verdean experience)—across national and diasporic socio-spatial contexts. This account of locality provides the key to her appeal, her "authenticity" as a World Musician. There are a number of intertwined elements.

First, the circumstances of Evora's life and career mirror a wider problematic about global postmodernism and celebrity. Few singers and artists in the non-Western world are successful outside of a specific local cultural/regional space. The workings of global capital they may surmise are capricious, arbitrary, and implausible—any kind of success is seen not as an entitlement but something both wondrous and implausible. As Joao Mendes, a Cape Verdean musician puts it "we were always outside the current. Just about every Cape Verdean we know is working in a factory, and we're doing this music" (Wald, 2007, p. 50).

Evora presents in life and song, a reflexive engagement with the trajectory of her own life. The "sound" of her music and her presence in performance which critics observe is often detached and somber—an understanding of her circumstance, as not something given but a case of happenstance. While a reflexive engagement with career is a common element in western celebrity discourse—often through close attention to the presentation of self in public forums (reflected iconically in the red carpet procession at award ceremonies)—what is different in the case of Evora is that it takes center stage in her sonic construct, assumes a *postcolonial value* if you will, signaling a part of the world, where hunger can often mean death (rather than food stamps), where rootlessness is a given, life itself is not.

Second, Evora's "text" speaks in concrete ways about the personal and sociological experience of being Cape Verdean (and African), a nation where most of its population has left for émigré communities in Europe and the United States. It is a national culture that is in a real sense, completely diasporic, where its relationship to "Africa" is lived *primarily in the imagination*, fueled by both a sense of acute loss and profound belonging. Her best known songs reflect this concern directly. I will discuss two of them—*Besame Mucho* and *Sodade*.

Besame Mucho speaks to the experience of dislocation and suggests that leaving things behind is as much a fact of global culture as it is of the Cape Verdean/African experience. There is a central value accorded to departure itself and to the substantial personal loss that it entails. What provides contextual and deeply emotive meaning to the song is the performative index of Evora. Watching her performance of *Besame Mucho* on video, what stands out is her mode of address: Her brow is written in perpetual anxiety, there is none of the practiced genuflections (of western artists) to audiences, little or no sense of her own presence on the stage. This is not the carefully calculated neglect of a Bob Dylan or the shy acknowledgment of mastery of Eric Clapton, but the expression of what is undeniably, loss. Leaving, going far from home, being kissed for the last time, are elements of the common place. It is hard not to read into the text of Cesaria Evora's version of the song a lament for the nation, a signature moment of collective dispersal with no return date—the nation in its moment of fragmentation holds no promise of a future—this experience is *common* to the emigration of populations from the third world to the first.

Evora's other signature song is *Sodade*, a famous *morna*. "What the *corrido* is to Mexico or the tango to Argentina, the *morna* is to Cape Verde. This national song form is at least a century and a half old and is part of nearly every Cape Verdean band's repertoire. *Mornas* have minor key melodies and are slow, often with a beat similar to that of a Cuban *habanera*. But their lyrics are at the heart of the matter. The lyrics of a *morna* can stand alone as a poetic form. Lyrics usually speak of love and longing for ones distant *cretcheu* or beloved. The *morna* shares common and mournful roots in the Gulf of Guinea slave plantation islands of Sao Tome and Principle, where a rhythm called *lundum* originated" (Broughton et al., 1999, p. 271).

Watching Evora sing *Sodade* on video is profoundly moving—in the live concert version I watched, the song itself is bookended by long acoustic interludes—where Evora shuffles on the floor, sits smoking in a chair, and seems lost in contemplation of the very mood she is creating. It is a masterful rendition—the pacing, the movement, the punctuated equilibrium between the instruments and the singer are perfectly balanced. *In sum, the discursive experience of alienation is mediated through her presence—which* succeeds in doing the impossible—being simultaneously taciturn and effervescent, alone and commensual, emotional and detached. She represents being in the moment and being disembodied better than any other musician I have seen. She makes the rendition of each line of the song, a thick metaphor for the lived experience of immigration. The song reflects the question asked by most migrants—What drew them away from their homes? A question that segments the many others that drive them all their lives: What did they leave behind? When can they return? What did they gain? What did they lose? She locates the wider question about belonging and migration to the specificities of the Cape Verdean/African experience with its references to the Island of Sao Nicolau. The song also provides a vision/experience of personal/national agency—represented in the idea of writing and forgetting—that most migrants feel. There is a dislocation, a coming apart of the old, and a sense of both arrival and departure that those leaving and those being left behind enter into. The possibility of becoming something else (or) somebody else. Here the desire to connect depends on what point in the journey you are in—where relationships (may) continue with the act of renewal (writing) but the other event is much more likely—"if you forget me, I'll forget you." For many modern migrants this experience is revisited throughout their lives—from the moment of departure, to periodic return, to death, at home or abroad. It is an experience that is constantly relieved—through the rendition of music, literature, festivals, and the texts of mediated experience (e.g., YouTube videos). In sum, *Sodade* speaks to the complex set of emotions that make up the immigrant experience, a key recurring element of global post modernity.

Three, Cesario Evora can be assessed as an element of the expression of African locality by her own self-definition as a musician. This refers primarily to her resistance to moving outside the musical ambit of Cape Verdean music. Her album *Voz D'Amor* (Voice of Love) has songs like *Isolada*, a *morna* that Plougastel says "conveys all of the despondency in the world, the sorrows of caresses cut short and love lost, but also a great affection for an arid, rough country that forces many of its children into exile" (2004, p. 1). The song *Jardim Prometido* (promised garden) transforms a song about youth and rural life into "an anthem full of hope for the future of a rainless country that will be forever verdant in the hearts of its people" (Plougastel, 2004, p. 1). The song *Monte Cara* speaks of the mountain overlooking the port of Mindalo. Perhaps the most famous song from this album is *Velocidade*, a song written for Cesaria by a legendary Cape Verdean musician Luis Morais before his death in 2002. A simple song, it "is a striking portrait of one of the pretty young girls to be admired on the terraces of Mindelo's café" (Plougastel, 2004, p. 2). Similarly, *Miss Perfumado*, the album considered her most important work, is a rendition of classic Cape Verde *morna* songs including *Sodade, Angola, Lua nha Testemunha*, and, of course, *Miss Perfumado*. Her latest album *Rogamar* (Prayer to the Sea) speaks of the presence of the sea, the love of the sea for the people of Cape Verde, the perils of the sea when crossing between the islands.

In speaking from a place, a locality, Evora creates a marketing opportunity for herself, but equally importantly also mediates an understanding of African locality through her music. It needs to be emphasized that this measure of locality is produced relationally, through the active movement of people—of a culture in transition. People who stay in one place do not need to be reminded of locality, they embody it. Evora's music and songs, and her insistence on a tightly constructed narrative of locality (a landscape, a city, a bar, a certain rendition of authenticity of experience) is part of her magic—she constructs a landscape of belonging— and in doing so, she taps into the needs of the world marked by the postmodern condition—a condition defined quintessentially by migration (local, national, and global) and its resultant feelings of alienation, separation, and personal/collective angst.

Finally, Evora represents her locality through a "persona" that reflects her identity as a poor African women and a Cape Verdean. Press reports continually speak of her as "the barefoot diva" pointing to this as both a fact, born out of the experience of growing up poor and barefoot, and of her current decision, to use her barefoot presence, as a sign of support for the poor and disenfranchised women of her homeland. The same themes are emergent in her responses to interviews by Western critics and scholars. The questions they ask are often constructed around the paradigms of celebrity, personality, and promotion. Her responses are almost always about locality, authenticity, and her identity as a Cape Verdean woman. Here are some examples from an interview with Fred Bouchard. When asked, "What singers or other musicians have influenced your style or evolution," She answered, "Nobody really. I am singing the same Cape Verdean songs now that I was when I was 16. I can put some Spanish and Brazilian songs on my records, but that doesn't mean anything, because they are songs I like and understand. People like me best for my Cape Verdean music." Her response is at odds, with the idea of personal development, of innovation, of individualism that firmly anchors corporate cultural expression. In speaking of continuity of performance, unchanged since sixteen, and presumably of a tradition much earlier, she constructs a presence that amplifies the need for tradition, a center, in a fractured world. When she effaces the Spanish and Brazilian influences in her songs, with "but that doesn't mean anything," it signals a clear intent to not problematize, to not deconstruct a narrative but to state—simply—that "they are songs I like and understand," suggesting a sense of her own agency ("People like me best for my Cape Verdean music").

One exchange is particularly telling for the purpose at hand here—locality/authenticity/gender (and is being reproduced below in its entirety):

Q: Has fame and money affected you?

A: When I was singing in Cape Verde, I had no resources. Now, my career is bigger and I have more money. But that is all: My life is the same; I see the same people and sing the same songs. I think my singing hasn't changed.

Q: Do you live inside your songs, inhabit them?

A: You can say that I sing about myself and about others too. These things can happen to anyone. I am not singing about things that happen to me, but you might say they happened to you. I sing about love, immigration, and politics. It's a mix of day-to-day things. Its simple as that, nothing complicated.

Q: What do you want to do next in your career?

A: When this tour ends, I'll go home to São Vicente and take rest for eight months. And then we'll see.

Q: What do you do at home?

A: I open my house to my friends and neighbors and visitors from abroad. I garden and I cook. You can come and visit if you like.

(Interview with Bouchard, 2000, pp. 52–54).

Her response to the first question (about fame) is predicated around the key rubrics of performance and lived experience—in each case, she does not reach out to a rhetoric of excellence or effect but of personal intimacy and local culture, especially around interaction and relationships, More crucially, she does not see her performativity to have changed and developed along new lines that often accompany ideas about impact that are central in the Western star's relationship to celebrity. This is at the heart of her authenticity, a sense of unchanged tradition, her feet (barefoot) grounded in the dirt. Her response to the second question (about artist reflexivity) is astonishingly revealing. The question assumes a certain kind of response—about the process of creation, a finely developed sense of reflection and creation that most serious artists love to talk about, how they might as the question asks, "inhabit" the song. Instead, what Evora gives is a response grounded in a postcolonial taciturnity—a direct and unproblematic assertion of the facts of life, which are about "love, immigration, and politics." This is not merely a statement about the global postmodern condition—one marked by movement (of money, people, and ideas) but of the loss of agency as a woman (and the centering of the personal as political) and always, of an understanding (through moments of arrival and departure as also of loss and gain) of emotion, as a guiding principle in the life of individuals and communities. These facts of life, she asserts are "day to day things" simple and uncomplicated. This too is at the heart of her presence as a signifier of authenticity. Her response to the third question (future plans) like the first one about fame is not what you expect from a celebrity within corporate media environments, who would use such a question to talk about their future projects, ("plug them so to speak") with a treatment of the themes they will address, or the personal space they will explore. Rather, Evora says she will rest up for eight months and then decide. In response to the last question, Evora tells us she meets friends, gardens and cooks, and opens her house to visitors— here too, the need for personal isolation that is a prequisite for celebrity life is missing, in favor of the authentic, grounded in the performance of a traditional gender politics—cooking, gardening, meeting friends.

In sum, I would like to suggest that making sense of Evora as a signifier of global postmodernism implies an examination of authenticity through the range of ways in which she mobilizes ideas about African locality. Evora mobilizes through the work of her song/performance, a key element of the global postmodern—a feeling of reaching back, of engaging with a tradition, of seeking texts that speak to this condition—and finding them in performances (like those by Evora) where they become coterminous with the artist—and understood through the kinesthetic appeal of their presence. It needs to be emphasized that this is not an understanding of tradition grounded in sociological rules and rituals (around say food, religion, or clothes) but an *emotion*, a feeling of being in the presence of an elder, somebody grounded in a different time and place, but able to see through the aesthetics of expression to embody a collective loss, that is simultaneously Cape Verdean/African and universal in its address.

Bueno Vista Social Club and Ibrahim Ferrer: Locality, Age, and Authenticity

An important landmark in the development of World Music came with the hugely successful album of Cuban music *Bueno Vista Social Club* and specifically in the identity construct of its most well-known performer, Ibrahim Ferrer. I will turn to a general discussion of this album followed by a detailed discussion of Ferrer and some of the songs in the album,

suggesting that the album articulates issues of authenticity through a mobilization of "old age" as a text of global postmodernity along with deeply
felt nostalgia for a "lost" locality—Cuba before Castro.

The *Buena Vista Social Club* album is an evocative, transformative listening experience—it has the balance, nuance, and verisimilitude of something
simultaneously granular and polished. Much like listening to Cesaria
Evora, you don't have to know the language or know that the songs in this
album are fully realized, the work of a lifetime of immersion in music and
a full complement of the vicissitudes of life, both personal and sociological.
The album was the brainchild of Ry Cooder, the well-known American musician, and Nick Gold, his producer. They were in Cuba working on a different project that fell through. At the last minute they decided to produce
an album of older, traditional Cuban folk music. Musicians long retired and
mostly forgotten were contacted at short notice—some like Ibrahim Ferrer
were literally taken from the street during his daily walk. Ferrer would later
say, "An angel came and picked me up and said, 'Chico, come and do this
record.' I didn't want to do it, because I had given up on music." They managed to put together "a galaxy of some of Havana's most experienced ex-
ponents of *son* (the predominant musical force in traditional Cuban song
and dance and the root of *salsa*) *guajira* (a Spanish-derived, slow, acoustic
form associated with Cuban farmers) and *bolero* (one of the most European
styles of traditional Cuban music)" (Williamson, 1997, p. 83).

The album was recorded in the old RCA victor studio in Havana (built
in the 1940s before the trade embargo/blockade that followed the 1959
revolution). The likes of Nat King Cole and Cab Calloway recorded there.
"It's the best studio I have been in," said Cooder. "Its big, but it's a very
sensitive room" (Williamson, 1997, p. 83). In this sensitive room were as-
sembled eighty-nine-year-old guitarist Compay Segundo, seventy-seven-
year-old pianist Rueben Gonzalez, the fifty-six-year-old Eliades Ochoa,
and, above all, the seventy-three-year-old vocalist Ibrahim Ferrer. The
songs were packaged as the *Buena Vista Social Club*, named for a former
hotel in Havana. The album was a hit, selling several million copies
worldwide, leading to a documentary by the well-known director Wim
Wenders (it was nominated for an Oscar). In the years to come, the album
sparked a revival in Cuban music, and solo discs by most of the major
players (Nickson, 2006; Gonzalez, 2003; Moon, 1999).

What explains the albums success? I will suggest that there are two interrelated elements around authenticity, old age, and locality that worked
to create the impact it made on the World Music scene. These elements
were the cultural/historical construct of all the singers and the iconography of Ibrahim Ferrer.

The cultural/historical construct of the singers: Simply put, the age and
"voice" of the singers on the album became a stand-in for history itself.

Writing in *Jazzis*, Holston (2000) suggested that the sound's segmented history was part of its appeal: "The Buena Vista's elder musicians represent a virtual history of Cuban musical styles. For most, the *son*'s classic Afro-Cuban idiom is the stylistic reference point originating in the orient (eastern) region of Cuba, the *son*'s basic *tres* (Cuban guitar), guitar, and *maracas* traveled to Havana, then gradually took on more of an African flavor with the addition of bongos. Later, the incorporation of bass, cloves, and two trumpets began to point the way to the *salsa*, bongo, and *timba* of today" (Holston, 2000, p. 53).

From an industry perspective, the success of the album lay in the audience that was ready for a new sound. As David Bither, a senior VP at Nonesuch records put it, "these are infectious records, and there has been increasing evidence in the last ten years that there is an audience for music from different parts of the world. There is growing enthusiasm amongst a variety of musical communities for this type of music. The fact that the record has been produced and features Ry Cooder gives American audiences a doorway into this music who might not otherwise be familiar with the great richness of music and some of the remarkable musicians who have been living and working in Cuba for the past half century" (Williamson, 1997, p. 10). On a similar note, Raul Fernandez, who worked on the Smithsonian Institute's Oral History project, suggested that "the Cuban *son* is very powerful. The appeal [of the album] has much to do with the audiences tiring of the heavily electronic, stylistic simple music that's being produced for the global market. [In contrast] Buena Vista synthesizes centuries of history and musical fusion. It's not just an aural peanut-butter and jelly sandwich" (Moon, 1999, p. 29).

Finally, The singers and the album were marketed as evocative of a specific time and place, as was the documentary that followed it. As the website for the music/documentary puts it:

Havana, Cuba, circa 1949: A dance club resplendent with the elegance of the island's nightlife before the Revolution. Sparkling chandeliers, bow-tied waiters, couples dressed to the nines. On stage, a big, brassy band fronted by a slick-haired heart-throb. There is the kind of gaiety in the air that can only brew in the company of young people and everyone here is young. There is drinking and dancing and flirting. The ambience is a curious mix of abandon and formality. When a young man asks a young woman to dance, the gesture is rendered with great respect and formality; the young man gently extends an upturned hand. But on the dance floor, things are considerably looser. The rhythms echoing in the hall play the bodies like marionettes, a ritual unleashing of desire. And yet, for all the seemingly spontaneous force of the music and dancing, there are clearly defined patterns. The bodies pace and twirl to the music's 6/8 rhythm, and even more specifically, to five accented beats within that signature, what is known as the clave, the root of tropical music. There is plenty of room for improvisation among both musicians and dancers, but the limits are known to all. It is exuberant, even "dangerous" music, kind of tropical rock 'n' roll where the sexuality is barely, if at all, contained.

Both the specificities of the historical moment the album was evoking and the singers—became part of the mythology/marketing of the album. Cuba's history—and its complex, troubled relationship with America—was part of the narrative of the album. The question of whether the old musicians still had it became tied to whether Cuba's past (before the 1959 revolution) could be recovered. The liner notes on the album/documentary oriented listeners/viewers to how this moment could be narratively constructed:

> Just about everyone involved in the project remembers the moment that Rubén González showed up at Egrem for an "audition." Nick Gold, Juan de Marcos González and Ry Cooder watched from the control room as the diminutive, plaintive-faced González sat at the piano in the booth. The lights were dimmed. González caressed the keys, executing a tumbao progression. Without prompting, Orlando "Cachaito" López joined in on bass. After several minutes, the lights came up; González took it as a bad sign. "I thought they wanted me to stop playing," he recalled. Just the opposite: everyone in the control booth was keenly aware that the master still had "it." And so it was with the rest of the cast.

This self-reflexive engagement with musical history and history making was a central part of the album's appeal. Once again the liner notes puts this square and center: "If you'd been at the Buena Vista Social Club in Havana, circa 1949, history itself would have danced before your eyes. And it does so once again, through the music and the film. We return to the proscribed Island, a place that was rendered at once mythic and hopelessly superficial through the lens of the Cold War. We also return to a past that was virtually proscribed in Cuba itself."

For critics of the album/documentary, the last statement "a past that was virtually proscribed in Cuba" speaks to the album's placement within a specific political narrative that has dominated American perceptions of Cuba—one of death, or stagnation—in Cuba after the 1959 revolution. As the island became closed to Americans, it also became a site for a relatively stable set of discourses around identity that drew on the Cold War, the Cuban Missile Crisis, and the construct of Castro as a dictator. They pointed out that the music seems to be outside of history—that what happened after 1959 did not matter—"not a word about the blockade of Cuba, not a word about the fact that all the musical and cultural roots together with the old repertoire were jealously kept by the people, not a word about the other kinds of music that, in claiming to draw their inspiration from the old rhythms, use the instruments and means that musical training after the revolution made available to them. "Modernism," a key word amongst young Cubans, is not mentioned at any time in the film, while any member of the younger generation could have explained what they owe musically to the tradition and what they were breaking away from (Roy, 2002, pp. 194–195).

The Icongraphy of Ibrahim Ferrer: The construct of Ibrahim Ferrer as a singer and a media text was central to the phenomena that became the *Buena Vista Social Club*. Part of his importance lay in the narrative trajectory of his life. Ibrahim Ferrer was born on February 20, 1927, when his mother went into labor during a dance in the Cuban village of San Luis. By twelve, Ferrer was an orphan, surviving by selling newspapers and produce on the street. He began his singing career at fourteen and was part of numerous bands and groups including Pancho Alonso, with whom he sang on and off for three decades proving himself a master of the energetic, up-tempo *guarachas* and *sones* but also a sublime bolero singer with an uncommon sense of space and silence (Star plus.com/ music/Ferrer_ibrahim biography). He retired from active singing in 1991, living off a state pension and making money on the side shining shoes and selling lottery tickets. When approached for the album, he refused the invitation, but eventually relented, grumbling that he did not even "have time to take a shower." The rest as they say is history. As Gonzalez puts it,

> of the accompanying tales that contributed to the *Buena Vista Social Club*'s success, the story of Ibrahim Ferrer was a particularly compelling one. Here was a retired, forgotten, never-quite-a-star singer called for a small walk-on part and ending up on eight of the fourteen tracks on Buena Vista, five as a lead vocal, leading to his first album as a leader and international star status. (Gonzalez, 2003)

Ferrer emerged as the star in the documentary shot by Wender who accompanied Cooder back on his next trip to Cuba, followed by the success of his two solo albums *Bueno Vista Presents Ibrahim Ferrer* and *Buenos Hermanos* which featured Cooder, trumpeter Jon Hassell, and the gospel group the Blind Boys of Alabama. Critics suggested that Ferrer's album offered an informal history of classic Cuban singing from lovelorn romantic ballads, to stately, slithering dance numbers built on the *son* rhythm and Cooder in interviews emphasized that "Cuban music is a vocal music. If you don't sing it right, it doesn't happen. Ibrahim is one of the few who understand how to sing it. He possess the great sad top end of the voice that you need" (Moon, 1999, p. 40).

At the heart of Ferrer's appeal was his voice, a strange indefinable entity, both subtle and powerful. As Gonzalez (2003) put it, "Ferrer has a peculiar voice—a light worn out tenor, not particularly rich, powerful or commanding. In spite of it, perhaps precisely because of it, Ferrer still sounds tailor-made to convey loss and heartbreak. And whatever is lacking in his instrument, Ferrer more than makes up with his instincts, knowledge and guile. Cooder sets up compact, unsentimental grooves and Ferrer, as good singers do, phrases as if skating over them, creating tension by laying back then rushing" (p. 71).

The iconic image on the album cover that the listener is centrally oriented to is that of Ferrer, walking on the streets of Havana. This is an image that provides the foundational narrative of the album. It is at the heart, an image about locality. Arrayed on one side of the street are old American cars (the Studebakers) that are a staple of American iconography as it relates to Cuba, a residual of both history and continual estrangement. The cars and Ferrer are arranged on either side of the street and work together to create a segmented construct—a rendition of history, that it turns out is not lost, but is recoverable—and infact has been recovered in the songs and image of Ibrahim Ferrer.

The songs that Ibrahim sings in the documentary extend and segment the iconic image on the album cover. I immersed myself in repeated viewing of the songs/documentary and came up with four recurrent elements: The use of the urban landscape of Santiago; the placement of local people within that landscape; the use of cars as a key referent and finally, the use of the natural environment. Each element had a specific thematic orientation—the urban landscape focused on was the decaying, sepia toned buildings of Old Santiago on which are found faded posters of the revolution—Che Guevara, most noticeably; the people that live in these old buildings are shown as extensions of the buildings—a woman, smoking a large cigar, men huddled around a broken down Studebaker, shopkeepers, children looking quizzically at the camera. The old, colorful Studebakers are a central recurring leitmotif of the documentary—they are stars in their own right—and punctuate the narrative of the entire documentary appearing as both bookends to songs, and as ghosts of the living past. The car's work as segmented metaphors for both history and indigenous experience—they are splashed by the sea as it crashes on the embankment; they grace the covers of albums and photo's that stitch together different parts of the documentary. The cars even appear as part of the natural environment, lying under green, dirty, and drooping trees, crowded under the decaying natural landscape. Ibrahim Ferrer appears as a construct across these visual images, drawing sustenance from them but equally crucially *framing* the landscape. The documentary is not a critique of Cuba but a love letter to a place frozen in time and Ferrer *becomes that moment*. As the *New York Times* wrote in his obituary, "besides offering American audiences a musician's eye view of Cuba, the film set up Mr. Ferrer as a particularly sympathetic figure tall, distinguished, and lively, an excellent bolero singer who used space and silence in his relaxed elegant delivery to increase the drama, a man who had been rolled over by history and was now simply trying to enjoy an absurdly lucky situation."

The songs with their themes of love, redemption, personal life and fate are tied in to the visual metonymies of the documentary. Each song is located within a historical tradition. *De Camin a La Verada*, is in the tradition of a religious hymn; *El Curato de Tula*, an example of a *descarga* (Cuban jam style); and *Dos Gardenias*, a *bolero*. In its lyrics *De Camin a La Verada* represents an interesting collapse of the secular and the religious—working through the expected progression of the vicissitudes of love, through a call for a religious intervention/encounter. *El Curato de Tula*, is wonderfully inventive, evoking both locality and personal wit, coupled with a generous dose of sexual innuendo. Its self-referentiality (with the actions of Ferrer and Eliade as actors within the narrative of the song) become a sign of its authenticity, signaling the listener to both the pleasure of its immediate construction (the improvisation of the lyrics) and to the source of such improvisation—the presence of these old men, and their obvious ineptitude in such matters. As Eliades Ochoa, said in an interview about the album, "there is a saying in my country. The soup from an old hen is better than from a young one. Also rum and urine—better with age. And that's what's happening to our music" (Holston, 2000, p. 54). Finally, the *bolero* needs little introduction. *Dos Gardenias* is a bottomless treasure in the search for the authentic—and Ferrer's rendition of the song is memorable. Ry Cooder suggests that "the *bolero* conveys both the innocence of another time and a true musical sophistication. It doesn't mean anything if you can't sing it for real, with a certain depth and beauty that has to be heard to be believed. Ibrahim is one of those great voices" (Cantor, 1999, p. 12).

I would like to suggest that each of these songs (and the others on the album) work to create, a consistency of discursive intent, around issues of authenticity mediated by a fullness of presence (of both song and the singer, Ferrer) and a sense of pleasure, both as personal expression and as part of a global humanism. This latter expression of the (presumed) unity of creative intent is central to the authenticity that World Music inculcates. As the liner notes for the album/documentary put it, "Through this story, then, we return to the Island, one that we really all inhabit: The island of history, with all its twists and turns, its ironies and cruelties. This is the story of a dozen or so musicians that were trapped by history but who were also ultimately granted a reprieve, very late in their lives, from it." World Music, works through texts like Ferrer to recover history, to reach out to a space of cultural and national authenticity, creating both a market for such music and for a certain narrative about history itself.

In sum, the album lends itself to analysis along the lines of the excavation of a native authenticity, marked through a shrewd rendition of a certain topos—the streetscape of Santiago with its iconic cover—with the textual imprint of Ferrer (as a stand in for history) walking in his trademark golf hat, between the shade and the light, between modernity and tradition, lending both voice and figurative presence to the rebirth of prerevolutionary musical form under the nose of the communist state.

Ali Farka Toure: Locality, (African) Ethnicity, and Authenticity

I want to engage with Ali Farka Toure's life/work as embodying three elements of the discursive imprint of global postmodernism—a nuanced but emphatic assertion of African ethnicity—seen through three intertwined thematic elements—the construction of the "rural"; a subaltern reading of (American) blues music; and finally, music as a negotiation of the religious/spiritual in the text of modernity. Each of these intertwined elements shape ideas about African locality and authenticity that he represents in World Music. First, a brief biography.

Ali Farka Touré was born in 1939, on the banks of the Niger River in northeastern Mali, near Timbuktu. His mother's nine previous children had all died in childhood, and the nickname "Farka," or donkey, was given him as a form of protection, a symbol of endurance. At times he would wryly joke about this, telling one interviewer, "Let me make one thing clear: I'm the donkey that nobody climbs on!" (Duran, 2004). Ali had no formal schooling and his childhood was shaped by life in a small farming community. He grew up entranced by the music played at spirit ceremonies in the villages along the banks of the Niger. He would sit and listen as musicians sang and played the favored instruments of the spirits: *jurukele* (single string guitar), *n'jarka* (single string violin), and *n'goni* (four string lute). His family did not consider music as an honorable occupation and the boy's interest was not encouraged. Ali was a fiercely independent boy and at the age of twelve built his first instrument, a *jurukele* (Duran, 2004). He became known as the "Bluesman of Africa" reflecting a style that combined elements of the American blues tradition and Arab-influenced Malian traditional music. After Mali's independence, he served as director of the Niafounke artistic troupe from 1962 to 1971. With the troupe he performed for the first time in Europe, appearing at a 1968 international festival in Sofiya. He recorded extensively in France during the 1970s and began returning to his roots in the 1980s with a series of collaborative efforts, working with Taj Mahal on *Source* and Ry Cooder on *Talking Timbuktu* (Barz, 2007). He was never to make an album outside Africa again. He released *Niafunké* in 1999 and his collaboration with *kora* player Toumani Diabate, *In the Heart of the Moon*, in 2005 (Duran, 2004). He won two Grammy's during his career, the only African artist to be so honored. He retired from his career as a musician shortly afterwards focusing on farming and eventually becoming the mayor of his town. In 2003, he participated in the documentary *Feel Like Going Home*. Directed by Martin Scorsese, the film traces the history of the blues from the banks of the Niger to the Mississippi Delta, and would bring Ali to an even wider audience. He worked on one final album, *Savane*, but did not live to the see its release. He died on March 7, 2006, succumbing to bone cancer. Ali was accorded a posthumous Commandeur de l'Ordre National du Mali (the country's highest honor) and a state funeral attended by all the country's senior politicians and major music stars as well as thousands of ordinary people (Duran, 2004).

The "Rural"

Ali first and foremost defined himself through the idiom of village and local African culture. This is not to suggest that he did not occupy an important place within the national iconography of Mali (he did as can be attested by both the presence of the politicians at his funeral) and of the African continent more generally (as seen in the moniker—"African bluesman"). Rather, it is the concreteness of his songs and his persistent efforts at self-definition within the regional context of his village and region that stands out. He chose to live in his village, for most of his life, placed farming and taking care of his town people (when he became mayor) above music. He was often quoted as saying, "for some people, Timbuktu is a place at the end of nowhere, but that's not true, I'm from Timbuktu, and I can tell you that it's right in the centre of the world" (news.bbc.co.uk/go/pr/fr/-/2/hi/africa/4782176).

The "rural" that Farka came to represent was the "desert"—where the discursive imprint of the Sahara and West Africa, with its arid landscape dotted by mud mosques, colorfully decked camels, and nomads became fused with his music. Much of this fusion came from his involvement and development of a "festival of the desert" (also known as the Essakane Music Festival) in his hometown of Niafunke. The festival was an old tradition, going back over a century, as a gathering of the nomadic Turaeg for a festival that celebrated their culture and music. Ali Farka Toure was a central figure in the "reimagination" of the modern version of this festival beginning in 2001. In 2003, the festival was filmed by a French documentary maker, Lionel Brouet and included former Led Zeppelin singer Robert Plant, Ali Farka Toure, Tinariwen, Oumou Sangare, and many others. The documentary focused on both the acts and the history and modern reassembling on an old tradition. In the years to come, the festival has become a tourist destination for fans of World Music and Afro-Pop, and is seen as a continuing legacy of Ali Farka Toure.

I want to spend some time discussing the construct of this festival drawing on viewings of songs from the documentary and on online diaries and images of the festival by music journalists. The festival's website (www.festivalinthedesert.org/) outlines the self-reflexive intent—both political and cultural—that the festival attempts to achieve:

> The Essakane Music festival was developed by a Tamashek (Touareg) association whose aim is to develop the region. It hit on the idea of grafting the Festival onto the great traditional gatherings of the Tamashek people on a grand scale. For centuries these gatherings have provided an invaluable opportunity for the nomadic Tamasheks to meet and celebrate with various forms of Tamashek song, dance, poetry, ritual sword fighting, games, and other ancient cultural traditions. The association opened the event to the entire desert region, to the whole of Mali, and eventually to the world. The festival celebrates the 1996 "Flame of Peace," in which 3000 guns were publicly burned to signify the beginning of the reconciliation between the nomadic and sedentary communities of the southern Sahara.

Music journalists and critics who have visited and reported from the concert usually frame the music through the prism of the desert and the local Tureg culture. Sean Barlow who reported on the festival in 2003 for a number of outlets (Afropop.com, NPR, CBC, allAfrica.com visitors, World Link TV) described the experience as follows:

> Just getting to the festival was a three-day adventure. The first legs of the journey covered familiar air space—New York to Paris to the Malian capital Bamako to Timbuktu in the north of the country. But then we drove northwest of ancient Timbuktu in a caravan of "quatre-quatres" (4x4s) across the rolling desert terrain. No road, just a track in the beige sand that suddenly turned into a fine pearl white. We passed groups of blue-turbaned Tuareg men heading to the Festival on their sprightly camels. Those camels! What dandies decked out in their Tuareg leather finery! Every toubab ("white person") amongst us seemed to fall under their spell. We arrived a day early at the Festival in the Desert's magnificent site, spread over gleaming white sand dunes under a cobalt blue sky . . . Camping out with the royalty of Malian music in the Sahara Desert north of Timbuktu under a sky full of blazing stars . . . meeting new artists from Mali, Mauritania, Niger, and beyond . . . without a doubt, the third annual Festival was the most thrilling music festival experience of my life. Over the next four days, I would visit the tents of familiar and emerging artists to film and record their groups performing informal, acoustic sessions and to interview them. Whenever a group started to play for us, local kids would flock to the tent opening and watch intently. (www.afropop.org/multi/feature/ID/193/Festival+in+the+Desert+2003:+Dispatch+1)

Songs from the documentary simultaneously evoke both the rural and the process of cultural revival that the festival undertook. In one remarkable clip, Ali is tightly framed as he introduces the festival by smiling hugely into the camera and saying "the festival was organized for the pleasure of those who had never heard the word, 'festival'—and they are very happy about it." The crowd of listeners squat on the ground, laughing and singing along with Farka and the other musicians—a number of people stand and dance on the stage. There are critical diacritical markers of the local—African clothes, local instruments (calabash, njarka), and dance (a slow, controlled gyration with deft hand movements). One reviewer of the CD (from the documentary) suggests that "Mr. Toure exhibits some serious guitar chops across a wide swath of tempos, rhythms and styles. Most important, his seemingly effortless yet complex guitar playing is employed over beautiful compositions, vocal melodies, percussion, and singing. The first track, *Goye Kur* is a tour de force with ringing, fluid chorused guitar, a bright bold vocal chant and melody, rumbling and precise calabash percussion and a haunting *njarka* line that anchors the whole shabang" (Douglas Watkins, www.amazon.com/Source-Ali-Farka-Touré/dp/B000000628).

It is a performance that evokes specific ideas about the nature of African music, one which is centrally located within an account of locality but reaches out toward a global humanism—a discourse that often accompanies ideas about Africa as "original home of humanity." Agawu's (2003) general analysis about African music is appropriate for what Ali's music came to stand for:

> What is African music? It is communal and inviting, drawing in a range of consumers young and old, skilled and unskilled. It allows for the spontaneous and authentic expression of emotion. It is integrated with social life rather than set apart, natural rather than artificial, and deeply human in its material significance. Its themes are topical and sharp contemporary relevance, sometimes humorous and satirical, sometimes sad and affecting, often profound. (Agawu, 2003, p. xi)

Ali's close ties to the land (the rural) led him to turn down very lucrative offers to perform overseas. He remained uncompromisingly wedded to his traditional music, refusing to "go commercial." He invested in the development and innovation of local languages and showed an understanding that language and politics were deeply intertwined. During the 1990s rebellion by the Tuareg people of northern Mali, he was seen a peacemaker singing in all of the region's languages—*Songhai, Fulani,* and the Tuareg's *Tamashek.* He pioneered and perfected the adaptation of *Sonrai, Peul,* and *Tamascheq* musical singing styles to the guitar. His songs celebrated both universal themes (love, friendship, peace) and those specific to the village where he was born and raised—they spoke of the land, the spirits, and the river. When he was awarded his first Grammy, he refused to come to the United States for the ceremony, saying: "I don't know what a Grammy means but if someone has something for me, they can come and give it to me here in Niafunké, where I was singing when nobody knew me" (Winters, 2006).

African Bluesman

Ali's relationship with American Blues was a source of considerable ambivalence to him. "*The Times* of London, in its obituary noted that he didn't imitate the work of blues and soul giants like John Lee Hooker and Otis Redding, but rather 'claimed to recognize African roots (in those forms) and derived confidence and affirmation of his own art from the fact.' Certainly his international fame, which coincided with a growing Western interest in 'World Music,' led to such comparisons and to the 'bluesman' moniker" (Winters, 2006).

Touré was hailed as the "Malian bluesman," and for a time seemed pleased at the comparison, but as the years passed he found the simplistic labeling an annoyance. "The journalists always ask me the same questions," he would say. "They always want to know about blues. I say, the word 'blues' means nothing to me. I do not know blues, I know the African tradition. The music that you call blues, I can call by its proper name. I can call it *agnani*, I can call it *djaba*. I can call it *amandrai* or *amakari*, the music played on the indigenous guitar, the one-string or the three-string. I can also call it *kakamba*. There are many names for this legendary art. I respect [Hooker] and appreciate his genius as the translator of African music in the United States, but my music is the roots and the trunk, and he is only the branches and the leaves" (Wald, 2007).

Nevertheless, he admired and was inspired by American music, just as American music had been enriched by the music of his homeland. He kept a picture of himself with Jimi Hendrix on display in his home, presumably from his 1960s international tours with a cultural group from Niafunké (Winters, 2006). Toure's music falls into a stream-of-consciousness groove, deftly employing repetition and chanting over a lilting beat. The mournful singing and string bending betrays his collection of American blues and soul cassettes (traces of Otis Redding, Lightnin' Hopkins, John Lee Hooker, and others abound). But the western influences seem but one guidepost, rather than a starting point, for Toure's deeply rooted, spiritual music. Not so much spiritual in the conventional sense, but more in worship of family, heritage, hard work, and struggles on the land (McCord, 2005).

What stands out is not just the terms of the postmodern encounter that Ali negotiates in his rendition of the blues, but his remarkable accuracy in reading it, as a text about subalternity, focused equally on the cultural/

economic ghettoization of the African American experience and on his own mission, as the act of recovery, of an art form and the identity of politics it represents. In this, Ali is perhaps unique, in understanding and assessing the ideological import of the blues, across both sides of the Atlantic. In an interview Ali sits under the shade of tree, harmonizing with a visiting African blues musician. He provides a very personal vision of the work of global music, one marked by the burden of history and (simultaneously) a global humanism:

> Blacks left (for the United States) with their culture, but the biography, the ethnicity, the legends they did lose. Still their music is African. Whether in the United States or in Mali, I think that there are only cities and distances separating us but our souls, our spirits are the same, there is no difference. There is no difference at all. I have never felt it. I feel sorry, why? Because they are people who should be united. The first time I heard John Lee Hooker, I said, I heard his music but I said, I don't understand this music—where did they come up with this? This is something that belongs to us, but its different—because he had to play to make a living. Otherwise this music is not made for whisky, or for scotch, or for beer. When a black American comes to Africa, he should not feel like a foreigner, because he has left his home. It's your territory. It's your navel.

Religion and Spiritualism

Finally, Ali spoke from a very specific religious/spiritual space—a hybrid form of Islam and Animism. In today's atmosphere of the "war on terrorism" and the radicalization of Islam in many parts of the world, Ali's work and life attests to a syncretic African Muslim identity. As a child, he was seen as a "child of the river." This had a very specific powerful connotation:

> In Niafunke, as in most of Mali, the dominant religion was Islam and Ali was a devout Muslim. But in this part of the world Islam coexists with a much older indigenous belief system connected with the mysterious power of the Niger. People believe that under the water there is a whole world of spirits called *Ghimbala*—male and female djinns with their own character and history and symbolic colors and ritual object; all this is vividly portrayed in the local mythology. These djinns control both the spiritual and temporal world. When the harmony of these two worlds go wrong, as it inevitably happens in this harsh, unpredictable climate, when there are unexplained illnesses or sudden natural disasters, then people get together to hold spirit ceremonies, in which music and dance are the central activity. Then thanks to music, spirits may accept the gifts, and if so, it is considered as an auspicious sign. Those who have the ability to communicate with the spirits are called "children of the river." Consequently, Ali's was intensely personal and spiritual, sacred and common at the same time. Though he won a Grammy this year for *In the*

Heart of the Moon, an album of duets with Toumani Diabate, one of the masters of Mali's *griot*, or court music, tradition, he always distanced his own style from that of the griots. Theirs was made for money, he would explain, while his was a way of communicating with the genii or spirits: "It speaks of cows, of greenery, of a man with his animals in the wilderness who hears certain sounds which do not come from the animals, but from nature. It speaks of love and of harmony in the family. All of these tunes have their words, their legend, and their story." In the end, he would turn away from his music when he felt it was getting too commercialized and instead focus on what he thought mattered—the land, the village, the local. When Touré became Niafunke's mayor, children flocked around him, [and] locals looked to him for leadership, advice, employment, and financial support. . . . He committed himself to community and commercial development, and even played shows in France to fund initiatives to develop the town. A reasonably well-off man, he nonetheless spoke of poverty (*pauvreté*) as being the true path to happiness. (adapted from Duran, 2004)

In sum, one may see the life/work of Ali, as imbued with specific notions of African authenticity—his sonic construct tied to a specific identity politics—based on patrimony, religion and a hybrid Islam on one hand, and a humanistic, environmentally centered (almost Gandhian politics) of space on the other. In between these discourses lies his (uneasy) but key alliance with American blues.[3] Understanding his place as a global music text is important precisely because he exemplifies the kinds of ruptures and absences that mark the working of a global postmodernism—a process neither usefully tracked with accounts of cultural homogenization nor of cultural bricolage—rather his work represents an act of strategic imagination and cultural recovery that is often ignored.

Nusrat Fateh Ali Khan: Authenticity, Locality, and Religion

My mother's family is from the city of Ajmer, India, the site of perhaps the most famous of all Sufi tombs (Sufism is a mystical branch of Islam focused on the idea of reaching God through forms of personal enchantment, like music). The tomb of Nizamuddin Auliya is the focus of an annual pilgrimage that brings thousands to Ajmer. As a child, I would go to this annual pilgrimage, called the *Urs Mela*, and spend most of the night with my cousins, listening to *Qawwali*, a devotional music intimately tied to the Sufi faith (its roots are in ancient Turko-Persian poetry sung with male choruses, *tabla*, harmonium, and handclapping). The singing would start around nine at night and continue till about two or three in the morning, when we would stumble out of compound of the *Dargah Sharif* (the tomb), onto the waiting rickshaws that would take us home. I have memories of swaying to the music, transfixed by the beauty and surrender of the singers, the overwhelming smell of roses, the cool night air. Everything it seemed would be forgotten, when a famous *Qawal* (a *Qawwali* singer) and his party came onstage—elbowing a cousin to get a better view, the sheer beauty of the song offsetting the exhaustion and hunger pangs in the middle of the night. The *Qawwali* would always be sung in a large building attached to the tomb—painted green and gold in the holy colors of Islam—nobody was allowed to sing inside the tomb itself—it was too sacred a space for even devotional music to be sung. This was a tradition, hundreds of years old—that was put aside, for a singer, of unparalleled eloquence and profound grace—Nusrat Fateh Ali Khan.

Known as the greatest exponent of the *Qawwali* (he died at the age of forty eight in 1997), Khan had a dream, that he was singing inside the tomb of Nizamuddin Auliya—a dream, that the *Khadims* (keepers) of the tomb made possible, in this one (and only) exception. In doing so, he began a career that was to take him from regional (and religious) prominence to a preeminent place in the World Music firmament—and for the purpose at hand, here to exemplify the development of a language that married the secular to the sacred; the theological to the sociological. Khan's career can be read as an text that imagines a social/political future that was simultaneous grounded in religion and humanism; empathy and devotion—all framed through a reworking of the question of "love" taken from its assumed place in the realm of romance, and placing it firmly in the space of religion. In all of this, Khan represents, an unusual journey in the presentation/development of authenticity. Following a biographical overview, I will focus on a discussion of the role of religion (Sufism) in Khan's performances—which is at the heart of his "authenticity." (Please note that my discussion of Khan will be abbreviated as compared to the other singers, since many of the same themes that inform Evora, Ferrer, and Toure can be applied to Khan, the exception being the centering of religion—which I will focus on.)

Nusrat Fateh Ali Khan was born October 13, 1948, into a family with a 600-year history in *Qawwali*: The art is family-based and hierarchical, and Nusrat was well placed. His father was the eminent singer Ustad Fateh Ali Khan. Intended by his family to be a doctor, Nusrat grew up in Punjab, Pakistan, eavesdropping on his father's singing classes and later studying. His first performance was at his father's funeral in 1964. The singer has said he dreamed of his father placing his hand on his throat, awakening his voice. After this his reputation grew quickly in Pakistan, where he released more than 100 albums and achieved a status as the *ShaheShan*, the king of *Qawwali* singers. In 1985, he performed in England at the Annual World of Art, Music, and Dance Festival organized by Peter Gabriel (Spencer, 1997, p. 29).[4] He died of heart failure August 6, 1997, in London. He was forty-eight. At 350 pounds, Khan had long suffered from health problems related to his weight (Kemp, 1997, p. 20). I want to suggest that Khan was a complex, multilayered figure, his life and work mobilizing two interrelated elements of the "authentic." These elements are those of performativity and Sufism/mysticism—each element making up Khan's place in the working of the global postmodern.

Performivity

I never got to see Khan in concert—something I have always regretted. Understanding Khan as a mobilizer of the "authentic" must necessarily begin with the performative index of his songs and the singer as a "text." *The Boston Globe* described his concerts as "having the energy of a rock 'n'roll show, the loose attitude of a house party and the spiritual power of a religious event all rolled into one" (Wald, 2007, p. 229). His mystique and appeal was centered by the celebratory discourse around his "presence"—this was not unique to Khan, many of the famous *Qawwal's* I had listened to in the *Dargah Sahrif* shared this attribute. There were *Qawal's* who did not hold your attention—and you could trade punches with a cousin—and then there were the stars that stirred something strange, uncomfortable and wondrous inside you—it was quite literally intoxicating. The experience was fundamentally visceral and mystical at the same time. In sum, assessing the Qawal as a symbol of the authentic is inseparable from the singer's performative index (or to put it differently, the messenger is the message). Viewer accounts of Nusrat reveal a mastery of form and performance:

> In performance, Khan, who would sit cross-legged at the center of his backing singers, harmonium players and percussionists, was a prodigious presence, both physically and spiritually. As he sang, he would lift his hands, palms upward, higher with each reach of his voice and curl his fingers into visual representations of the music's snaky twists and turns. His acrobatic voice was at times gruff and edgy; at other times, it soared gracefully over the hypnotic, droning music until it reached undulating, white-hot peaks that transported listeners to another realm. (Kemp, 1997, p. 20)

> To be in the presence of Nusrat Fateh Ali Khan is a mystical experience in itself. A short, heavy man, Khan sits on the stage with his party, made up of his younger brother Farukh, his nephew Rahat and half a dozen cousins. Waiting for the right moment to sing, he stares intently at the floor. His eyes close as he slowly gestures his hand in front of him, as if to say "The song is about to begin. Please join me and listen." As the spirit of the music grows, his excitement grows—ever so slightly. Khan, now swaying his large, majestic torso back and forth, winces while his left hand flails in front of him. The hypnotized audience rests on each syllable of his words. (Carvin, 2007, p.1)

Performativity is an integral part of popular culture—as seen across genre (rock 'n' roll, rap, country music) and in this central sense, Khan's cross over appeal in the West can be assessed along predictable lines—rapport, intimacy, and engagement. But what Khan seems to inspire is in equal part, something that is not usually part of the ambit of performativity in popular culture—a pedagogy derived from a specific liturgical and theological vision, that of Sufi Islam. Here, singing itself is a form of worship, a focus of the authentic that I now turn to Sufism and mysticism.

Sufism and Mysticism

The most famous of Nusrat's *Qawwalis* include those that are directly aligned with a Sufi/mystical framework for understanding religious experience. "*Qawwali* is a religious institution, invented to spread the religion of Islam," said Khan in an interview. "The message is unity of God, praise of the Prophet, and other mystical and spiritual themes. We recite mystic poetry and in this poetry our elders have said that a human being can reach the state of God. Because God is in us, and if we can cleanse ourselves from the inside, through the qawwali medium a human being can travel through all those stages and reach that elevated stage which we would probably not be able to reach even through years and years of worship" (Wald, 2007, pp. 229–230).

There are songs like *Shams Ud Doha, Badar Ud Doja* (titles for the Prophet Mohammad) that evoke the links between the singer, Mohammad, and Allah. In a similar vein, *Ali Maula, Ali Maula*, is a paean to the cousin and son-in-law of the Prophet Mohammad, a figure revered by Sufis. The song has a intoxicating refrain, sung in cycles of increasing velocity.

Sufism is fundamentally humanistic, rather than theological and uses the language of "love" in some significant ways. One key element is the use of the language of "intoxication" itself—where the lines between love for a woman, the love for god, and the love of being in love—are constantly blurred. Many of the other famous *Qawwali's* by Khan represent this using dense metaphors from a range of influences—cultural, architectural, ecological, experiential. In *Aa Bhi Ja Rut Badal Jayegi*, he compares/collapses the pleasures of architecture (the murals of the Ajanta caves in India) to those of a woman, and of nature itself. In *Aadmi Aadmi Se Milta hai*, there are some deeply felt expressions of moving beyond the petty, to the universal, a reaching of mutual respect and personal redemption.

My favorite Qawwalii remains *Kali kali zulfoh ke phande na dalo* which is a stirring lament to the fate of all humans—the coming of old age, the beauty and arrogance of youth, the love for something in the past. In the tone and rendition of the song there is an acceptance of one's life and even a resigned pleasure of the future—a coming to terms with death and the ultimate union with God.

The language of mysticism is fundamentally at odds with institutionalized religion. As Khan put it, "our elders created this medium that goes beyond religion—its is basically regarding the relationship between a human being and God. Anybody (not just a Muslim) can strive to reach God, and *Qawwali* is a medium to do it" (Wald, 2007, p. 231). What makes Sufism perhaps unique is in the terminological and sociological collapse of the categories of "love"—where each *Qawwali* works at two levels—the personal and the divine, where to speak of love for one's partner is also to speak of love for the divine. The search for meaning rather than its uncritical acceptance is a central to the both Sufi and mystical inquiry— separating it from mainstream theological expression (which assumes an unknowable God). The *Qawwali* offers a polemic that for the lack of a better word is "political"—engaging with the superficiality of religious ritual—the bedrock of its institutional practice—and assurance of the true value of religion—its groundedness in the reality of personal emotion. It is this simultaneous personalization and universalization of religion that is at the heart of Khan's authenticity—and which connects him to the meditative and spiritual practices of the modern world.

It is not surprising then that the discourse-surrounding Khan—in both interviews by him and commentaries by other artists—the mystical/ spiritual context is closely related to issues of performance. "I have never heard so much spirit in a voice," Peter Gabriel said in a prepared statement released two days after Khan's death. "My two main singing inspirations, Nusrat and Otis Redding, have been the supreme examples of how far and deep a voice can go in finding, touching, and moving the soul" (Kemp, 1997, p. 20). In an interview, Khan said, "To be a *Qawwal* is more than being a performer, more than being an artist. One must be willing to release one's mind and soul from one's body to achieve ecstasy through music. *Qawwali* is enlightenment itself" (Carvin, 2007, p. 1). What makes Khan different from other *Qawwal's* of the past is his use of the mystical tradition of Sufism, to speak a global language. As Kemp (1997) put it, "for a musician so deeply rooted in tradition, Khan was surprisingly open to experimenting with contemporary technology and Western styles in order to get his music to larger audiences. Although he sang in his native Urdu, Khan wanted his music to communicate in a way that transcended language. Khan likened his music to a bridge that brings different cultures, different religions and people of different ethnic groups to the same central point" (Kemp, 1997, p. 20).

In sum, I would like to suggest that Khan centered performativity as a liturgical experience that transcended the specific religious idiom and became a language of its own—by not just engaging the viewer as an audience but as a participant, invoking a kind of "high" that resonated across the cultural and linguistic boundaries that separated him from many of his listeners. Under Sufi doctrine, the performer is the instrument through which a conversation between the divine and the secular are created, maintained, and sustained. Here the collective engagement of the audience is not the practiced body movement of rock concerts, but the manifestation of an energy that for the lack of a better (more sociological) category, can be called "spiritual." This *experience* was the heart of his "authenticity."

To summarize, the four artists here represent different trajectories in how the discursive construct of "authenticity" is played out in World Music, illustrative of the wider working of global postmodernism. Each singer represents authenticity through a rendition of "locality"—Cape Verdan, Cuba, Africa, and Pakistan—but with substantial difference— issues of gender, age, ethnicity and religion, shape the form and substance of the "authentic" as it is played out in the lives and texts of these performers. My goal in this chapter has been primarily descriptive, focusing on a mapping out the vast range of contexts that make up the narrative of "authenticity" in World Music. There are at least three interrelated generalizations about authenticity that can be made across these artists—as steps to a broader subaltern theory of the global postmodern.

First, the "authentic" is not a monolithic construct, made up of a fixed set of cultural binaries of West/rest, self/other, modern/traditional, but is mobilized through a *specific account of locality*. The "local" remains an important sociological category. Rather than mere agents of global capitalism or indigenous elites, these artists exemplify the sheer *empiricality* of the local as an element of global postmodernism. The local, speaks in and through many contexts (gender, age, ethnicity, and religion) and it is its imbrication within and across these multiple areas that allows for its viability in the modern world. To put it another way, the global (postmodern) cannot exist without the local.

Second, the "authentic" in World Music is tied intimately to the kinesthetic and psychological experience of the artist. What connects each of these artists is the *pleasure* of watching, listening, and experiencing their music. The voice and presence of Evora, Ferrer, Ali, and Khan are eloquent testimony to the return of the "authentic" in an age of global mass production. To put this more speculatively, the centering of *performativity as authenticity* separates World Music from the mass produced genuflections that structure celebrity performance elsewhere. The (global) postmodern is not reducible to the language of the marketplace (even as it must speak through it) but takes center stage through the language of performance.

Finally, the "authentic" in the work of World Music allows for a contextual, localized *and* transcultural account of identity in the modern world. In the end, what connects each of the artists is the cultural work they perform. If global postmodernism is the discursive centering and movement of identity politics, then these artists represent—through the biographical and discursive imprint of their music—the *performance of identity*.

Needless to add, a number of research questions around "tracking" authenticity remain unanswered, and a few can be posed for future work: How can authenticity be "tracked" in other spatial contexts (Asian, Latin American, Caribbean, Middle Eastern, East European)? How is "gender" as a construct about "authenticity" framed across historical contexts? How is "religion" recast in contemporary narratives about political life, as seen for example in patriotic songs and films? Why has "youth culture" (as opposed to old age) become the standard bearer for musical expression?

CONCLUSIONS AND DIRECTIONS:
AUTHENTICITY, APPROPRIATION, HYBRIDITY

Since this chapter has been narrowly focused on "tracking" authenticity, I want to conclude with a change of focus, discussing the issues not addressed in this chapter—those of appropriation and hybridity and how authenticity is related to these questions. Peter Gabriel puts the ideas behind these issues succinctly: "There are two jobs to be done," he says. "One is to protect and preserve the seed stock as wide and varied a base as you can keep alive. The other is to try out as many hybrid possibilities as you can that will give you the most vibrant, pulsating, new life forms" (Taylor, 1997, 12). Bohlman (2002) put this more formally:

> There are two contradictory ways in which World Music is understood today
> . . . For many, World Music represents much that is right in the world, indeed,
> the very possibility that music and music-making bring people together . . .
> There's also the darker side to World Music. World Music can raise fears that
> we are losing much that is close to home. Its homogenizing effect threatens
> village practices as it privileges the spaces of the global village. Its dissemi-
> nation across the globe depends on the appropriation of transnational
> recording companies, whose primary interests are to exploit cultural re-
> sources. Fusion and border-crossing may enrich some world-music styles,
> but they impoverish others. (p. xii)

While space does not allow for a detailed consideration of each of the above artists as they relate to issues of appropriation[5] and hybridity, what follows is a brief engagement with Ry Cooder (as a stand in for other important western artists like Paul Simon and Peter Gabriel) and the success of the *Bueno Vista Social Club*. The role of Ry Cooder as an artist (and producer) of the album cannot be overstated. He appears throughout the documentary (along with his son, Joachim) as a key element in the narrative, playing instruments, smiling, being completely engaged in the music. There is a famous long segment in the documentary where he and his son drive a motorcycle through the streets of old Havana. Most of the shots in that sequence are shot by Joachim Cooder sitting in the tandem. The liner notes on the documentary explicitly address issues of appropriation:

Often times with such first-third world co-productions, the stars wind up being the first world "discoverers" of the third world talent. But Ry Cooder's dealings in this arena are of an entirely different nature. His name does not appear on the covers of the albums. Indeed, he seems no more than a session player that merely lends a hand on a couple of numbers. He is more than that, of course his obvious joy at communing with the Cubans was one of the driving passions of the project but he chose, consciously or not, to be a highly self-effacing presence in every way. There are probably more people in the United States and Europe who've heard of *The Buena Vista Social Club* family of albums than of Ry Cooder, the American slide-guitarist. Credit has gone where credit was due.

Critics of the album/documentary disagree with this assessment. As Roy (2002) puts it, "the fact remains that movie audiences (in Cuba) found the ubiquitous presence of Ry Cooder and his son irritating, and even found the sound of the 'Hawaiian' guitar regrettable, as it fills the silences that were so important to the balance of the original music" (p. 194). My viewing of the documentary suggests a similar reading—both the Cooders appear frequently, often unnecessarily, placed one presumes to orient the American listener and viewer to *their* presence in the production of this "new" music. Holston (2000) extends this criticism and suggests that Album's like Bueno Vista structure specific relationships between third World Musicians and first world promoters: "Perhaps in any given country, long-neglected musicians are waiting for a David Byrne, Paul Simon, Peter Gabriel, or Ry Cooder; to arrive at the town square in a shiny white Land Rover to rescue them from obscurity and sweep them away to fame and fortune" (p. 55).

Outside of issues of personal intent and profit, critics point to the consequences of the success of the album: "The essential criticism (of the film) deals with the fact that the one-sided vision conveyed by the film confines Cuban music within the myth of the 'golden age' of the 1950s, in a supposed purity of the past against which the innovations of recent years can only be considered a deviation. This marginalization into a type of 'exotic ghetto,' removed from the current reality, presents the advantage of satisfying the 'retro' nostalgia of foreigners who find those octogenarians and nonagenarians, so natural and full of energy, to be 'extraordinarily moving' and who even find the dilapidated apartment buildings of Havana so 'marvelously picturesque'" (Roy, 2002, p. 194). Roy also argues that "many musicians have resented this musical boom for the performers of the old-style music—as a negation of their struggles to keep their musical heritage while at the same time renewing it, and finally as a desire to deny the existence of musical life in Cuba after the revolution, even a denial of the revolution itself" (Roy, 2002, p. 195).

An important element in understanding appropriation is of course the agency of the third world artists themselves. For Turino (2005), the issues of agency is more or less absent since these artists are only allowed entry into the capitalist markets if they "fit" expectations about narrative authenticity of cultural others. World Music, he argues is "defined most importantly by the use of styles that index foreign or exotic difference . . . the indices of foreign societies are either selected because they already include aesthetic familiarity within the style, or foreign stylistic differences are tempered by transformations which make them accessible to cosmopolitans" (Turino, 2000, p. 335). Ali Farka Toure offers a counterpoint to such a perspective when he says, "Yes, but if I say I want to record with European musicians, its not to say that I want to learn European music. No, no, I will write the songs and they will play them" (Duran, 2004). The underlying question, rarely addressed is of the role such authenticities play in the role of World Music within the *national* spaces they occupy (rather than transnational, corporate market). Taylor (1997) examines the role of band Lady Smith Black Mambazo within the history of South African culture and politics:

> Perhaps Black Mambazo resist apartheid because they sometimes refuse to engage with it, refuse to allow apartheid to infiltrate every corner of their consciousness. Their lives are made by their music, their church and their friends and families. Ladysmith Black Mambazo's music is neither an example of resistance or complicity, but an attempt to escape the very grounds of the oppressor/oppressed paradigm that European colonialism imposed on them. (cited in Taylor, 1997, p. 81)

The wider questions that can be extrapolated include: What is the role of the authenticities of World Music in contemporary times? Do they offer a space within global capitalism that allows for indigenous identities to remain intact? If the world is increasingly driven by global capital and there are few cultural zones left that are not in some ways tied to the marketplace, what better place to retain authenticity than to make it a commodity? Is World Music a space for cultural rejuvenation and the retaining of authentic cultural traditions *through* global capitalism? The paradox in making such a assumption are obvious: One can easily argue that by virtue of working with the system, it reinforces it, rather than critiques it, despite the agency that artists subscribe to their work. This question of authenticity as appropriation can be best tackled by examining the *specific textual strategies through which World Music is constructed* and the ways in which they are received. While outside the purview of this chapter, such an exercise would need to focus on the genre's avowed "hybridity." How hybrid is the music of cross-cultural collaborations? Studies that track the specific textual signatures of each of the collaborative artists; the overall range of hybrid sonic constructs and the quantitative and qualitative assessment of whose "voice" speaks through the text would address some of these questions. The question could also be addressed as simply, an issue of production and distribution—who produces these albums and who gets to be involved in such productions? The recent success of the *Putumayo* line of World Music raises this issue beyond the role of individual artists and producers and needs to be addressed at the macro-industry level—again questions outside the purview of this chapter.

I want to conclude with two quotes from scholars with different perspectives on the future of World Music. These quotes can be the starting point for future studies of authenticity, appropriation, and hybridity. Aubert (2007) argues that while World Music is often

> seen as humanist, generous and revolutionary . . . as the crucible of a new age, of a regained paradise in which each has the freedom to express him or her difference. However its humanism is technocratic and its generosity dyed in mercantilism, qualities, which inevitably qualify and even tarnish its reach. World Music looks for consensus: it tries to satisfy the largest number of people with a product of synthesis. (Aubert, 2007, p. 54)

Kassabian (2004), on the other hand suggests that listening to World Music encourages a "distributed subjectivity" and that

> listening is a significant terrain for the summoning and engagement of distributed subjectivity. It is a central, defining feature of life in the industrialized world of postmodernity. It is not simply a commodity exchange, nor is it simply a production of subjectivity. Nor is it simply an aesthetic experience. It is a simultaneous, coextensive condition of almost every act and activity, a constant flow. (p. 222)

NOTES

1. International Communication scholars have not systematically addressed "World Music." For a broad accounting of the different artists and music that comprise World Music see Wald (2007), Bordowitz (2004), and the excellent but now dated *World Music: The Rough Guide* (Broughteon et al., 1999). A comprehensive search on LexisNexis for both World Music and the individual artists netted numerous articles in *Billboard, The Village Voice, Jazziz,* and *National Geographic.* Fanzines for these artists were an additional source of music, lyrics, and links to some reviews. For a scholarly (but broad) accounting of the World Music see Taylor (1997), Tenzer (1996), Feld (1994), Keil and Feld (1994), and Bohlman (2002). For studies on World Music within the field of cultural studies, see Barrett (1996), Goodwin and Gore (1990), and Erlmann (1996). For studies focusing on issues of communication, see Colista and Leshner's (1998), Garafalo (1993), and Laing (1986). An important essay on the role of music journalists and World Music is Avant-Mier and Furisch (2008) which examines how the discourse of World Music is constructed using the language of authenticity, exoticism, and cultural difference. I am grateful to them for sharing this paper.

2. There is an embarrassing wealth of World Musicians for future studies to address. Using just one of the contexts I addressed in the chapter—gender—here is a (partial) list of women singers/performers with an expected focus of analysis for each of them: Oumou Sangare from Mali; Mercades Sosa (Argentina), Violette Parra (Chile), Silvio Rodriguez (Cuba), Susana Baca can all be engaged with issues of gender and women's empowerment (and local, often marginalized ethnicities) within a regional (Latin American) and national context. The songs/music of Emeline Michel (Haiti), Sandra Luna (Argentina), Daniela Mercury (Brazil), and Carmen Linares (Spain) are interesting points for departure for studies looking at artists that have both retained and reworked traditional musicians' forms such as *tango, fado, chanson, flamenco,* and *rhumba.* Studies of postcolonial identity and gender can examine singers such as Umm Kalthum (Egypt), Hadia Talsam (Egypt), DjurDjur (Algeria), Angeline Kidjo (Benin), Sheila Chandra (UK), and Aap Mama (Belgium). Naturally, this is a very small sample of the many women of World Music.

3. The desire of World Music fans to see Ali as a "Mali Bluesman" can be seen as part of a wider marketing/discursive strategy that has a long history. As Wald (2007) puts it, "the World Music boom has to a great extent been sparked by the quest of western musicians to reconnect their music with its roots, and for a hundred years quests for the root of pop have tended to lead back to Africa. Ragtime, jazz, blues, rock, salsa, reggae, hip-hop—the rhythms of Africa have been the engine of virtually all-modern international styles" (p. 1).

4. Khan's soundtrack work brought him the most attention among Westerners. In 1994, his voice was layered into the score for Oliver Stone's *Natural Born Killers.* Perhaps the most famous of Khan's soundtrack contributions were his duets with Vedder on two songs, "The Face of Love" and "The Long Road," for the score of Tim Robbins's 1996 film, *Dead Man Walking.* Khan also sang on Gabriel's soundtrack to Martin Scorsese's *The Last Temptation of Christ.*

5. A key illustration of this process is the oft-cited case of Paul Simon's album *Graceland,* which was seen as a process of "rejuvenation" and the "creative rebirth"

of Paul Simon through his collaboration with South African artists (who came to represent an "authentic" essentialized African voice). Many critics, especially in the academia (a documentary on the subject shows Simon being criticized by students at the largely African American Howard University in Washington, DC) suggesting that this was a form of sonic exploitation, if not evidence of contemporary cultural imperialism. "It's hard to know if you are being attacked as an artist or as a person, said Simon about the *Graceland* controversy, and this is the point: as a person he was resolutely anti-apartheid, as an artist, his western, voracious aesthetic allowed him to appropriate anything and do anything with it" (Taylor, 1997, p. 22).

From a cultural studies perspective, issues of appropriation are related to the idea that "popular music texts can be analyzed as institutionally produced commercial commodities that function as cultural artifacts inscribed with meanings which are then consumed and interpreted by fans and audiences. For Theodor Adorno the holistic, critical analysis of popular music as it moved through the circuits of production, textualization, and audience reception was central to understanding the politics of mass culture in modern capitalism. Popular music was a rationalized, standardized, and pseudo-individualized artifact that produced rationalized and standardized responses of emotional sentimentality and false consciousness in the consuming public . . . within cultural studies, the theoretical counterpoint to Adorno has been the Gramscian emphasis on the resistance to hegemony among the 'people' and their capacity to produce their own meanings of popular texts and artifacts through ritual, recontextualization and alternate readings" (Herman, Swiss, and Sloop, 1998, p. 5).

Among the "people" that a Gramscian reading refers to might include the musicians that produce World Music. McLeod, K. (1999), for example, details the case for hip-hop culture that can be applied to World Music artists as well.

> The multiple invocations of authenticity made by hip-hop community members are a direct and conscious reaction to the threat of the assimilation and the colonization of this self-identified, resistive subculture. Authenticity claims are a way of establishing in-group/out-group distinctions. Therefore, by invoking authenticity, one is affirming that, even though hip-hop music was the top-selling music format in 1998, hip-hop culture's core remains pure and relatively untouched by mainstream American culture. Hip-hop can balance large sales and mainstream success with a carefully constructed authentic self. (p. 146)

A middle ground in this debate would assume that "appropriation is rarely just appropriation . . . any sort of cross-cultural musical interaction is an appropriation with multiple implications. According to Steven Feld, 'musical appropriation sings a double line with one voice. One of those lines is admiration, respect, the other is appropriation'" (Taylor, 1997, p. 40).

REFERENCES

Agawu, K. (2003). *Representing African music*. London: Routledge.

Aubert, L. (2007). *The music of the other: New challenges for ethnomusicology in a global age*. Aldershot, UK: Ashgate.

Avant-Mier, R., & Fursich, E. (2008). The authenticity dilemma: World music in the popular press. Unpublished paper.

Barrett, J. (1996). World music, nation, and postcolonialism. *Cultural Studies, 10*(2), 237–247.

Barz, G. (2007). Ali Farka Tour, Grove Music Online. Retrieved on May 20, 2007, from www.grovemusic.com.

Bobey, J. (2001, August/September). Cesaria Evora. *Dirty Linen*, 95, 66.

Bohlman, P. V. (2002). *World music: A very short introduction*. Oxford: Oxford University Press.

Bordowitz, H. (2004). *Noise of the world: Non-western musicians in their own words*. Brooklyn, NY: Soft Skull Press.

Bouchard, F. (2000). Genuine Cape Verdean Soul (Interview with Cesaria Evora). *Down Beat: Jazz, Blues, and Beyond, 67*(2), 52–53.

Broughton, S., Ellingham, M., & Trillo, R. (Eds.) (1999). *World music: The rough guide*. London: Rough Guides.

Cantor, J. (1999, June 26). Ibrahim Ferrer: Veteran Cuban singer stays youthfully nimble. *Billboard*, 12, 26.

Carvin, A. (2007). The spirit of Nusrat Fateh Ali Khan. Retrieved on May 15, 2007, from edwebproject.org/nusrat.html.

Coetzer, D. (1997, October 25). Evora top winner at S. Africa's Kora's. *Billboard*, 60, 83.

Colista, C., & Leshner, G. (1998). Traveling music: Following the path of music through the global market. *Critical Studies in Mass Communication, 15*, 181–194.

Duran, L. (2004). Ali Farka Tour (World Circuit Biography). Retrieved from mali music.com/cat/cata/aft/aftbioa.html.

Erlmann, V. (1996). The aesthetics of the global imagination: Reflections on world music in the 1990s. *Public Culture, 8*, 467–487.

Feld, S. (1994). Notes on "world beat." In C. Keil & S. Feld (Eds.), *Music grooves*. Chicago: University of Chicago Press.

Feld, S. (2000). A sweet lullaby for world music. *Public Culture, 12*(1), 145–171.

Garofalo, R. (1993). Whose world, what beat: The transnational music industry, identity, and cultural imperialism. *The World of Music, 35*(2), 16–32.

Gonzalez, F. (2003). Ibrahim Ferrer: Buenos Hermanos. *DownBeat: Jazz, Blues, and Beyond, 7*(7), 71.

Goodwin, A., & Gore, J. (1990). World beat and the cultural imperialism debate. *Socialist Review, 20*(3), 63–80.

Graham, E. (2003). The international country of Cesaria Evora. Retrieved from www.boheme-magzine.net/php/modules/107.

Herman, A., Swiss, T., & Sloop, J. (1998). Mapping the beat: Spaces of noise and places of music. In A. Herman, T. Swiss, & J. Sloop (Eds.), *Mapping the beat: popular music and contemporary theory* (p. 330). Oxford: Blackwell.

Holston, M. (2000). Beyond Buena Vista. *Jazziz, 17*(5), 52–55.

Jensen, J. (2002). Taking Country Music Seriously: Coverage of the 1990s boom. In S. Jones (Ed.), *Pop music and the press* (pp. 183–201). Philadelphia: Temple University Press.

Kassabian, A. (2004). Would you like some world music with your latte? Starbucks, Putumayo, and distributed tourism. *Twentieth Century Music, 2*(1), 209–223.

Keil, C., & Feld, S. (1994). *Music grooves*. Chicago: University of Chicago Press.

Kemp, M. (1997, February 10). Star of Pakistan dead at 48: Nusrat Fateh Ali Khan. *Rolling Stone*, 20.

Laing, D. (1986). The music industry and the "cultural imperialism" thesis. *Media, Culture & Society, 8*, 331–341.

McCord, J. (2005). Ali Farka Tour: Red and Green. *World Circuit Review*. Mahler Publications Division. Retrieved from gateway.proquest.com (Review of Red and Green).

McLeod, K. (1999). Authenticity within hip-hop and other cultures threatened with assimilation. *Journal of Communication, 49*, 134–150.

Moon, T. (1999, February 9). The Cuban Invasion. *Rolling Stone, 82*, 29, 40.

Nickson, C. (2006). Last chorus: Ibrahim Ferrer, 1927–2005. *Sing Out! The Folk Song Magazine, 49*(4), 210–211.

NPR (2007). Cesaria Evora: At home on the road. *All Things Considered* (Radio Show). Retrieved from npr.org/templates/story/story11426375.

Plougastel, Y. (2004). Cesaria Evora: Review of Voz D'Amor. Retrieved on May 20, 2007, from www.lusafrica.fr/focus/cesaria/voz_d_amor.asp?language=en.

Roy, M. (2002). *Cuban Music: From son and rhumba to Buena Vista Social Club*. Princeton, NJ: Markus Wiener Publishers.

Spencer, P. (1997). Nusrat Fateh Ali Khan, 1948–1997. *Sing Out! The Folk Song Magazine, 42*(3), 29.

Stokes, M. (1994). *Ethnicity, identity, and music: The musical construction of place*. Oxford: Berg.

Taylor, T. (1997). *Global pop: World music, world markets*. New York: Routledge.

Tenzer, M. (2006). *Analytical studies in world music*. New York: Oxford University Press.

Trebay, G. (1996, November 19). Cape Verde drive. *The Village Voice, 41*, 47.

Turino, T. (2000). *Nationalists, cosmpolitans, and popular music in Zimbabwe*. Chicago: University of Chicago Press.

Wald, E. (2007). *Global minstrels*. London: Routledge.

Williamson, N. (1997, August 30). Industry pays tribute to Qawwali master Khan. *Billboard*, 10, 96.

5

Playing with Postcoloniality:
Four Moments
in Indian Cricket

Cricket civilizes people and creates good gentleman. I want everyone in
Zimbabwe to play cricket. I want ours to be a nation of gentleman.

—Robert Mugabe

Cricket is not an addition or a decoration that one adds to what really
constitutes the history of a period. It does not reflect the age. It is the age.

—C. L. R. James

Pause and Decide.

—Swaroop Kishen, Indian cricket umpire,
autograph to author

There are two positions that one can assume about cricket (the game, not
the insect!). For the fan (especially in India and the subcontinent),
cricket is a passion like no other—it produces a surrender that is complete
and abiding; it rejects critical attention, it is at the heart of national subjectivity (whether it be Indian or Pakistani) and is determined in its grasp of
the subaltern—positioning itself in ways that weave around the contours
of local and national identity politics—that have historically divided postcolonial societies. For the scholar, cricket, like all sports, "is a relational idiom, a sphere of activity which expresses, in concentrated forms, the values, prejudices, divisions, and unifying symbols of a society . . . sport is a
microcosm of the fissures and tensions of a deeply divided society: fissures
that it both reflects and plays upon, mitigates as well as intensifies" (Guha,

1998, p. 157). In this chapter, I will try and a walk a line between these two positions—a task that is fraught with danger—both theoretical (assuming that one can be a fan *and* a critic) and personal—I may stop loving the one thing that I have loved (always)!

Cricket is a cultural form (and media practice) that is fundamentally shaped by colonialism and its aftermath—a sociological condition that centers my discussion here. After a "framing" section drawing on important trends in postcolonial theory, I will do a broad accounting of four key "moments" in Indian cricketing history and development, focusing my analysis on issues of the male subject—the cricketer—as an icon of wider sociopolitical processes and changing models of masculinity. A brief conclusion and directions section will engage with research questions and issues not addressed in the bulk of the chapter.

FRAMING POSTCOLONIALISM AND CRICKET

What is postcolonialism? There are two immediate referents that the term recalls. It attempts to identify conditions of contemporary globality as something that has links with processes of colonialism and imperialism—a historical process that has provided spatial, social and cultural maps for most modern societies. It is also an attempt to define the contours of contemporary social formations that live in the aftermath of colonialism and struggle to define alternate set of maps as they function in new global structures. Simply put, I use the word, "postcolonialism" as the long-term process of diffusion, acculturation and negotiation (along both nationalist and subaltern lines) that begins when the "colonizing power inscribes itself onto the body and space of its others and which continues as an often occluded tradition into the modern theater of neocolonialist international relations" (Williams and Chrisman, 1994, p. 13).

The postcolonial project in literary and historical studies (which saw numerous writings from the mid to late 1990s) as relevant to the study of international communication is an attempt to move to make sense of a confused world, a world made up of

> crises-crossed economies, intersecting systems of meanings and fragmented identities. Suddenly, the comforting modern imagery of nation-states and national languages, of coherent communities and consistent subjectivities, of dominant centers and distant margins no longer seem adequate . . . we have all moved irrevocably to a new kind of social space. (Rouse, 1991, p. 8)

Synthezing a large (and often convoluted) body of literature, one can identify three major strands in postcolonial theory[1] that have relevance for an understanding of cultural/media forms such as cricket. These include issues of theory, power, and identity.

Theory

Postcolonial theory developed in opposition to traditional models of what can be broadly defined as categories of "modernism"—macro theories of Marxism and functionalism that tried to create overarching frameworks (around issues of class or social structure) that could be applied across national, cultural, and political contexts. Postcolonial theory is an attempt at developing what Ulf Hannerz called "cultural complexity," the different ways in which national cultures developed across the world. Such an approach toward "theory" was also (by definition) counter to understanding the non-Western world as "third" or "developing" world—where their definitions of self were always made in relation to the typologies developed by the west (first/second/third world; developed/undeveloped). The approach rejected the linear and evolutionary logic that often accompanied such typologies. As Arif Dirlik puts it "Postcoloniality represents a genuine need, the need to overcome a crises of understanding produced by the inability of old categories to account for the world. The meta-narrative of progress that underlies two centuries of thinking is in deep crises. Whether they be fixed geographically, or structurally, the Three Worlds are no longer tenable. The globe has become as jumbled up spatially as the ideology of progress has temporally" (1994, p. 352).

Power

While eschewing macro theories or models of global structuration, postcolonial theory does not suggest that the world is bereft of concerns of power—quite the opposite—drawing on the influential work of Michel Foucault, postcolonial theorists argue that issues of power are fundamental to the understanding of postcolonial societies. They see power as a inherent, subjective and subaltern process in these societies, whose analysis can be best undertaken by understanding the constitutive processes by which these societies come into being. These constitutive processes are best examined, postcolonial critics suggest, by looking at the very construct of "culture" and "nation" in these societies. Drawing on the influential work of Benedict Anderson on "imagined communities," they argue that cultures (French, Indian, Algerian, etc.) and "nations" are "imagined" and "co-constructed" by rulers and subjects working together in unbidden ways. Cultural practices (with media as a central agent) are intimately tied in to the creation of such "nations" from a precolonial core that often consisted of kingdoms, tribal states, or village structures. At the heart of this position is the idea that "culture" is "always relational, an inscription of communicative processes that exist historically between subjects in relations of power" (Clifford, 1986, p. 15) and that the idea of the "nation" and "nationalism" is "a contradictory discourse with internal contradictions that need to be unpacked in their historical specificity. As Radhakrishnan (1992), puts it "the historical agency of nationalism has been sometimes hegemonic, though often merely dominant, sometimes emancipatory though often repressive, sometimes progressive, though often traditional and reactionary" (p. 82).

Identity

Since postcolonial scholars use a conceptual lens that is not oriented toward examination of macro-sociological frames (such as marxist theories of labor or functionalist theories of social structure), but on the microprocesses of tracking power and complexity, it should come as no surprise that an issue of personhood and self are at the heart of postcolonial inquiry. The key analytical category becomes that of "identity." Identity for postcolonial critics is not a static unitary entity. It is "neither continuous nor continually interrupted but constantly framed between simultaneous vectors of similarity, continuity and difference" (Stuart Hall quoted in Frankenberg and Mani, 1993, p. 295).

Framed with such strokes, one may assume that for postcolonial theorists, identity is amenable to any kind of construction that individuals may choose—quite the opposite—identity as *the* defining element of culture requires (paradoxically), a reliance on structural categories of most modern societies—categories that have a "politics of location"—where the identity of the speaker from a certain space defines the value/impact of what he or she says (or the texts they construct). These points of entry defined typically by one's national origin, race, class, gender, ethnicity, sexuality, have far reaching consequences for the cultural work that individuals perform. A variety of conceptual terms including "hybridity," "creolization," "mimics" are used to understand the complex relations between the different identity formations in any society, the focus in each case being the idea that "there is no such thing as an independent cultural identity but that every identity must define and position itself in relation to the cultural frames affirmed by the world system" (Ang, 1991, p. 253). Chandra Mohanty (1987) argues that developing a politics of location requires exploration of the "historical, geographical, cultural, psychic, and imaginative boundaries, which provide ground for political definition and self-definition" (p. 3). Location is not seen as something rigid but as a "temporality of struggle" (Mohanty, 1987, p. 40) characterized by "multiple locations and asynchronous processes of movement between cultures, languages, and complex configurations of meaning and power (Mani, 1989, p. 26).

These three sets of issues (theory, power, and identity) inform much of postcolonial theory and will constitute the background around which I discuss cricket. In addition, there is now an emerging body of literature[2] examining the role of cricket as an institutional force in the project of colonialism and its work in the postcolonial era and I will use insights from those essays in an attempt to locate the "four moments of cricket," using a narrative style that is simultaneously personal and sociological. Each moment is referenced with the personal/national experience of cricket in India and the Diaspora, There is a single claim that runs through the account to follow: cricket in some elemental sense, provides a script for social relations in the former British colony of India and can be used as a text through which the logic of postcolonialism can be analyzed. Following Guha (2002), I work with the assumption that "the history of this English game in the Indian sub-continent can be told through (Indian) cricketers" (p. 438). My own analysis, while focused on the broad cultural currents that the five moments of cricket suggest, is also different in that I squarely locate these moments as fundamentally mediated (through radio, print, television, film, and now the Internet). I focus on one category of "identity" as it reflects discourses about the postcolonial—the construct of masculinity in key Indian batsman. While space does not allow for a full rendition of the literature of men's studies, three key themes can be identified. First, masculinity is a social construct, working and animating the specific vectors of the historical moment in which it is occurs. To put this another way, what it means to be a "man" changes with time and modes of social organization (much as the "farmer" is different from the factory "worker"). Second, ideas about masculinity are developed through the institutional structures that govern discourse in any society (what Althusser calls the institutional state apparatus of a society). In other words, churches, schools, offices, and the mass media are ways in which dominant ideas about masculinity are circulated. Three, masculinity is "performed"—the most visible of these performances occur in participatory arenas—such as sports—whether it is the local school or community team or giant sporting spectacles involving national, and global spectatorship. Cricket shares all of these ideas with other sports, but also some key differences—it's lineage is fundamentally tied to the experience of colonialism—and it is colonialism's very masculinist determination that I track in this chapter.

What is cricket? Cricket emerged out of rural preindustrial England as a village game, eventually became part of English class structure, played at Oxford and Cambridge, and as the English empire grew in its global reach, became part of the political, civilizing mission of colonialism. Central to the game's performativity was the idea of "fair play" and "sportsman-ship," where both stoic reserve and hard work represented wider dis-courses about industrial power and Victorian values. The game itself was complex, its rules intricately learned through socialization—a process that took shape both in public schools and in the wider arenas of county and national cricket. It was from its beginning more than "just a game." The rules of the game to the extent that they can be simply defined include, two teams made of eleven players each. Each side has a number of specialist batsman and bowlers (both fast and spin bowlers); the goal is to score as many runs as possible in two innings. The bowlers meanwhile take "wick-ets" or get the batsman out in a number of ways—bowling them out by hit-ting the wickets (three wooden stumps that the batsman stands in front of); having a fielder catching a ball hit into the air; having them run out or al-ternately having them LBW or leg before wicket (where the ball hits their pads in line with the wickets). Most games last five days and end in a "draw"—with neither team winning (a situation that is often pointed out is much like life!) In recent years, the five-day game is complemented by a one-day version and now an even shorter version, called the Twenty20. Fielders stand in a complex set of fielding arrangements, depending on the type of bowler, the situational context of the game and the reputation of the batsman. Players, historically only wore white clothes, and in the five day version still do. In the one-day and Twenty20 version, teams dress in a range of "national" colors.

Cricket is a "batsman's" game (unlike baseball, which is dominated by the pitcher)—the high number of runs in an innings (200 plus) provide a quantitative sense of his centrality—but do not do justice to this claim. Spectatorship of a cricket game is visually focused on the performative ability of the batsman—whether it is the viewer's eye or the camera, the batsman is at the heart of the narrative action that mobilizes wider dis-courses about masculinity.

FOUR POSTCOLONIAL (MEDIA) MOMENTS: SPORTS AND MASCULINITY FROM RANJITSINGHJI TO MAHENDER SINGH DHONI

The First Moment: Learning from *Lagaan* or Falling in (Postcolonial) Love

This memory could have come from elsewhere—maybe out of an R. K. Narayan novel but I am certain its mine: A dusty street, a dustier boy, walking barefoot in the hot sun. Darting between clumps of shade as he makes his way to the nearby store to get *nankatai* for tea. He clutches a

Sony transistor (bought recently, it's a prized possession that belongs to his father) close to his ear. India is playing Australia. The boy weaves in tandem with the rise and fall of the crescendo of static. As the sound fades, but the faint, tinny sound of the announcer gets animated, the boy knows that something has happened, something bad. He clutches his head, sinks down under a tree—pushing the transistor fiercely against his ear. Slowly, he gets up, swings up on the tree's limb and swings his feet, waiting for the score. In his head he imagines the cricketer's whose faces and postures he knows from the special color issue of *Illustrated Weekly* that the *newspaperwallah* brought. Sitting in the tree, he surrenders to the world of cricket, suspended by the sounds of a distant world. To put it in a more contemporary way, love does not have to be a digital connection; radio and print can do the job just as well.

How does a nation fall in love with an alien cultural practice? In the critically acclaimed and Oscar nominated Bollywood film *Lagaan* (Land Tax, 2001), cricket is an instrument of both colonial expression and subaltern desire. I want to use the film as the conceptual lens through which to understand the first (mediated) moment of India's encounter with cricket. Majumdar (2002), provides both summary and an analytic frame for assessing the film:

> Set in 1833, *Lagaan* is the tale of a team of village men playing cricket against an oppressive, colonial regime in the village of Champaner to save their lives, families and land. At the outset of the film, Captain Russell, the arrogant British army officer in charge of the cantonment at Champaner is outraged that a young, spirited, peasant boy, Bhuvan, describes cricket as a *feringhee* version of *gulli danda* (an indigenous game played with two sticks), a game that he, Bhuvan has played since he was a child. Captain Russell challenges Bhuvan in the presence of the provincial Rajah and the rest of the villagers to beat the English team in a cricket match, failing which the entire province would be charged three times their share of annual tax of *Lagaan*. Should these country bumpkins succeed in the impossible task of defeating the English team, their taxes, and those of the entire province shall be revoked for three years. The Cricket match thus becomes an arena for asserting indigenous strength against the might of the colonial state. The sporting prowess of the villagers and their ultimate victory helped them emphasize that their "Indian" identity was in no way inferior to the whites. Native mastery of the colonial sport of cricket had emerged as the leveler between the colonizer and the colonized. (Majumdar, 2002, p. 30)

Farred (2004) analyses the film as a text about postcolonial origins, the specific ways in which cricket came to "epitomize the complicated cultural bond—that locale where the history of colonization is ameliorated by the history of shared, often memorable and intensely combative, encounters on the cricket oval—between the colonizers and the colonized" (p. 94). Cricket, he suggests in time became a "cultural practice shared by the colonizer and the colonized alike" (Farred, 2004, p. 94) a practice shaped by the experience of *playing* cricket—a key ingredient of the film *Lagaan*: "With the final eighty minutes of an almost four hour movie dedicated to the cricket match, *Lagaan* dramatizes the historic role cricket plays in developing and expressing a subaltern Indian consciousness. In pitting the cultural familiarity of the English colonizers [with cricket] against the desperation and naiveté of the colonized, *Lagaan* implicitly pays tribute to the history of cricket in the Asian continent. [The film] honors the earliest generation of Indian cricketers; those who learned from and learned to beat the colonists at the game they [would come to] love so much. *Lagaan* locates itself within the originary moment—the late 19th century, that era when Indian cricket was born and in which its first accomplishments were recorded" (Farred, 2004, p. 94).

Majumdar suggests that *Lagaan* does more than just identify a historical moment, but is "a commentary in *the filmic and imaginative mode on the evolution and development* of cricket in colonial India. The cricket match thus became an arena for asserting indigenous strength against the might of the colonial state. Native mastery of the colonial sport in cricket [emerges] as the leveler between the colonizer and the colonized" (Majumdar, 2002, p. 29). Farred (2004) points out that in *Lagaan* "imaginary, India comes to cricket not through choice or idle mimicry but through historical and cultural necessity. *Lagaan* emerges out of the vulnerable psychic space created by the threat of subaltern existence . . . the film dramatizes the narrative disruption in thinking subaltern politics in colonial India" (p. 100). Sen (2001) develops this argument and connects the politics of postcoloniality with the emergence of nationalist identity politics: "the game of cricket in *Lagaan* functions as a metaphor for political adulthood: it is when the villagers learn the game that they become nationalist warriors" (p. 246).

What is the link between the film *Lagaan* and the image I began this section with? (The boy sitting in a tree.) Very simply, it is a statement about a communitarian identity. The boy represents spectatorship—much like the villagers in *Lagaan* who care nothing for the code of the game. They brag, jeer, laugh, and cry without shame. This emotionalism is precisely why nineteenth-century Englishmen doubted that Indians could play cricket, and why the cricketers of that ear were often ridiculed by English observers (Sen, p. 247). The cricket game that makes up the end of the film, features the entire village which has crowded around the field, sitting on rocks, on trees, shouting, sobbing, and getting hysterically happy or flamboyantly forlorn with each turn of the game. There is a line that connects the villagers raised in the colonial moment to fans like me, raised a generation after independence. That line is continuous and unbroken, representing the (continual) emergence of a national "self," both before and after colonialism—a process that is simultaneously sociological and personal. It is a specific kind longing and loving, representative of the fact that "cricket is the repository of overburdened cultural links. It is the defining cultural practice, the Indian national obsession, the Indian national pathology that contains within it the Indian poetic" (Farred, 2004, p. 94).

The Second Moment: Making Love, Watching Vishwanath

Gundappa Vishwanath is a short man, absurdly short even by Indian standards. There is nothing of the modern day athlete about him—the bulging muscles, the tall frame. In the years to come he will look positively rotund. But on this day, when I see him, he is merely stocky. His wrists are huge—I have gaped at them as he came around signing autographs after batting at the nets in New Delhi's Ferozshah Kotla Cricket ground. India is playing Pakistan and I watch Vishwanath come in to bat at one drop. He walks in to bat in his usual unhurried fashion, as if this was not the most important thing to be happening in the nation right now. Sikander Bakht, an eminently forgettable Pakistani bowler, comes into bowl. His first ball is outside the off stump, and Vishwanath moves onto the back foot, his bat goes up rapier like and he executes the shot that has come to define him—the square cut. The ball races to the boundary. Four runs off the first ball. Vishwanath, it is well known never takes time to settle in; gauge the bowler, figure out the bounce in the pitch; adopt a tactic before starting an inning. He approaches every ball, with a single goal—to hit it with elegance, beauty, and clarity. It is said that he never accumulates runs, he spends them. He is not a miser, but a spendthrift. He uses the bat like a lover, willing the public, his partner (so to speak), to reach more fully into themselves, to participate with increasing abandon—and paradoxically control—in the act of making love. In this way, am I seduced by Vishwanath, and like all first loves, there has never been any other that can take its place. Vishwanath remains the (national) center of my cricketing imagination, centered on an etiology of performance that simply put is about only one thing: art.

Farred (2004) suggests that through "charting the history of cricket in the sub-continent we can also map, for want of a better phrase, the genealogy of a national essence" (p. 94). This essence, I would suggest is located within the kinds of spectatorship that watching Vishwanath engenders—a mode of nationalist viewing that is firmly rooted in the praxis and poetics of performance. Appadurai (1996) suggests that playing, watching, remembering, and fantasizing about cricket are all related to the erotics of Indian nationalism. "The erotic pleasure of watching cricket for Indian male subjects is the pleasure of agency in an imagined community, which in many others arenas is violently contested. This pleasure is neither wholly cathartic nor vicarious because playing cricket is close to, or part of, the experience of many Indian males. It is however, magnified, politicized, and spectacularized without losing its links to the lived experience of bodily competence and agnostic bonding" (p. 111) There is he asserts a complex link "between gender, fantasy, nation, and excitement" (p. 111).

Appadurai goes on to suggest that mass media played an important part in the development of such—this relationship between gender, nation, and fandom: "In the process of vernacularization (through books, newspapers, radio, and television) it became an emblem of Indian nationhood at the same time that it became inscribed, as practice, onto the Indian (male) body. Decolonization in this case not only involves the creation of imagined communities through the workings of print capitalism . . . but it also involves the appropriation of agnostic body skills that can further lend passion and purpose to the community so imagined" (1997, p. 112).

I would like to suggest that Vishwanath is emblematic of a certain kind of imagined community—one tied to a orientalist vision of Indian masculinity, that takes sustenance from early media (radio, print, and state run television) in India. Specifically, I would like to argue that Vishwanath represents one textual moment in a series of texts that begin with Ranjitsinghji and continued through players like C. K. Nayadu, M. A. K. Pataudi, Salim Durrani, Mohammad Azharuddin, and V. V. S. Laxman. Different generations fall in love with different texts (Vishwanath in my case) but *within the same nationalist conjuncture*, one predicated on a specific praxis/poetics of performance. In this sense, there is not a temporal synchrony at work here, but a diffused, spatial, and aesthetic principle that governs this moment. A moment that began with Ranjitsinghji, where one must necessarily begin. Simply put, what Ranjitsinghji began was a way of *performing* Indian-ness.

His batting was not only about getting runs but the manner in which he got them. "He was seen in cricket circles as carrying a peculiar oriental glow. The great C. B. Fry said of him that "he moved as if he had no bones; one would not be surprised to see brown curves burning in the grass where one of his cuts had traveled or blue flame shimmering round his bat, as he made one of his strokes." Neville Cardus said "when he batted, strange light was seen for the first time on English fields" (Appadurai, 1996, p. 96).

Ranjitsinghji was accepted by England as a particular kind of oriental. Nowhere is this more evident than in how he was covered by two generations of English journalists. Neville Cardus wrote, "Ranji was the most remarkable instance in all of cricket's history of a man expressing through his game not only his individual genius but the genius of his race. No Englishmen could have batted like Ranji. In 1896, the *Daily Telegraph* compared Ranjitsinji's wrists to jungle creepers and declared that he had turned cricket into an "oriental poem of action." References to jugglery, wizardry, and black magic became ubiquitous in contemporary articles about the man and his batting (Sen, 2001, p. 242).

What began as orientalist trope became social fact—the batting of Vishwanath and his descendents are part of the process of decolonization—the power of subaltern agency—making the terms of the masters their own. It is the willing participation of the spectator in such viewership (through radio, print, and television) and in the willing disposition of the performer to present such a bodily agency that completes the pact between nation, gender, and passion that Appadurai suggests. I am not, however, suggesting that there is a uniformity of expression or agency in each of the players identified above, or even that they are received with the exact same language that framed Ranji—I am, however, suggesting that they are *trajectories* that take sustenance from the colonial imagination and in due course animate the narrative of the nation—helping frame moments of national reconstruction. Needless to add, none of this becomes possible without the talent (technical and cultural) of the cricket players and teams themselves.

Mansour Ali Khan Pataudi, also known as the "Nawab of Pataudi" (a royal title—his family ruled the seat of Pataudi) was perhaps the closest in both educational heritage (he studied at Oxford) and colonial affiliation (his father played for England) to the legacy of Ranjitsinghji. Nicknamed "Tiger," his place in the annals of Indian cricket rest firmly in his leadership of India, a task that made him in the words of Wisden, the English Cricket Almanac,

> Unarguably, India's greatest captain ever. Taking over the reins of the Indian team at the age of 21, barely months after being involved in a car accident that would impair the sight in his right eye forever, he led India in 40 of 46 Tests he played in, and won 12 of them. But more than anything else, he led Indian cricket out of its morass of defeatism and instilled in his fellow cricketers a belief that winning was possible. Under him, India achieved their first overseas Test victory against New Zealand in 1967. This he achieved by playing, as had become customary with him, three spinners, because he reckoned, against conventional thinking, that India's only chance lay in playing to their strengths. As a batsman he was boldly adventurous and unorthodox for his times, and unafraid to loft the ball over the infield. His Test average was a modest 34, but what he could have achieved with complete sight is a matter of conjecture. (cricinfo.com/india/content/player/32222.html)

The text of Pataudi has three synecdochical elements—the nickname, "Tiger" begetting a constitutive bearing—"royal"; a batting style that became condensed with being blind in one eye, and a defining shot, the leg-glance (where the ball is flicked off the legs). This construct emerges in a world before television—primarily in black and white newspapers (where his image often blurs with the historical memory/imagery of his father) and later in color magazines. Tiger emerges as a specific kind of postcolonial text, where the mastery of the indigenous (ruler) to combat both personal circumstance (the loss of his feudal lands and his right eye) and take on the task of the national reconstruction using an indigenous language—the three spinners—who in turn can be read as continuous within the narrative history of orientalism where guile and wonder (the snake charmer, the Indian rope trick, and so forth) mix unproblematically with the exotic and wondrous. The cultural work that Pataudi performed was *reinscribing* the colonial imagination, along lines already established by Ranjitsinghji. Like the former, who was often afflicted with poor health (asthma) but played on pluckily, so was Pataudi cast in a similar vein—as somebody who could overcome the limitations of his (and his nations) lot by sheer will—a trait that drew squarely on existing notions about Victorian masculinity, a trait often used as a model to emulate by the indigenous elite (to which Pataudi belonged). However, Pataudi was not merely the extension of a colonial logic, he also began an important personal (and national) journey. He married a film star, Sharmila Tagore, and in the process married cricket and Bollywood, the two defining media and cultural practices of Indian (public) life. It is also significant that as a Muslim, leading India in the post-partition era (after India was divided into a largely Hindu India and a Muslim Pakistan), he embodied a specific kind of agency—where the bonds of religion were simultaneously confirmed and effaced in the envelope of royalty that surrounded him as a player. His work as a text of secularism worked paradoxically, through the twin narratives of royalty and celebrity culture—he combined them both on the cricket field, where he led a team of mainly middle-class (and some working-class) Indians *into* national consciousness.

Mohammad Azharuddin, the magnificent Indian batsman, and former captain, exemplified the same discursive range, as is evident from this biography on Cricinfo (a widely used cricket news and analysis website):

> Those who saw this supreme batting artist at his peak will never forget him—sinewy wrists transforming a slender piece of willow into a magician's wand. Azhar's leg-side play was reminiscent of a Michelangelo in the midst of housepainters. In later years, he expanded his off-side repertoire, and conjured some of the finest innings played in the modern era—his 121 at Lord's in 1990 was one for the gods. His technique was suspect against the short stuff, a deficiency he sought to overcome through instinctive stroke play, sometimes with cavalier disregard for the team situation. As captain, Azhar

enjoyed tremendous success on made-to-order home pitches, while right to the end of his career he was peerless in the field, whether prowling the covers or pouching catches at slip. He announced his arrival, against England in 1984–85, with three hundreds in his first three Tests, a feat that has never been matched, while his last Test innings also bore him a hundred. (Premchandran; contentusa.cricinfo.com/india/content/player/26329.html)

I was lucky to see (and cover as a reporter) Azharuddin's batting in a regional cricket match, before his debut for India. In addition to the leg glance, he showed a penchant for a shot that came to define his career. This was a cover drive off his back foot. He hit then Indian captain Kapil Dev (who was bowling to him) for a succession of boundaries. It was a shot unlike any other because he was clearly breaking some rules. He hit the cover drive not with his shoulders (like most batsman) but largely with his wrists. He would lean back, move his feet marginally (as opposed to classic full step back) and then swoop down over the ball in a short graceful arc that would guide more than smash the ball between the gully and cover for four runs. It was clearly an endeavor that spoke to a special gift and those of us in the press box knew immediately that we were watching something extraordinary. We got out of our seats and crowded around the balcony. Shortly after this inning, Azhar made his debut for India and scored three consecutive centuries, but I have always had a certain satisfaction in knowing that I saw him bat, before he became a national and global cricketing icon—watched him, in a sense, construct the persona and performative text that he became in later life.

Azharuddin's orientalist/nationalist performance arrived at a historical postcolonial moment—the emergence of satellite television in the early to mid-1980s and the development of what Appadurai refers to as "the means of modernity." Azharuddin's textual history can be intimately tied to early globalization (or using the banal label of the times—"market liberalization") and deregulatory changes in the nature of the Indian state. Specifically, Azharuddin was the first beneficiary of a new kind of television aesthetic—the use of multiple cameras. A key element was the use of one camera exclusively focused on a close-up of the batsman. The images from this camera were used for the other key narrative element from this time period—the slow motion replay. This allowed the viewer to participate fully, with the batsman. Watching Azharuddin meant taking part, with his masculinity, with an erotic immersion in his square drive.

The orientalist moment today lives on in a batsman, Azharuddin closely mentored—V. V. S. Laxman. Cricinfo has the following biography of the batsman:

Wristy, willowy, and sinuous . . . His on-side game is comparable to his idol Azharuddin's and yet he is decidedly more assured on the off side, and has the rare gift of being able to hit the same ball to either side. The Australians, who have suffered more than most, paid the highest compliment after India's 2003–2004 tour Down Under by admitting they did not know where to bowl to him. Laxman, a one-time medical student, finally showed signs of coming to terms with his considerable gifts in March 2001, as he tormented Steve Waugh's thought-to-be-invincible Australians with a majestic 281 to stand the Kolkata Test on its head. But even though he had another wonderful series against the Australians in 2004–2005 with two centuries, one of them involving back-from-the-dead, match-winning, 300-plus partnership with Kolkata ally Rahul Dravid at Adelaide, he hasn't quite managed the consistency that could have turned him into a batting great. (Sambit Bal; content usa.cricinfo.com/india/content/player/30750.html)

Laxman is a complex, contradictory text embodying the cultural and economic circumstance in which he performs. He represents a *completeness* in orientalist expression—he has all the shots—the glance, the drive, the cut, the hook, and he plays all of them with the consummate timing and minimal force. But he is also the least successful of the batsman that preceded him within this discursive ambit—unlike Vishwanath, Pataudi, and Azharuddin he is not a consistent part of the Indian side. Frequently seen as inconsistent he is known primarily for his few iconic innings. Reading Laxman last (in this section) is appropriate, because I would like to suggest that Laxman represents the end point of a certain kind of discursive functionality around national identity—he speaks in a dying language. The context of the game of cricket has been fundamentally altered—cricket is now primarily a medium of rational accounting and corporate expression (seen in the accumulation of runs, the taking of wickets) using a model of masculinity predicated on power and consistency. The kinds of visual aesthetics and physical performance that Laxman represents, has not necessarily gone out of fashion—the five-day test match is an arena where it still exists, but even there the needs of run accumulation take primacy over the ways in which they are scored. In this fundamental sense, the "failure" of Laxman can be seen as part of wider problematic about postcoloniality—the emergence of a national order, framed through the prism of corporate performativity; the development of a theory of the body and perhaps most crucially, an engagement with the demands of accountability—"you are only as good as your last innings," rather than a performance outside of time and necessity, the kinds of aesthetics that underlay the orientalist vision of cricketing. It is indeed an end of this "moment" of cricket, where the love of watching a performance takes second place to the love of accumulation, the focus of the next "moment."

The Third Moment: Moving Nations, Making Money

Cricket as a "means of modernity" reached its full development through the media/cultural work of two of India's greatest batsman, both cast in almost identical physical and technical mold—Sunil Gavaskar and Sachin Tendulkar. Gavaskar's career spanned the 1970s and 1980s and Tendulkar (who played his first test at the age of sixteen) has been the leading batsman for India since the 1990s. Dominating the last four decades of cricket in India, these two batsmen have come to define the postcolonial conjuncture of Indian cricket with the nation-state in modern times. I will discuss both these batsman together, but first a brief biography on each of them:

> Sunil Gavaskar was one of the greatest opening batsmen of all time, and certainly the most successful. His game was built around a near perfect technique and enormous powers of concentration. It is hard to visualize a more beautiful defense: virtually unbreachable, it made his wicket among the hardest to earn. He played with equal felicity off both front and back foot, had an excellent judgment of length and line and was beautifully balanced. He had virtually every stroke in the book but traded flair for the solidity his side needed more. His record for the highest number of Test hundreds was recently overtaken by Sachin Tendulkar, but statistics alone don't reveal Gavaskar's true value to India. He earned respect for Indian cricket and he taught his team-mates the virtue of professionalism. The self-actualization of Indian cricket began under him. (Sambit Bal; content-usa.cricinfo.com/india/content/player/28794.html)

> Sachin Tendulkar has been the most wholesome batsman of his time, and arguably the biggest cricket icon as well. His batting is based on the purest principles: perfect balance, economy of movement, precision in stroke-making, and that intangible quality given only to geniuses, anticipation. If he doesn't have a signature stroke—the upright, back-foot punch comes close—it is because he is equally proficient in each of the full range of orthodox shots (and plenty of improvised ones as well) and can pull them out at will. Though he has adopted a noticeably conservative approach in the last quarter of his career, there are no apparent weaknesses in Tendulkar's game. He can score all around the wicket, off both front foot and back, and has made runs in all parts of the world in all conditions. In 2000, he became the first batsman to have scored 50 international hundreds, and he currently holds the record for most hundreds in both Tests and one-day games. (Sambit Bal; content-usa.cricinfo.com/india/content/player/35320.html)

Watching Gavaskar as a teenager, I was struck by much of what the above account details—the technical excellence, the mastery of performance. It is this single, fundamentally constitutive element in his batting that exemplified the self-determination of the modern Indian nation-state. It is a moment of postcolonial de-linking, where the tools of the masters are not dismantled but revisited, through the *discourse of mastery* in place of mimicry. Gone is the exotic, orientalist construct of an Indian aesthetic in batting, gone too is the fundamental anxiety about identity that bedevils the postcolonial when the master leaves. Here the postcolonial moment is manifest in a fully realized model of performance and reconstituted authenticity. Gavaskar is never compared to any English batsman; if there is a parallel drawn it is to Don Bradman, the greatest batsman to have played the game. (He played for Australia, his identity marked not by nationality but by his technical perfection and a relentless pursuit of runs.) The 1970s were a decade of change and turbulence, as Indian democracy under Prime Minister Indira Gandhi went through a period of corruption, political strife, war with Pakistan, and the imposition of emergency rule. It was a period of fundamental changes in the workings of the Indian state, from an era of Nehruvian Socialism to the travails of a mixed economy and the entrenchment of political corruption. These fundamental changes found expression in popular culture through the emergence of a Bollywood star, Amitab Bachchan, as an "angry young man" and Sunil Gavaskar, as the Indian "anchor" on whose shoulder much of India's journey of national self-realization (through cricket) rested. Gavaskar showed the way in ways that is hard to describe today—growing up in India in the 1970s, the fate of India was tied in a profound way to how Gavaskar performed in a test. When Gavaskar got out early, a despondency descended on the nation, who knew that the rest of the team were incapable of scoring runs, doing what was necessary to stave off defeat. It appeared as if the terms of the social contract with destiny—success or failure—rested on his bat. Vishwanath, Gavaskar's contemporary (and brother-in-law) was deeply loved, but we understood that he could not be relied on. He belonged to a different time and place, a different cultural and political aesthetic—where India and other postcolonial nations were marked with extraordinary individual gifts but lacking the grit and backbone to succeed in a world of (masculine) industrialism (both personal and sociological) that the developed west had a monopoly on—with one exception—Gavaskar. Gavaskar became in a very real sense, the nation, each time he walked out to bat. While later Indian teams had other stars, in the 1970s and early 1980s, India only had one. What was equally significant about Gavaskar was his complete understanding of his role—he realized that he embodied a new kind of identity politics to cricket—it was a based on a regional (Bombay), cultural (Hindu, middle class), and national (Indian) identity. He also belonged to the marketplace, a place almost never visited by Vishwanath. One of the first cricketers to understand the power of advertising, he was frequently seen on magazines, newspapers, and later on television. One particular advertisement for a shaving cream was memorable: it showed a close-up of Gavaskar shaving. With each stroke of the razor, the cream was wiped off, revealing his smooth skin. Appearing on this arc of smoothly shaved skin was an image of Gavaskar playing a cricketing shot. When I began shaving, I was a willing participant, in this aesthetic, imagining (and coalescing) images of Gavaskar and my own shaving with his batting. It was not uncommon for me after shaving to pick up a cricket bat in my bedroom and practice a few shots before the mirror! The power of performativity that Gavaskar represented lay precisely in his ability to capture the paradoxes of the moment—a moment of a nation-state in transition, a period of regeneration of identity politics, that prefigured the rise of both the corporate state and the rise of the Hindu centered national politics in the 1990s. Gavaskar gave rise to a specific kind of national identity—working successfully in the divide between nation and market, past and present. It was an identity that Tendulkar who followed him was to fully realize, both on and off the cricket field.

The similarities between Gavaskar and Tendulkar are often pointed out—they are both from Bombay, both short and compact, both share a nickname—"the little master." Tendulkar fulfills the cultural work begun by Gavaskar in three interrelated ways—his batting reveals not just the discourse of mastery, but a new (corporate) language for recasting the cultural practice of cricket in the postcolonial world. This is tied to the genre of cricket in which each batsman played. Gavaskar's batting revolved around the five-day test match. The one-day game was still in its infancy when he finished his career. Tendulkar established his credentials in both the one-day game and the test match. An entire generation of batsman's techniques were caught in the paradigmatic change that the one-day game format represented but not Tendulkar. He became a point of origin—fashioning a style of batting that has been copied by batsman around the world—a sound defense and a mode of attack, predicated on that defense. For this reason, while (like Gavaskar) he is called "the little master," he alone is called "master blaster." The kind of aggressive intent that Tendulkar shows was rarely evident in the career of Gavaskar. A certain kind of batsman died with the emergence and dominance of the one day game—the classic purist—and a certain kind of batsman was born—the unorthodox hitter, who could change the game in a few overs. Tendulkar, by contrast, has excelled in both versions—he is not a transitional figure, who can straddle both worlds, but the embodiment of classical practices married to modern means. In this sense, he is *sui generis*. Tendulkar is also a brand—his cherubic face, often likened to the Indian god Krishna, is everywhere in India's urban/media landscape—on billboards, plastered to the side of telephone poles, and through advertising (television, print, new media) where he pitches everything from soft drinks to cars to shoes and everything in between. In his complete embrace of the moment of market liberalization, he represents a clear break from both the past (that Gavaskar still represents) marked by fealty to the state, region, nation (and test cricket), and ideas about postcolonial affiliation (such as the "commonwealth" or even "third world"). Instead, Tendulkar's rise to stardom is centered on the rise of the Hindu subject—and Tendulkar is squarely constructed as a national Hindu text. The rise of the Bharatiya Janata Party (BJP) to national power and its political philosophy of Hindutva (centered on the idea of India as a land of and for Hindus—a philosophy in direct opposition to Nehruvian secularism, the founding doctrine of Indian democracy) are parallel texts to the cricketing performance of Tendulkar—a practice that while not codeterminative, speaks to a larger paradigmatic shift in Indian culture and politics, a centering of a certain kind of postcolonial identity—at home in the world of modern industrialism and (simultaneously) a regressive, essentialized Hinduism.

I want to conclude with a brief consideration of another contemporary Indian batsman Virender Sehwag who rounds out the narrative contingencies of this postcolonial moment. Sehwag is perhaps the most potent opening batsman of the contemporary era, having the capacity to destroy the best fast bowlers of the world. He is a fascinating player/text to deconstruct in that he has consciously modeled himself after his idol, Sachin Tendulkar. His conscious participation in this act of (collective/national) determination is central to the pleasure that Sehwag offers to the postcolonial subject. When he first appeared on the scene, he looked eerily like Tendulkar. Built almost identically, he dressed, walked, and copied all the mannerisms of Tendulkar. In one memorable magazine spread, the two players were positioned side by side, with the writer, detailing the minute similarities and differences between the two players. His narrative trajectory was constituted around a single question—would he be able to become another little master? There were a set of related questions that followed—could he ever be as good as Tendulkar? Was he a mere mimic, a poor man's Tendulkar? This fundamentally postmodern concern (the relationship between the real and the facsimile; between authenticity and imitation) has been the central defining feature of Sehwag's career—and he has fashioned a compelling narrative, that engages with contemporary Indian postcoloniality. His biography on Cricinfo points to key moments:

> Virender Sehwag is a primal talent whose rough edges make him all the more appealing. By the time he had scored his first centuries in one-day cricket (off 70 balls, against New Zealand) and Test cricket (on debut, against South Africa, from 68 for 4), he was already eliciting comparisons with his idol Sachin Tendulkar. It is half true. Like Tendulkar, he is short and square with curly hair, plays the straight drive, back foot punch and whip off the hips identically, but leaves Tendulkar in the shade when it comes to audacity. Asked to open the innings in Tests on the tour of England in 2002, Sehwag proved an instant hit, cracking an 80 and a 100 in the first two matches. Regularly thereafter, he kept conjuring pivotal innings at the top of the order, none as significant as India's first 300 (which he bought up, characteristically, with a six), at Multan against Pakistan in early 2004. (content-usa.cricinfo .com/india/content/player/35263.html#Profile)

Sehwag works through the frame of mimicry and imitation but stretches the performative frame of Indian batting styles in new and unpredictable ways. By matching Tendulkar stroke for stroke when they open the innings for India, and often surpassing him, the Tendulkar-Sehwag show has been the most entertaining opening partnership in all of contemporary cricket. Watching them together, the pleasure of critical comparison becomes a national obsession—each moment of their individual expression—is an entry point into a conversation about Indian masculinity and identity. There are two key elements in most comparisons—the first is the element of classicism. Each shot, the punch of the back foot, the cover drive, the lofted shot over the slips, and perhaps most crucially, the hook shot that both batsman employ frequently are compared by fans with attention played to minute deviations from the classic posture and rendition of each shot. Tendulkar, it is always noted, rarely wavers from his classic elementalism. Even when he improvises, the beginning of each shot is anchored by a strict adherence to the axioms of tradition—playing in the V (an expression referring to batting straight, rather than across the line of the ball), playing the ball down, rather than in the air. Sehwag, on the other hand begins with the same classic orientation, but at the last minute changes the trajectory of the shot and its rendition. The commentary that surrounds the batting of each player is also usually focused on just such an analysis—the slow motion replays of shots allow for the minute examination of how each player presents a different rendition. Television is central to the pleasure that both Tendulkar and Sehwag accord. They emerged into the national and global scene as the Indian media market settled into a stable pattern of market liberalization, bringing in television companies like ESPN, and establishing media voyeurship as a primary mechanism for establishing a relationship between a sport and nation. In doing so, the primary agency for understanding cricket moved from the outside to the inside, from the trees and maidan to the large screen TV and the darkened (preferably air conditioned) room. Cricket became part of a familiar place (for the west), a place shaped by the entertainment-political complex, a place with a shared language about identity, celebrity, and consumption.

Sehwag moves the national conversation about cricket in a different direction from Tendulkar, whose performance is predicated on his resting place—as the icon of a modern (Hindu) India. Sehwag is an innovative, audacious performer who belongs clearly in the arena of the spectacle—he is a child of the commodity-world, rather than arena of cultural, religious, and national revival. When he bats, the Indian nation sits at the edge of their seats, waiting to see the next extravagance of expression that Sehwag provides. When Tendulakar bats, they sit back, with the pleasure of watching something powerful and nuanced, assured and dependable. Put another way, if Tendulkar is the resting place of contemporary Indian modernity, Sehwag is the force that pushes it forward to a place that is still taking shape—whose form is being determined by two contemporary texts—the former captain Sourav Ganguly and the current one-day captain, Mahinder Singh Dhoni. The cultural context these two captains perform are constitutive elements of the last moment of Indian postcoloniality, one marked by increasing importance into the global market economy, and a sense of arrival of the nation-state (to which I now turn).

The Fourth Moment: Global Missions, National Icons

The contemporary period of postcoloniality and Indian cricket is marked by four interrelated elements—a sustained discourse of aggressive masculinity—paralleling the rise of the Indian economy and its central role in global information industries (brought to marginal attention in news about outsourcing); a paradigmatic shift in media/collective discourse, from within the nation to its diasporic constituents; a complete embrace of corporate fashioned identity politics, with attention focused on the male body as an index of (national) sexual expression and finally, and most crucially, a corporate philosophy ("winning is everything") representing a complete break from the history/discourse of fair play and the gentleman's game. These four elements introduced by the Indian captain Saurav Ganguly have come to full fruition under Mahender Singh Dhoni.

Ganguly was India's most successful captain, leading the side much as he batted—with intuition, arrogance, and unstinted aggression. India won tests at a steady pace, went to the World Cup finals in 2003 and was the only team to put up a fight against Australia, the dominant (and overbearing) team of the last two decades in the cricketing world. A controversial figure, for picking fights with opponents, he bred a culture of complete allegiance to his team *and* complete contempt toward the opposition. He bred a similar culture of spectatorship and membership in national identity. This often put him at odds with older Indians and parts of the media establishment. The child equally of television and the Internet, Ganguly's every move and score is fodder for feverish debate and passion. A century by him at Australia brought the following passionate blog:

> What I say is those critics and so called "purists" can go have a walk because not in years has India had a captain whom everyone in the side could proverbially die for. He stands by them no matter what happens, and is returned the favor by the team, which stands by their skipper through thick and thin. So why bother about the critics when Ganguly is one of the very few skippers India has had who are naturally aggressive, who back the youngsters and who, for a change, don't take a step back when aroused verbally. Urgent, emotional, doubtlessly decisive, and arrogant to the core. Ganguly is the man most of India loves to hate. Why? Because he chews nails on the field. Be-

cause he doesn't follow tradition. Because he wants to lead the side dictator style. Because he doesn't give a sorry damn to what critics think. Because he wears his heart on his sleeve. Because he doesn't take a step back when confronted. Because he takes his shirt off and flaunts it after an unbelievable win at Lord's. (www.cricketfundas.com/indplayers/ganguly.html)

The scene described at the end of this blog entry has became iconic of the postcolonial moment that Ganguly represents—standing on the balcony at Lord's, the home of cricketing tradition, taking off his shirt and waving it in the air. His lean, muscled body is arched in arrogance, the gold chains and hirsute masculinity, inviting erotic attention. This match, a one-day international game between England and India played on July 14, 2002, is worth dwelling on. It represents a paradigmatic moment in India's national engagement with cricket (embodying each of the four elements identified above). Excerpts from a media account of the day:

London, July 14. Indian captain Saurav Ganguly said India's sensational two-wicket win over England at Lord's yesterday erased the painful memories of the one-day series against that team at home early this year. "I have no words to explain. It has been outstanding," said Ganguly of India's victory after having remained literally glued to his seat throughout India's epic run chase in the afternoon. It was clear that not clinching the home series against England after leading 2–1 had rankled Ganguly. For, soon after Kaif and Zaheer completed the winning run, he took off his shirt in the manner Andrew Flintoff had done in Mumbai as England won the nerve-wrecker of a match in the final Ganguly ran on to the field after India won, straight to Mohammad Kaif and pinned the youngster down on the field in an overt display of emotion with a hint of tears in his eyes. The team popped up champagne in the dressing room and everybody, including team manager Rajeev Shukla, drenched themselves completely. The celebrations continued late in the night after the team returned to their rooms as the hotel authorities had arranged a party on their own. Later, Shukla took the boys out for dinner but not to an Indian restaurant—the team had a raucous dinner in an Italian joint. After completing one of the most audacious run-chases in the history of the game, Kaif ran up to the sightscreen, shouting himself hoarse with helmet in one hand and bat in the other as he looked at a bunch of supporters and a few friends sitting in the stands. (www.tribuneindia.com/2002/20020715/sports.htm-top)

The relevance of this game cannot be overemphasized in the annals of modern Indian cricket. It is often seen as the turning point in how Indian cricket has been played. Before this game, the "old guard" of Sachin Tendulkar and Rahul Dravid dominated discussion of India's batting. After this game, Virender Sehwag and two new faces—Mohammad Kaif and Yuvraj Singh—became central figures in the cricketing imagination. Both, in their twenties, they represented *identical* cricketing styles—quick, direct, aggressive, and both were fundamentally shaped in the image of their maker—the captain, Saurav Ganguly. Kaif and Yuvraj are often spoken as if they are two sides of the same coin—a one-two punch, whose identities are anchored not in their Muslim or Hindu/Sikh heritages but in their mobilization of a certain style of playing, one uniquely suited to both an image of the Indian nation taking its place on the world stage (and the television screen). This game being played at Lords can manifestly be read as a "revenge of the colonies" narrative and it was in a sense some of that. An English paper, *The Observer*, for example said of the match, "In the past many [of the Indians] have enchanted us with the wristy magic of their batsmen. This Indian side contains plenty of those, but there is also a steel and an athleticism that was often absent from their predecessors." But equally, it was played before a large Indian diasporic population in England. It also became one of the most popular videos sold in DVD form and visited online. My younger son, a cricket devotee, first came to the power of cricket watching this game—as Kaif and Yuvraj chased the England total, I could sense in his involvement—something sociological—he was experiencing something new—a diasporic pleasure—made up by the desire to participate (from afar and on one's terms) with the idea of personal/national origin.

When the game was over and India had won, one image remained burned in the national imagination—the image of Ganguly, his shirt removed, waving it in the face of tradition, of history, willing the nation, it seemed, to embrace its new history. It is hard not to read this as a text about postcolonial arrival—an arrival that speaks fundamentally to a deeply masculinized identity, one predicated on the presentation of self as an object of consumption—an object that is simultaneously indigenous (in the ethnic construct of the brown body) and global (in its posture, the presentation of the body as an object of lust and desire). As further evidence of the moment's postcoloniality was what the team did after its win—it went to an Italian restaurant—this in London, the home, as is often noted, of the best Indian restaurants in the world! There can be little more that needs to be said—this moment of arrival, presumes not just an awareness of "Italian food" as a marker of a wider, Western practice of consumption, but of the value of "choice" as a symbol of victory. The Indian team not only wins on a world stage, but it consumes on a world stage as well—it does not stay ghettoized within its own diasporic/ethnic space/restaurant but like the "masters" it has agency—sampling the menus of different cultures—in the spirit of a colonial experiment. The past has indeed become the present.

This present now is a new more frenzied version of the game, called the Twenty20 with its own World Cup held in 2007, which was won by India's under its young captain Mahinder Singh Dhoni. Somini Sengupta writing in the *New York Times* captured the postcoloniality of the moment perfectly (an excerpt):

> New Delhi, Sept. 24, 2007. Cricket, always more allegory than sport in this country, is very often the screen on which India's anxieties and aspirations are projected. That is why the Indian cricket team's victory over Pakistan on Monday in a new lean, swift version of the elegant old game came to signify something far larger than itself. The captain, a longhaired 26-year-old wicketkeeper named Mahendra Singh Dhoni, boldly told his teammates to shake off the burden of history, and they did. Fans and pundits seized on the team's success in the first tournament of Twenty20, a radically compressed new cricket format, to celebrate the ascendance of a brash and confident new generation, rising from far-flung small-town India, free of pedigree and custom.
>
> Think of Twenty20 as cricket on Red Bull. Or as the historian Mukul Kesavan put it, "kamikaze cricket." The whole point is to go for it, and keep going for it," said Mr. Kesavan. Not least, Twenty20 served to redeem cricket in both countries, after the humiliation and scandal that the teams suffered in April at the Cricket World Cup in Jamaica. In that tournament, India was trounced by its neighbor Bangladesh. The Pakistani team faced the death of its coach, Bob Woolmer. Redemption, along with the new demographics, promised to breathe new life into cricket, already a big business. A 10-second television spot during a match easily goes for $10,000 in this country, and Twenty20 matches broadcast here have been spliced with advertisements unabashedly chasing the youth market. "Next-generation cricket, next-generation bike," went one advertisement for an Indian-made motorcycle. Much was made of the fact that the captain, Mr. Dhoni, grew up in an uncelebrated eastern city called Ranchi. Near the end of the close and tension-filled game, India beat Pakistan by five runs. Minutes later, apparently in a moment of abandon, Mr. Dhoni took off his jersey, gave it to a young fan and marched topless before the crowd.

It is significant that in his first moment of triumph as a captain, Dhoni chose the rhetorical gesture used by his mentor on the balcony at Lord's—the removal of his shirt. One can freely speculate that Ganguly's gesture must have been on his (and the nation's) mind, when he removed his shirt. Dhoni's gesture brought to fruition, the presentation of a certain masculinist aesthetic—one that I have suggested revolves around the presentation of the naked male body, as the text on which the nation's collective fantasies about global success and personal agency can be written—this is certainly a beginning point for deconstructing Dhoni.

On a concluding note, I spent the summer of 2007 teaching at Oxford University and my two sons and I took the train up to watch a Twenty20 game in Birmingham between two counties—the games were exciting, participating in the act of watching even more so. The English crowd, made up of a multiracial Britain—white, black, Asian, was enjoying the game, singing a range of colorful songs, enjoying the spectacle of big hits and frequent dismissals. It was an experience that was quintessentially similar to watching a game of basketball or football in the United States. In this fundamental sense, the Twenty20 version brings cricket in complete compliance with the norms, rules and conventions of mass produced entertainment content—in other words, the domain of popular culture, which has always been anchored around youth culture and marketed identities. What matters in the commodity world is the recasting of local/national texts into this global language. My younger son, who was deeply disappointed with India's performance in the one-day World Cup, rediscovered his love for cricket through the Twenty20 World Cup. Even my older son, barely interested in any sport, saw some redeeming features (it was over quickly!). India's performance in the Twenty20 World Cup and the emergence of Dhoni as the latest face of Indian cricket, represents not only the extension of the cultural practices of masculinity, performance, and accountability inaugurated by Ganguly, but something more—the assured presence of a *national* identity—even as it becomes part of the language of global corporate expression. In this sense, Dhoni represents an expression of cultural dispersal—the idea of "diaspora"—expressed not only through rituals of cultural revival (such as religious festivals by immigrant groups) but equally in the space of sporting performance and participation that connects the playing fields of Ranchi (the city where Dhoni comes from), Birmingham, and even my hometown—Athens, Georgia. (The "field" is our backyard with a brick path serving as the pitch. The gate serves as the wickets. Hits to the picket fence yield four runs, hits over, a six.) The Twenty20 World Cup and the text of Dhoni is at the heart of the discursive work that connects these different parts of the postcolonial world. Specifically, what Dhoni offers is a comfort with hybridity, with both corporate expression and the easy mobilization of local, national, and global vocabularies to express both personal identity and collective agency. A visit to Dhoni's official website (dhoni.com) reveals the contours of this expression—he is described as the "Ranchi Rocket," as somebody who combines "rock-star cool and down to earth humility," somebody who owns ten bikes; loves hip-hop and Kishore Kumar; loves home cooked food and chicken tikka pizza, Amitab Bachachan, and Angelina Jolie; and is an avid gamer (favorite game: *Counter-Strike*). The image on his "lifestyle" page shows him in a black leather jacket and pants (the jacket has a *Los Angeles Raiders* logo on it). His corporate sponsors we learn include the global (Exide, Pepsi, Reebok) and the national/local (Siyarams, Godrej, Parle Milk Shakti). In all of these ways, Dhoni represents a language of postcoloniality, which speaks equally in obscure corners of the world like Athens, Georgia, and Ranchi, India, through the cult of celebrity and an aesthetic of performance. My younger son, has long hair like Dhoni, clearly mimics his batting style—only sixes satisfy him. I think back to a young boy, bespectacled, clutching a transistor to his ear, wondering whether India would survive its cricketing journey in a far-off land. And I surmise: it has, and more.

CONCLUSIONS AND DIRECTIONS

In this concluding section, I want to address some research questions (around postcoloniality and cricket) not undertaken in the above analysis, and offer them as important avenues for future projects to explore.

First, what modes of discursive accountability account for the fact that there have been very few genuinely fast bowlers to have emerged out of the Indian encounter with cricket? When Indian cricket first came of international age, its opening attack was headed by Mohammad Nissar, by all accounts a genuinely fast bowler. But after him, Indian cricket for the next several decades, was dominated by spin bowlers, the opening spells was undertaken by bowlers who were slow-medium bowlers (at best) and part-time acts until the Indian spin bowlers came on. It was not until the 1980s when Kapil Dev emerged on the scene that India got a genuine fast bowler. Throughout my childhood, there was a recurrent complaint about Indian diet and temperament that did not allow for the emergence of fast bowlers. One of my uncles had a pet theory—it was the lack of meat and alcohol in India's dietary arsenal, he argued, that did not give them muscle power and mental aggression to bowl fast. A not so subtle subtext here was the idea that "Hindu" culture and temperament was unsuited to the kinds of performativity and masculinity that cultures where meat and alcohol were part of the diet could easily undertake. The Hindu temperament it was implicit was at its best at the art of spinning, weaving webs of confusion in the batsman's mind. Such discursive frames invite obvious points of entry: was the orientalist discourse (guile, suppleness) that informed Indian batting, a discursive limit for young fast bowlers (of that era) and more importantly an advantage for the emergence of spin bowlers? If so, in what ways, did the spin bowlers (Gupte, Bedi, Chandrashkethar, Prassana, Venkat) that dominated India through three decades (1960s–1980s) draw on the orientalist frame, and equally crucially, in what ways did they refashion them within the nationalist juncture of postcolonial India? Each of these bowlers, were thick, segmented narratives about the Indian nation—Bedi, a symbol of effortless guise; Prasanna, the artist of the flighted ball; Venkat, the poor man's Prasanna; and above all the polio-afflicted Chandrasekhar, an odd, subaltern subject, given to both brilliance and erratic energy—and armed with the most orientalist of weapons—an unreadable googly (a kind of delivery by a spin bowler) that took strategic energy from his polio-withered arm and a fragile, temperamental mind. A research project that undertakes both the performative poetics of these spinners and their discursive underpinnings would be an important contribution to tracking the work of both orientalism and subaltern agency.

Second, there is a complete absence in scholarship of cricket examining the history and sociology of fielding. Batsmen dominate both the sport and its study. How do certain modes of masculinity affect fielding performance? Historically, in the Indian context, fielding was always seen as something unimportant. This changed as the game became competitive, becoming a key element in contemporary cricket. A historical inquiry, could be focused on at least three four key figures in the narrative development of Indian fielding—the fielders Salim Durrani, Ramnath Parkar, Eknath Solkar, and Mohammad Azharuddin. A fan favorite in the 1970s, Salim Durrani, who was a brilliant batsman, who it was often joked, was too bored with fielding to bend down and field the ball. He would lazily jog after it. He epitomized a wider discourse about Indian efficacy and productivity—the nation was able in sporadic effort to beat the opposition, but on the whole, it preferred a draw, and getting back to doing just enough to get by. Ramnath Parkar, who played in just a few tests for India in the 1970s, along with Eknath Solkar were two figures that stand out for their brilliant fielding—Parkar fielded in the covers (where many of the batsman's shot are hit) while Solkar was known for fielding at short leg (a dangerous place where you could be hit by a batsman). I remember watching both of them live in matches played at the stadium in Delhi, the crowd hushed into silence as Parkar would run toward (in place of waiting for) a fully hit ball, swooping it up in one quick movement and throwing it to the wicket keeper. He always wore a blue cricket cap and always had his sleeves rolled down—he was intuitively aware of fielding as a spectacle, rather than a chore to be performed. Both figures came into the fan's consciousness through still photography. Solkar, especially is archived in one's mind purely through photos of a series of brilliant catches he took at short leg, his arms and legs stretched out in effort. Azharuddin, brilliant both in the slips (behind the batsman) and in the covers created a vocabulary for technical excellence (in fielding) and as India's captain helped operationalize it into the language of nationalist excellence. He managed to do what other captains before him—Gavaskar, Pataudi, and Kapi Dev—could not do on a consistent basis—the creation of a new technical and discursive standard for Indian fielding performance. Subsequent captains—Ganguly, Rahul Dravid, and now Mahender Dhoni have built on this, but not always as successfully. In the contemporary era, the wider theoretical question that fielding seems to be especially suited to answer is that of the transference of corporate pedagogies into nationalist vocabularies. Informed by management theories about accountability and collective participation, fielding has emerged as a key element in the performative index by which players, teams, and success is now determined. Australia, the dominant team of the contemporary era, exemplifies this philosophy with its complete, total embrace of fielding as the building block of team and national aspiration. Here too, the emergence of Indian cricketers, as a foil to the Australians has been fundamentally related to their adopting the Australian pedagogy of performance (and having Australian coaches). These issues obviously are only the initial entry point for a wider history of fielding as a text on which national and global aspirations can be read into.

Finally, the women's question is virtually unexamined in the study of cricket. Postcolonial scholars have focused on how the project of nationalism works in a hegemonic fashion within the boundaries of the nation—specifically examining how public culture is often synonymous with male culture. Scholars of feminist historiography have examined the question of "why it is that nationalism achieves the ideological effect of an inclusive and putatively macro-political discourse, whereas the women's question—unable to achieve its own autonomous macro-political identity—remains ghettoized within its specific and regional space" (Radhakrishnan, 1992, p. 78).

In recovering the "women's question" for an understanding of cricket, I would suggest at least two separate areas of (initial) inquiry. The first is a history of women's cricket in India (focusing especially on the iconic figures of Shanta Rangaswami and Sudha Shah). Here, questions of the religious, domestic, and national roles of women as mobilized within the arena of the emergence of cricket as the dominant Indian sport needs to be examined. Of particular interest should be the (lack) of public participation and state and corporate sponsorship of women's cricket. The second is the question of sports fandom as applied to Indian women's cricket. How is spectatorship amongst Indian women viewers of cricket different from those of men? Historically, women were almost completely absent in the stadiums, which were crowded with men—shouting obscenity-laden attacks at the players on the field. With television, the woman as spectator is now an integral part of the sporting narrative—the camera takes breaks between each over to cut to women, who sit gaily attired, fanning themselves, smiling demurely, and on occasion jumping in excitement along with their friends and families who seem to accompany them. How do domestic ideologies about wife, sister, and mother play out in the public arena? Finally, a recent film, *Chuk De India*, is worth mentioning in this context. The film, about the embattled Indian women's hockey team, is a tender, moving parable about hard work, nationalist energy, and secular integrity in the making of a new Indian nation. It draws on the performance of a number of players/trajectories of Indian women's identity—stubborn, sexy, upper class, minority, untouchable, tribal—as they take on two sets of institutional and cultural constraints—those facing the nation from the outside as it struggles to become a global player (in field hockey)—and those facing the nation from the inside—as it threatens to break apart from its internal divisions. The team's Muslim coach (played by Shah Rukh Khan) and his team become the site on which these tensions are played out, predictably with success, in the manner of Bollywood, but there are important pedagogical lessons to be learned—cricket appears throughout the film as a dominant, hegemonic discourse displacing the trajectory of both the women's question and the wider one of national identity. While space does not allow for a more complete discussion here, the film has a clear subtext: How might a film about the Indian *women's* cricket team be narrativized? How might it counter the masculinized story of cricket in India? And to which one might add a broader narrative question—How might the Indian nation have developed *without* cricket?

NOTES

1. Postcolonial theory came into prominence in the 1990s with key writings from Homi Bhabha and Gayatri Spivak with subsequent application of their ideas in literary criticism, comparative literature, history, and cultural studies. Key publications in this time period include Ahmed (1994); Breckenridge and Veer (1993); Dirlik (1994); Williams and Chrisman (1994); Radhakrishnan (1996); Spivak (1990); Ashcroft, Griffiths, and Tiffin (1989); Grewal and Kaplan (1994); Bhabha (1992); Mishra and Hodge (1991); and Prakash (1992). In the field of international communication (for the same time period) see Shome (1995, 1996) and the debate between Kavoori and Shome in *Critical Studies in Mass Communication* (June 1998). For a more contemporary iteration see Shome and Hedge (2002a, 2002b), Parmeswaran (2006, 2008), and Kavoori (2006).

2. For a general history of cricket amongst many candidates see, Allen (1990) and Bowen (1970). For a history of English cricket see Brooks (1978), Birley (1999), Sandiford (1994), and the different essays in Stoddart and Sandiford (1998). For an overview of the global spread of cricket see Kaufman and Patterson (2005). My readings were narrowly focused on the colonial and postcolonial experience and cricket. There is now an emerging literature on the subject. For a representative account of cricket and the West Indian experience, in addition to the seminal writings of C. L. R. James (whose legacy is engaged within Farred, 1996) see Beckles and Stoddard (1995), the two volume history of West Indian cricket (Beckles, 1995, 1998), Griggs (2006), and Cozier (1978). A sense of the South African experience and cricket can be seen in Vahed (2001, 2002) and Padayachee, Desai, and Vahed (2004). For histories of Indian cricket see Docker (1976), Cashman (1980), Bose (1990), and most recently Guha (2002) and Majumdar (2005). Related essays on the colonial experience and cricket include Malcolm (2001), Nandy (2000), and

Williams (2001). For cultural analysis of the one-day cricket world cup see the case studies in Majumdar (2004) and Gemmel and Majumdar (2008).

REFERENCES

Ahmed, A. (1994). *In theory: Classes, nations, literatures*. London: Verso.

Allen, D. (1990). *Cricket: An illustrated history*. Oxford: Phaidon Press.

Ang, I. (1991). *Desperately seeking the audience*. London: Routledge.

Appadurai, A. (1996). *Modernity at large: Cultural dimensions of globalization*. Minneapolis: University of Minnesota Press.

Aschcroft, B., Griffiths, G., & Tiffin, H. (1989). *The empire strikes back: Theory and practice in postcolonial literatures*. London: Routledge.

Beckles, H. (1998). *The development of West Indies cricket* (Vols. 1–2). Barbados: University of the West Indies Press.

Beckles, H., & Stoddard, B. (1995). *Liberation cricket: West Indies cricket culture*. Manchester, UK: Manchester University Press.

Bhabha, H. (1992). Postcolonial criticism. In S. Greenbalt & G. Gunn (Eds.), *Redrawing the boundaries: The transformation of English and American literary studies*. New York: MLA.

Birley, D. (1999). *A social history of English cricket*. London: Aurum Press.

Bose, M. (1990). *History of Indian cricket*. London: Andre Deutsch.

Bowen, R. (1970). *Cricket: A history of its growth and development throughout the world*. London: Eyre and Spottiswoode.

Breckenridge, C., & Veer, V. (1993). *Orientalism and the postcolonial predicament*. Philadephia: University of Pennsylvania Press.

Brookes, C. (1978). *English cricket: The game and its players throughout the ages*. London: Weidenfeld and Nicholson.

Cashman, R. (1980). *Players, patrons, and the crowd: The phenomenon of Indian cricket*. Calcutta, India: Orient Longman.

Clifford, J. (1986). *Writing culture*. Berkeley: University of California Press.

Cozier, T. (1978). *The West Indies: Fifty years of test cricket*. Brighton: Angus and Robertson.

Docker, E. (1976). *A history of Indian cricket*. Delhi: Macmillan.

Dirlik, A. (1994). The post-colonial aura: Third world criticism in the age of global capitalism. *Critical Inquiry, 20*, 328–356.

Farred, G. (1996). *Rethinking C. L. R. James*. Oxford: Basil Blackwell.

Farred, G. (2004). The double temporality of *Lagaan*: Cultural struggle and post-colonialism. *Journal of Sport and Social Issues, 28*(2), 93–114.

Frankenberg, R., & Mani, L. (1993). Crosscurrents, crosstalks. *Cultural Studies, 7*, 292–310.

Gemmell, J., & Majumdar, B. (2008). *Cricket, race & the 2007 World Cup*. London: Routledge.

Grewal, I., & Kaplan, C. (1994). *Scattered hegemonies*. Minneapolis: University of Minnesota Press.

Griggs, G. (2006). Calypso to collapso: The decline of the West Indies as a cricketing super power. *Journal of Sport and Social Issues, 30*(3), 306–314.

Guha, R. (1998). Cricket and politics in colonial India. *Past and Present: A Journal of Historical Studies, November*(2), 157–161.

Guha, R. (2002). *A corner of a foreign field: The Indian history of a British sport*. London: Picador.

James, C. L. R. (1983). *Beyond a boundary*. New York: Pantheon Books.

Kaufman, J., & Patterson, O. (2005). Cross-national cultural diffusion: The global spread of cricket. *American Sociological Review, 70*, 82–110.

Kavoori, A (1998). Getting past the latest "post": Assessing the term "post-colonial." *Critical Studies in Mass Communication, 15*, 195–212.

Kavoori, A. (2006). International communication after terrorism: Toward a post-colonial dialectic. In A. Kavoori and T. Fraley (Eds.), *Media, terrorism, theory* (pp. 179–197). Lanham, MD: Rowman & Littlefield.

Majumdar, B. (2002). Cultural resistance and sport: Politics, leisure and colonialism, *Lagaan*, invoking lost history. *Culture, Sport, Society, 5*(2), 29–44.

Majumdar, B., & Mangan, J. (2005). *Indian cricket through the ages: A Reader*. New York: Oxford University Press.

Malcolm, D. (2001). It's not cricket: colonial legacies and contemporary inequalities. *Journal of Historical Sociology, 14*, 253–275.

Mani, L. (1989). Multiple mediations. *Inscriptions, 5*, 1–23.

Mishra, A., & Hodge, B (1991). What is post-colonialism? *Textual Practice, 5*, 400–411.

Mohanty, C. (1987). Under western eyes: Feminist scholarship and colonial discourses. *Feminist Review, 30*, 61–88.

Majumdar, B. (2004). *Cricketing cultures in conflict: Cricket World Cup 2003*. London: Routledge.

Nandy, A. (2000). *The Tao of cricket: On games of destiny, and destiny of games*. New Delhi: Oxford University Press.

Padayachee, V., Desai, A., & Vahed, G. (2004). Managing South African transformation: The story of cricket in KwaZulu Natal, 1994–2004. *Patterns of Prejudice, 38*(3), 253–278.

Parmeswaran, R. (2006). Military metaphors, masculine modes and orientalist others: Deconstructing journalists' inner tales of September 11. *Journal of Communication Inquiry, 30*(11), 42–64.

Parmeswaran, R. (2008). Reading the visual, tracking the global: Postcolonial feminist methodology and the chameleon codes of resistance. In N. Denzin et al. (Eds.), *Handbook of critical indigenous methodologies*. Newbury Park: Sage.

Prakash, G. (1992). Postcolonial criticism and Indian historiography. *Social Text, 31/32*, 8–19.

Radhakrishnan, R. (1992). Nationalism, gender, and the narrative of identity. In A. Parker, M. Russo, D. Sommer & P. Yeager (Eds.), *Nationalisms and sexualities* (pp. 77–95). New York: Routledge.

Radhakrishnan, R. (1996). *Diasporic mediations*. Minneapolis: University of Minnesota Press.

Rail, G. (1998). *Sport and postmodern times*. Albany: SUNY Press.

Rouse, R. (1991). Mexican migration and the social space of postmodernism. *Diaspora, 1*, 8–23.

Sandiford, K. (1994). *Cricket and the Victorians*. Aldershot, UK: Ashgate.

Sen, S. (2001). Enduring colonialism in cricket: From Ranjitsinghji to the Cronje affair. *Contemporary South Asia, 10*(2), 237–249.

Shome, R. (1995). Postcolonial interventions in the rhetorical canon: An "other" view. *Communication Theory, 6,* 40–59.

Shome, R. (1996). Race and popular cinema: The rhetorical strategies of whiteness in city of Joy. *Communication Quarterly, 44*(4), 502–518.

Shome, R., & Hegde, R. (2002a). Postcolonial approaches to communication: Charting the terrain, engaging the intersections. *Communication Theory, 12*(3), 249–270.

Shome, R., & Hegde, R. (2002b). Culture, communication, and the challenge of globalization. *Critical Studies in Media Communication, 17*(2), 172–189.

Spivak, G. (1990). *The postcolonial critic.* New York: Routledge.

Stoddart, B. (1988). Sports, cultural imperialism, and colonial response in the British Empire. *Comparative Studies in Society and History, 30,* 649–673.

Stoddart, B., & Sandiford, K. (1998). *The imperial game: Cricket, culture, and society.* Manchester, UK: Manchester University Press.

Vahed, G. (2001). What do they know of cricket, who only cricket know? Transformation of South African cricket, 1990–2000. *International Review for the sociology of sport, 36*(3), 319–336.

Vahed, G. (2002). Cultural confrontation: Race, politics, and cricket in South Africa in the 1970s and 1980s. *Culture, Sport, Society, 5*(2), 79–107.

Williams , C., & Chrisman, P. (1994). *Colonial discourse and postcolonial theory: A reader.* New York: Harvester.

Williams, J. (2001). *Cricket and race.* Oxford: Berg.

6

Consuming Technologies:
The Discourse of Cell Phone
Advertising in India

The spanking new Tata Sumo careened crazily through the traffic. On each side of the Sumo, smoke billowed from other cars, buses, and rickshaws. Through the smoke, one could see emblazoned on the sides of many vehicles bold claims of a new connectedness: cell phones. Similar advertisements hung everywhere: on crooked telephone poles, adorning the sides of slums, schools, railway stations, homes, and offices. The car driver clasped a cell phone to his ear as he narrowly missed a line of pigs heading straight for a garbage heap piled outside a tiny cell phone shop. The cultural vertigo was complete. (author field notes from visit to New Delhi)

In this chapter I examine how the cell phone is "mediated" in the developing world, using India as an example. Specifically, I want to focus on how advertising (the language of global capitalism) constructs culturally significant ways to think about and incorporate such media technologies into the fabric of social life—in other words, I want to suggest that understanding capitalism, must be centered in how it is *consumed*.

My approach differs from mainstream scholars of technological diffusion who traditionally use a "development communication" perspective that typically examines such technologies as a set of technological developments coordinated through policy prescriptions by politicians and institutional regulators. Rather than attempt such an exercise, I attempt to ask the more difficult—and perhaps more interesting question—how is the cell phone shaping issues of identity in the developing world? How

171

are such technologies a site for the articulation of a specific cultural consciousness that will both underpin and legitimize the future of economic and institutional development?

Recognizing that technologies are always understood in cultural contexts (Leonardi, 2003) and that each technology is fundamentally different in the way it is socially constructed by its users, I suggest that thinking about technology in this sense places communication in a position of importance rather than regarding it as ancillary to the "hardware." In other words, decentering technology at the interactional site allows it to be reconstructed as a social practice (Leonardi, 2003, p. 161). Taking seriously the idea that communication practices help to construct certain technologies, Jackson, Poole, and Kuhn (2002) encourage the promotion of communication as an "object of interest itself, rather than keying only to characteristics of communication that seem derivable from technology" (cited in Leonardi, 2003, pp. 161–162).

By taking this path to analysis, I am not saying that the cell phone cannot be understood by examining issues of technological innovation, state governance, or infrastructural development. I am saying, however, that an exclusive focus on the institutional and individual basis of assessing a media technology globally ignores how such technologies are mediated in cultural terms.[1] There are two important axioms that underlie the analysis to follow.

First, the role of a media technology can be better understood when you place it in a vision of a *cultural* future rather than an exclusively *technological* future. In other words, I propose that cell phones are *cultural technologies* that are appropriated and internalized by the culture within the matrix of global and cultural relations framed by processes of global capitalism.

Second, this process of appropriation of cultural technologies in the developing world takes place *through traditional media* rather than the "new" media technology itself (i.e., through computers or cell phones). These "traditional" media (magazines, newspapers, and television) still dominate the marketplace in developing countries (such as India) and it is through messages in these media that the cultural frame for understanding and selling media technologies is constructed. The selling is done through a well-worn form of persuasive communication—advertising. This chapter provides an in-depth examination of how advertising in traditional Indian media (newspapers and magazines)[2] constructs ideas about consumption, identity, and technology around these new technologies. In the next section (framing advertising), I provide an accounting of the general universe of ads in India that are related to how new technologies are framed, followed by a more detailed textual reading of selected advertisements (hereafter, ads) focusing on issues of identity, gender, and cell phone technology. The final section (conclusion) provides a contextual treatment of the wider question of the role of advertising in the developing world.

FRAMING ADVERTISING

Why advertising? Simply put, it's everywhere. Traveling in any of India's cities, the presence of cell phone advertising is overwhelming: banners hanging from telephone poles and trees; posters stuck on the walls of shops, homes, and hospitals; signs posted on rickshaws, buses, and cars; children holding up signs for Internet cafés; street vendors selling cell phone covers alongside combs, bangles, and rings. The research question about the function of advertising shouts at you from every intersection in India's urban landscape. As Ewen (1989) puts it, "urban imagery—advertising—bears the imprint of the lives of the people that they address. To approach an understanding of urban commercial imagery, images must be seen as engaged in a social-historical process, responsible to the changing terms of social life and of social institutions" (p. 83).

The commodity world: the images (and text) of advertising by cell phone companies needs to be first contextualized within a larger universe of ads articulating a fundamental shift in (the marketing of) cultural sensibilities in the developing world as it grapples with global capitalism. These ads—part of the entire "commodity world"—provide the contexts of interpretation; the "webs of signification" that frame consumption in countries like India. Every issue of the *Times of India*, for example, has at least two pages of full ads, where ads for cell phones appear alongside those for call center jobs, Internet service/companies, English language schools, computer schools, exam preparation centers (computers, law, MBA, SAT, GRE, MMAT), and for admissions to schools in Europe and the United States. These ads refer to both learning a new language (English) and a technological vocabulary (computers, Internet, call centers, etc.) thereby gaining entry into both the job market and a mode of consumption.

Let me illustrate with examples from a pervious study (Kavoori and Chadha, 2001) that provides a historical perspective to cell phones as the latest "new media." In this study focused on the "Internet" as a cultural technology, a colleague and I identified a range of such ads in the *Times of India*: Institute of Network Technology ("Get the head start in career: Java"), Career Makers ("Read and Write Fluent English"), National Center for World Languages ("Two months certificate courses in German,

French, Spanish, and Japanese"). The newsmagazine, *India Today* included ads from the Alps Cosmetic Clinic for Men and Women (the advertisement has a young man with a "cool" look with locks of hair casually strewn across the forehead. The text says "The real look for real men" which can be arrived at the "Gents Saloon and Barber shop" through "computerized hair styling"), Calorex Computer Finance (the advertisement has a computer with the text reading "Buy a computer with the easiest finance possible"), British School of Language (the school claims in the ads to be "India's largest and No. 1 English Teaching school" and lists the prices and locations for the latest classes of "academic English" for high school students), and finally, the law offices of Colin Singer which advertises "Canada Immigration."

Reading across these texts, it became clear that "linguistic acquisition" signaled both learning "English" and gaining entry into a mode of consumption. This included specific ideas—those focused on image mobilization (e.g., "computerized hair") and more general claims about Western/modern sensibilities (e.g., the computer as a tool for economic fulfillment, the direct referencing to immigration and the use of "Java" as emblematic of career opportunities).

In addition to issues of linguistic acquisition and consumer culture, other ads reflected another contextual theme, which was termed "technological national development." To illustrate, an ad by the Indian government's Ministry of Information Technology, advertised "Software Technology Parks of India," "Where dreams become a reality." It invited the reader to "join us for a giant leap into the IT millennium." A second ad from Venus Capital Management Company (a venture capitalist company based in the United States) announced the launch of "The India Technology Fund." The ad has a map of India with the words E-India emblazoned over it. The text of the ad included a statement by the director of the fund, which read, "In the next decade, technology, particularly software will mean to India what oil means to the Gulf countries." A third ad from Birlasoft (a software consulting company run by a leading family of Indian capitalists) had a male athlete pole-vaulting over a map of India centered on a graphic of the globe. The headline of the ad said "Whatever I.T. takes" while the text of the ad reiterated this message: "employ whatever I.T. takes to evolve as a leading software consulting company."

These same themes today inform the contextual reception of cell phones: An ad in *India Today* by the Indian government's Ministry of Information Technology, is focused on "Community Information Centers," "Where a new dawn of freedom—freedom from distance" is promised. It invokes the nationalist poet, Rabindranath Tagore and suggests that new technology will lead India "into that heaven of freedom" where "the minds is without fear and the head is held high, where knowledge is free." Another ad from Reliance Infocomm (one of India's leading industrial houses) entitled "Reliance India Mobile," frames the reader as a national subject: "Get Ready India." The text of the three-page advertisement is centered on the chairman and managing director Mukesh Ambani, who writes "A digital revolution is being unleashed in India today with the launch of Reliance Infocomm. I invite you to take part in this revolution." A third advertisement from the global media company, Samsung, has a cell phone being held by a number of young, attractive, and exuberant Indians who ask, "The future is calling. Are you there?"

Taken together each of these contextual categories (language acquisition, consumer culture and national technological development) represents the collective valorization of technology by three separate agents (the government, transnational capital, and indigenous capital). The valorization of this technology is tied to issues of reimagining the nation as a cell phone nation and the role of information technologies as the *economic* arm of nation building. Historically, media in much of the developing world was seen as the *cultural* arm of national building and media content was seen as fulfilling both entertainment and information functions. In sum, this frame for constructing cell phones mirrors and extends a process of cultural commodification and national reimagination already established by the Internet in India (Kavoori and Chadha, 2001).

ADVERTISING DISCOURSE(S) AND CELL PHONES

I now turn to a detailed textual reading of one set of advertisements that occurred across sites—billboards, newspapers, magazines, and television. These were the Motorola ads. The analysis here draws theoretical sustenance from a study of cell phone advertising in Slovenia by Pajnik and Tusek (2002) who examined issues of culture and technology using an Althusserian and structural-semiotic analysis and a research report by Motorola researcher Sadie Plant (2005), who conducted extensive field research for Motorola across the world in order to identify the sociological and ritual contexts for cell phone use.

Pajnik and Tusek's analysis (2002) focuses on cell phone advertising by Mobitel in Slovenia. They argue that cell phone advertising functions like most Advertising discourse, where ideology functions through the "interpellation of viewers." Interpellation is a process by which we organize ourselves into the position offered by advertising discourse in the presentation of a particular product. There is a discourse of the inner voice used in advertisements that is used in advertising that address the reader as "you" continuously telling you what it is you want and need (p. 279).

To counterpose, the Motorola report draws on a very different institutional and pedagogical discourse to make its case:

> We live in an age of intelligent machines that are in perpetual communication, creating new networks of knowledge, information and empowerment across the globe. At the heart of any technological change is the human experience. And its in understanding how the digital world is being experienced by all of us, as friends, colleagues and families, that we gain the most insight into the shape of things to come. (Plant, 2005, p. 1)

The Advertisements

The six ads from Motorola that I will focus on are part of a single advertising campaign using Indian models to frame the use of cell phone and the cultural discourses it interpellates viewers with. The six ads had the following titles: GlobalMoto, JetsetMoto, MastermindMoto, HeadsturnMoto, ColormeMoto, and TranceMoto. I saw these ads on posters, walls, newspapers, and magazines—in other words on both the media and urban landscape. The ads discussed here were all taken from the newsmagazine *India Today*.

Like the Mobitel ads in Slovenia, the Motorola ads, "were presented through the images of people, although they do not speak at all" (Pajnik and Tusek, 2002, p. 285) and created "the illusion of people connected, gaining friendship, love and social approval, while the phone as a technology stood as a substitute for personal communication" (Pajnik and Tusek, 2002, p. 297).

CULTURAL TECHNOLOGY AND MASCULINITY: ANALYSIS OF GLOBALMOTO, JETSETMOTO, MASTERMINDMOTO, AND HEADSTURNMOTO

Each of these ads are focused around different Indian male models that center the act of mobility and of the machine-body relationship that has come to characterize so much of the use of mobile technologies. The models hold up, flash, and "display" the phone as part of their body and the performance they enact. In this centering of both display and use, the cell phone ads replicate our general intimacy with machines. As Haraway (1990) put in a seminal article, "Late twentieth century machines have made thoroughly ambiguous the differences between the natural and the artificial, mind and body, self-developing and externally designed. Our machines are disturbingly lively, and we ourselves frighteningly inert" (p. 194).

In this sense, the cell phone is very clearly located within a wider matrix of technology relations seen for example in earlier narratives of beepers, cameras, watches, transistors, portable CD players, and even cars. Cell phones thus keep open the "technological determinism and ideological space opened up by the reconception of machines and organisms as coded text through which we engage in the play of reading and writing the world" (Haraway, 1990, p. 194).

Beyond this overall reiteration of a cultural positionality toward technology and body-machine relations, the Motorola ads do a lot more: they frame a gendered relationship to this technology.

GlobalMoto has the following elements: A slim, Indian male, dressed in a business suit holding a silver briefcase. He is on the go, he looks at the viewer in mid-stride, his expression a mixture of satisfaction and aloofness. His eyebrows are marginally quizzical; he conveys both assurance and a self-consciousness of the effect of his presence. This presence is framed with the accoutrements of being global—a blue jacket, unbuttoned and open; a cell phone receiver in his ear and the silver briefcase, with labels for five cities: Taipei, Tokyo, Mexico City, Sydney, and Montreal. It is an image where the idea of "mobility"—central to both the technological and discursive constitution of the cell phone is emphasized. As the Motorola report puts it:

> All around the world, the mobile has been become associated with a handful of phrases which recur like samples in a global dance track. These include "on my way," "on the bus," "on the train." If "where are you" is the perfect mobile question, the perfect mobile answer is "on the mobile." (Plant, 2005, p. 5)

Being on the mobile in the context of the GlobalMoto ads signals not just mobility but economic mobility—the ready inclusion of the Indian male presence within the work and cultural space of global capitalism. The man on the move in the advertisement is no ordinary man—his mobility is *both fashioned* by global capital and he is *made manifest* through its rearticulation in the context of a local masculinized presence.

The MastermindMoto ad extends the logic of mobility and corporate masculinized Indian identity and presents it with a narrative vehicle that is less tangential. It is focused on an Indian model that takes the value of globality and mobility and presents it in a direct mode of address. It shows a twenty something business executive wearing a shiny leather-look business suit with a pinstripe yellow tie. The model faces the camera, his head tilted up so that he is looking down at the reader. His expression is aloof, the disdain barely concealed. In his left hand, he holds an open cell phone, its screen lit up with colorful content (which is not decipherable). Behind him in small letters are the words "Pocket Internet Explorer" and "Windows

Media Player." The models legs are spread open; he leans forward, lightly balanced on a bright red sofa. His gaze (and by implication that of the cell phone) is emblematic of a wider logic offered by global capitalism: Get in the game or get left behind. Its sheer inexorability appears to inform the personification of these models. As Pajnik and Tusek (2002) put it, "the individuals in the advertisements are personified even if they are represented as members of a particular social group and the *individuality* is represented to be a *crucial new value*" (p. 297, emphasis added).

The last two advertisements, JetsetMoto and HeadsturnMoto, take the logic of corporate Indian masculinity and extend it into the realm of popular culture, youth identity politics and center the cell phone within the frame of cultural performance and play. JetsetMoto shows an Indian male model wearing a leather jacket and informal business shirt balanced on a skateboard. The picture is taken from the ground up, so that the businessman/skateboarder is flying over the viewer, who looks up at him. The model balances himself with barely outstretched hands, one of which holds a cell phone. He wears dark glasses; the graffiti under his skateboard says, "Switch." His gaze is away from the viewer; it is positioned at his destination (the point of landing or perhaps somewhere more abstract). What stands out from this corporate/popular culture performance is the effortless control and balance of the model. Unlike other skateboarding advertisements, the emphasis is not on contorted moves but rather on the almost unconscious pleasure that such control gives to the businessman/skateboarder. JetsetMoto is both an extension of the logic of GlobalMoto and MastermindMoto (in its reliance of the centering of corporate male masculinity) but it also articulates a more assured, comfortable and pleasurable set of uses of this technology. It personalizes the technology and links the critical new values of globalization with the promise of popular culture and personal enactment.

HeadsturnMoto takes the logic of Jetsetmoto and firmly places it within the realm of popular culture and an aggressive youth (identity) politics. It shows a young Indian male in his late teens, early twenties poised in stride. His legs are spread confidently apart as he looks intently and texts on his cell phone. His clothes serve as a diacritical sign for a new Indian masculinity. He wears tight black pants with shiny red markings running down each leg. His striped-black jacket swings open like a cape (Batman style) and his shirt is made of a thin black mesh through which his skin can be seen. His hair is carefully rumpled and his eyes invisible behind large, wraparound dark glasses. His expression is hostile, his gaze zeroed in on the cell phone that he cradles carefully as he texts. His shoes are shiny black leather and placed apart in a free-swinging but balanced style. HeadsturnMoto provides the viewer with a set of messages that draw on and take sustenance from the other Motorolo advertisements. They are firmly placed within the idea that the neoliberal global marketplace has arrived (and made possible) by the discursive strengths of a corporate male masculinity but there is more to HeadsturnMoto—it is the idea common to popular culture representations—that the moment also calls for a counterculture that uses technology to represent its identity politics—which like most corporate sponsored youth cultures is defiant, aggressive, flamboyant, and deliberative in its self-reflexivity and self-centeredness.

HeadsturnMoto is strikingly eye-catching and strikingly commonplace. It is easily placed within the MTV generated world of youth culture images that have now come to be synonymous with the face of global capitalism.

CULTURAL TECHNOLOGY AND FEMININITY: ANALYSIS OF COLORMEMOTO AND TRANCEMOTO

A beginning point for examining the two cell phone advertisements that used women models is the history of the use of women in advertising. There is an extensive body of feminist and postmodern analysis, which has focused on issues of patriarchy, marginality, and representation. While I do not reference this literature in this chapter, some of the key issues and concerns include:

> Research work has focused on the ways in which women in different regions and countries are represented through "cultural stereotypes," for example the mother, the virgin, the whore or the good daughter or wife. The media, from this perspective, is seen as playing a detrimental role by providing women with a limited number of role models which ignore the diverse character of women's lives. What is needed, it is argued, are more positive role models for women. (Reading, 1997, p. 2)

Connecting these issues with those of globalization and gender is important as one examines the representational import of using women in cell phones advertising. Following Sen and Stivens (1998), I suggest that scholars see consumption as a pivotal concept in thinking about the place of gender in the "newly affluent" cultures and the middle-class centered neoliberal marketplace. As they put it, "Consumption is central to the constant search for and the construction of new identities. Linking market and identity is important to think about gender and globalization in affluent Asia" (1998, p. 5).

In the context of the Motorola advertisements, ColormeMoto and TranceMoto, such consumption needs to be examined in the context of historical representations and the very politicized space of India's public sphere. As Sen and Stivens (1998) put it in the context of developing countries in Asia,

> Consumption patterns provide a way of tying gender directly into theorizing the connections between macro-level global processes and local complexities and specificities. In particular, the development of elaborate new femininities based on the consumer/wife/mother and the consumer/beautiful young women can be seen as central to the very development of these burgeoning economies. (p. 5)

The first advertisement, ColormeMoto has the following elements: An "oriental" model, her hair styled in a twist over her head, her neck adorned by a white lace collar holds up a cell phone to her left eye so that it becomes an instrument of viewing rather than use. Around her right eye is a tight arrangement of peacock feathers. The image on the cell phone is also that of a peacock. The peacock, a bird seen in the Indian context as a bird of beauty, color, and vanity is thus centered as a defining characteristic of this gendered use of technology. The "oriental" model evokes both Asian cosmopolitanism (as seen in the historically constituted "made in Japan") and Asian anxieties where the economic history of the "Asian tigers"—Japan, Korea, and Singapore are seen as the emulative model for other Asian countries. It is an unusual placement of discourses—the traditional geisha centered narrative (focused around sophisticated grace and sexual performance) is transferred to the Indian context, mirroring both national ambition and anxiety. Perhaps the key lies in the title of the ad: "Color*me* Moto" (my emphasis) where the agency is presumed to lie elsewhere, not in the woman herself but perhaps with one of the other male models for control of this technology or even more abstractedly in the idea of local subjects opening themselves willingly to be subjects of capitalist will—opening themselves to the pleasures of corporate sponsored performance.

The second advertisement "TranceMoto" parallels the discourses around popular culture and identity politics around "HeadsturnMoto." Here an Indian female model dressed in the skimpiest of clothes—a mesh, almost see through sleeveless top and shorts cradles a cell phone to her throat. Her legs are arched, her eyes look directly at the viewer, and her hair is in careful disarray. Her expression is hostile but sexually available, her lips and eyes immobile in the fixity of their expression. It is a familiar trope in corporate pop culture products—the young, hypersexual woman, available but hard to get. In the Indian context, it is a departure from the traditional symbols of sexuality—which are often coded with a repressed domestic sexuality (the submissive beautiful wife) or the voluptuous (Western) siren. What appears new is also the adoption of a kind of poverty chic (emaciated, thin women models) that mirror less the real poverty in India but the fashion based constructs of femininity that underwrites the Western beauty industry. TranceMoto, as the name suggests is a different animal—the trance is as much in its making—through the deliberate assumption of such a role by Indian women and in being entranced—through the possibilities presented and offered by capitalism.

CONCLUSION

The advertisements for the Motorola cell phone I have argued in the preceding section frames and constructs Indian consumers along a semantic/narrative storyline that centers individuality, references corporate sponsored identity formations and is reiterative of very specific modalities of identity formation in the Indian context in the wake of market liberalization. These findings mirror Pajnik and Tusek's analysis of Mobitel's advertising in the context of Slovenia. They see advertising as part and parcel of the formation and maintenance of class based ideological formations. In their words,

> Ideology functions in such a way that it recruits subjects amongst individuals or transforms the individuals into subjects—by interpellating or hailing. This is how the inner voice of advertising works. The rhetoric of Mobitel's advertising, both verbal and pictorial, is based on the inner voice. With shaping promises, assurances, and illusions, the voice promotes the good things about buying the product and also implicitly or explicitly warns the consumer what might happen if he or she does not buy the product. (2002, p. 279)

The idea of consumption is centered both in the case of India's Motorola advertisements and Slovenia's

> Mobitel's advertisements (which) speak to consumers about identity and appear to offer solutions—they open the path toward new and better identities. A new look can be synonymous with a new me (Jenkins, 1996, pp. 7–8). People in advertisements are not a realistic representation but an imaginary one. As Williamson (1978) suggested that if we buy the product we actually buy the image and at the same time contribute to the construction of identity—through consumption. (Pajnik and Tusek, 2002, p. 281)

But as I have suggested, the cell phone in the Indian context does not merely reproduce the reification of consumption, it also structures gendered identity formations that are symptomatic of wider structural/social divides that globalization generates. There are two clear implications.

First, the Motorola advertisements perpetuate a ghettoization of women within the realms of sexuality, ritual, enactment of tradition, and submissive performance while taking on the kind of technological accoutrements that corporate modernity signals as its *leitmotif*. The Motorola advertisements systematically restrict the mobility of women as players in the economic and political arena, even as they are centered unproblematically in the commodity world. There is considerable precedence for this in the developing world's historical engagement with media and advertising. To use one example, an analysis of women's representations on Ugandan media examined the press images of women in national newspapers over several months and discovered that women were rarely portrayed in relation to economic or political issues. They were also not included as experts on subjects outside the home (Reading, 1997, p. 2).

Second, the Motorola advertisements perpetuate an equation between masculinity and technology so that the relationship becomes durable (Faulkner, 2000, pp. 87–119). The use of cell phones by the Indian male subjects in the Motorola advertisements accentuate an assumption about male agency in processes of globalization but to this is added a very clear rearticulation of "the design cultures" of modern engineering and science (Oudshooron, Remes, and Stienstra, 2004) and in this overall sense the cell phone becomes both an agent of a regressive, powerfully gendered cultural technology.

In sum, the discourse of the cell phone in India reiterates problematics around gender.³ Mellstrom's (2004) work in Malaysia suggests that (much like in India) masculine bonds are mediated and communication through interactions with machines and where technologies become a means of embodied communication for male bonds. "These masculine practices continuously exclude women and perpetuate highly genderized social spheres where men form communities based on a passion for machines. Such passion transforms technologies into subjects in what might be termed a heterosexual, masculine, technical sociability, and subjectivity" (p. 368).

I want to conclude with some thoughts about the questions I began this analysis with—how do we assess the cell phone as a cultural technology? In addition, what do the discourses used by advertising tell us about the future blue print for society in the developing world? And perhaps, most crucially, what kind of ideological formation for a developing country is the cell phone? All these issues are relevant for future studies of the role of advertising in the developing world.

Grappling with these questions is difficult, especially, given the fact that India is often seen as an example of a third world country successfully encountering and dealing with new technologies such as the Internet, call centers, and cell phones. To understand the kinds of cultural "futures" the cell phone ads evoke one must first understand the role of the omnipotence of such advertisements in the urban-media landscape. With the evanescent nature of cell phone and call center companies (replacing the Dotcom's of just a few years ago) what is important as Berger (1977) says is to understand is that

> Publicity image belongs to the moment. We see it as we turn a page, a corner, on a vehicle as it passes by, on a television screen. Publicity images also belong to the moment in the sense that they must be continually renewed and made up to date. Yet they never speak of the present. Often they refer to the past and always they speak of the future . . . Publicity is not merely an assembly of competing messages: it is a language in itself, which is always being used to make the same general proposal. It proposes to each of us that we transform ourselves, or our lives by buying. (pp. 129–130)

The process of buying is simultaneously one of image making and of being absorbed into the image of advertising. This willing absorption by people and institutions of all economic and political backgrounds in India is indicative of the power of the cultural value of the new technologies such as the cell phone. Advertising simultaneously creates and masks the coming of the commodity world. As Jhally (1989) puts it:

> In advertising the commodity world interacts with the human world at the most fundamental levels: it performs magical feats of transformation and bewitchment, brings instant happiness and gratification, captures the forces of nature, and holds within itself the essence of important social relations (in fact, it substitutes for those relations). What is noteworthy about such scenes is not that they are concerned with daily life; it is the extent to which goods enter into the arrangements of daily life. (p. 218)

In sum, cell phone advertising is what advertising is always about: a form of persuasive communication that masks its true function in late capitalism: to sell commodities. It speaks to the interests of buyers rather than nations, to consumers rather than citizens. Historically, in the developing world, media technologies were seen as the cultural arm of nation building. They worked with the notion of informing and creating a citizenry rather than consumers. New technologies such as cell phones on the other hand create a culture of consumption and mask the cultural contradictions they create. As Schwoch, White, and Reilly (1992) put it

> Advertising for large corporations—especially those centered on the production and consumption of telecommunications, information, and computer services-present to viewers through their visual and verbal discourses the faith and beliefs that underlie what might be called "corporate soul" . . . [they work] through their dual epistles of technological utopianism and consumer culture. (p. 22)

Cell phone advertising in India (and perhaps in the rest of the developing world), then reflects the emergence of a fundamental change in market relations from a mixed economy to a capitalist one. Under current conditions of globalization, cell phone advertising (like other advertising in the developing world's urban-media scape) fills the discursive space created by the structural transformation of society. I conclude with two comments about other forms of advertising appear to be even truer about cell phone advertising:

> Capitalist production methods mean more than merely a new way to produce goods—it entailed a revolution in the cultural arrangements of traditional society . . . the world of goods in industrial society offers no meaning. The function of advertising is to refill the emptied commodity with meaning. (Jhally, 1989, pp. 220–221)

> While reinforcing the priorities of corporate production and marketing, advertising offers a symbolic empathy to its audience, criticizing alienation and offering transcendent alternatives. Needless to say, these "alternatives" are contained religiously, within the cosmology of the marketplace. (Ewen, 1989, p. 86)

NOTES

This chapter is coauthored by Kalyani Chadha and is based on our previous publications (Kavoori and Chadha, 2001; Kavoori and Chadha, 2006).

1. There is now a burgeoning literature on the sociology of the cell phone. A coedited book by this author (Kavoori and Arceneaux, 2006) entitled *The Cell Phone Reader: Essays in social transformation*, brings together essays by leading scholars examining the cell phone as cultural form. For overviews of the social import of the cell phone see Brown, Green, and Harper (2002); Horst and Miller (2006); Ling (2004). For cell phone and identity construction see Batista (2003), Katz (1999, 2003), Katz and Aakhus (2002), Kasesniemi (2003), Lemish and Cohen (2005), Moni and Uddin (2004). For international perspectives and the cell phone see Castells, Ardeval, Qiu, and Sey (2007); Banerjee and Ros (2004); Ozcan and Kocak (2003). For a historical perspective on telephones and culture see Rakow (1992) and Agar (2003).

2. This chapter is based on fieldwork in India during May 2004 during which I visited the cities of Bombay, New Delhi, Jaipur, and Mussouri in India and made a visual record of cell phone advertising in the urban landscape of New Delhi. Experience from this field experience was related to all cell phone related advertising in the newspaper, *Times of India* for the month of May 2004 and all cell phone related advertisements in the news-magazine *India Today* for preceding three months (March, April, May). Textual analysis of these advertisements was conducted with a focus on identifying emergent themes and recurrent motifs. These readings were related to the personal field experience in India. The specific examples of advertisements discussed in this chapter were chosen from this inductive process. Their function, thus, is both representative and illustrative within a textual and literary

analysis tradition rather than a social-scientific/content analysis tradition. No quantitative tabulation of these themes was made and none are offered here. This analysis remains in the end, a "reading" of ad texts. While no claims of objectivity can be made, there is no reason to suspect any systematic bias in interpretation. Parts of this chapter were developed in Kavoori and Chadha (2006).

3. Similar issues around gender and technology were evident in reference to the Internet (Kavoori and Chadha, 2001). In the ads examined in that study (advertisements on *Times of India* and *India Today* for the month of May, 2000), men were shown overwhelmingly as agents of/for the Internet. They appeared in a range of settings: Running across a keyboard as the text said "reach new heights in Java" (HMFL Infotech), peering diligently at computer screens (Aptech Computer Education), standing superimposed on a Leonard da Vinci painting (Tata Infotech Education), rock climbing (IIS Infotech Ltd.) and tight rope walking (Bisquare Technologies). In each of these advertisements, masculinity was articulated through the reiteration of discourses of male mastery over the environment (now transferred to the digital frontier). Other ads drew on a modernist discourse of technical competence, scientific judgment, and rational action. One example of this was the Aditi.com ad, where the model/engineer sits in a dark robe gazing into the distance, a picture of satisfied, meditative excellence. His gaze and pose is evocative of Rodin's thinker. The ad says "an Aditi engineer works at the absolute edge of technology. On the hottest e-commerce platforms . . . some people have the nerve to call it work." The model/engineer's qualifications and achievements are listed at the bottom of the ad, which end with the line: "When he isn't developing cutting-edge Internet applications, he's developing some serious muscle in the gym." The ad thus comes full circle encompassing both modernist competence with a direct reference to notions of traditional masculinity (muscle) but now strategized through an Internet based technological aesthetic, which assumes a specific kind of reification of the body (as a site for development) with an attendant discourse about masculinity far removed from traditional Indian society where images of masculinity are tied to filality and patriarchy.

REFERENCES

Agar, J. (2003). *Constant touch: A global history of the mobile phone*. UK: Icon Books.

Banerjee, A., & Ros, J. (2004). Patterns in global fixed and mobile telecommunications development. *Telecommunications Policy*, 28, 107–132.

Batista, E. (2003, May 3). She's gotta have it: Cell phone. *Wired News*.

Berger, J. (1977). *Ways of seeing*. London: BBC Penguin.

Brown, B., Green, N., & Harper, R. (Eds.) (2002). *Wireless world: Social and interactional aspects of the mobile age*. London: Springer.

Ewen, S. (1989). Advertising and the development of consumer society. In I. Angus & S. Jhally (Eds.), *Cultural politics in contemporary America* (pp. 82–95) London: Routledge.

Faulkner, W. (2000). The power and the pleasure? A research agenda for making gender stick to engineers. *Science, Technology & Human Values*, 25(1), 87–119.

Haraway, D. (1990). A manifesto for Cyborgs. In L. Nicholson (Ed.), *Feminism/postmodernism* (pp. 190–233). New York: Routledge.

Hardt, H. (1992). *Communication, history, and theory in America*. New York: Routledge.

Horst, H., & Miller, D. (2006). *The cell phone: Anthropology of communication*. Oxford: Berg.

Jackson, M. H., Poole, M. S., & Kuhn, T. (2002). The social construction of technology in studies of the workplace. In L. Lievrouw & S. Livingstone (Eds.), *Handbook of new media: Social shaping and consequences of ICTs*. London: Sage.

Jhally, S. (1989). Advertising as religion: The dialectic of technology and magic. In I. Angus & S. Jhally (Eds.), *Cultural politics in contemporary America* (pp. 217–229). London: Routledge.

Kasesniem, E.-L. (2003). *Mobile messages: Young people and a new communication culture*. Tampere: Tampere University Press.

Katz, J. (1999). *Connections: Social and cultural studies of the telephone in American life*. New Brunswick, NJ: Transaction.

Katz, J. (2003). *The social context of personal communication technology*. New Brunswick, NJ: Transactions.

Kavoori, A., & Arceneaux, N. (2006). *The cell phone reader: Essays in social transformation*. Oxford: Peter Lang.

Kavoori, A., & Chadha, K. (2001). Net tarot in New Delhi: Reading the future of the Internet in advertising. *Convergence: The Journal of Research into New Media Technologies, 6*(7), 82–95.

Kavoori, A., & Chadha, K. (2006). The discourse of cell phone advertising in India. In A. Kavoori and N. Arceneaux (Eds.), *The cell phone reader: Essays in social transformation*. Oxford: Peter Lang.

Lemish, D., & Cohen, A. (2005). On the gendered nature of mobile phone culture in Israel. *Sex Roles: A Journal of Research, 52*(7/8), 511–521.

Leonardi, P. (2003). Problematizing new media: Culturally based perceptions of cell phones, computers and the Internet amongst United States Latinos. *Critical Studies in Media Communication, 20*(2), 160–179.

Ling, R. (2004). *The mobile connection: The cell phone's impact on society*. San Francisco: Morgan Kaufmann.

McChesney, R. (1999). *Rich media, poor democracy: Communication politics in dubious times*. Champaign: University of Illinois Press.

Mellstrom, U. (2004). Machines and masculine subjectivity. *Men and Masculinities, 6*(4), 368–382.

Moni, M., & Uddin, M. (2004). Cellular phones for women's empowerment in rural Bangladesh. *Asian Journal of Women's Studies, 10*(1), 70.

Oudshoorn, N., Romes, E., & Stienstra, M. (2004). Configuring the user as everybody: Gender and design cultures in information and communication technologies. *Science, Technology & Human Values, 29*(1), 30–63.

Ozcan, Y., & Kocak, A. (2003). A need or status symbol? Use of cellular telephony in Turkey. *European Journal of Communication, 18*(2), 241–254.

Pajnik, M., & Tusek, P. (2002). Observing discourses of advertising: Mobitel's interpellation of potential consumers. *Journal of Communication Inquiry, 26*(3), 277–299.

Plant, S. (2005). On the mobile: The effects of mobile telephones on social and individual life. Motorola Company Report.

Price, M. (1999). Satellite broadcasting as trade routes in the sky. *Public Culture*, *11*(2), 69–85.

Rafael, V. (2003). The cell phone and the crowd: Messianic politics in the contemporary Philippines. *Public Culture*, *15*(3), 399–425.

Rakow, L. (1992). *Gender on the line: Women, the telephone and community life*. Urbana: University of Illinois Press.

Reading, A. (1997, September). Women, men and the mass media. Common Concern. Retrieved May 23, 2005, from www.worldywca.org/common_concern/sept1997.

Reeves, G. (1993). *Communications and the Third World*. New York: Routledge.

Schiller, D. (1999). *Digital capitalism: Networking the global market system*. New York: Routledge.

Schwoch, J., White, M., & Reilly, S. (1992). Television advertising, telecommunications discourse and contemporary American culture. In J. Schwoch, M. White & S. Reilly (Eds.), *Media knowledge: Readings in popular culture, pedagogy, and critical citizenship* (pp. 21–37). Albany: State University of New York Press.

Sen, K., & Stivens, M. (Eds.) (1998). *Gender and power in affluent Asia*. New York: Routledge.

Thussu, D. (2000). *International communication: Continuity and change*. London: Arnold.

Appendix A

Travel Journalism and the Logics of Globalization

Elfriede Fursich and Anandam Kavoori

Most traditional international mass communication research examines news journalism such as the work of wire agencies, foreign correspondents, or television news crews. One field of journalism that equally constructs representations of others, but has been mostly ignored, is that of travel journalism. In this article, we ask for increased attention of communication scholars to this genre. We argue that travel journalism is an important site for studying the ideological dimensions of tourism and transcultural encounters, as well as the ongoing dynamics of media globalization. We first analyze why tourism and travel journalism has remained under-explored as a field of study. Then, based on the literature on travel and tourism in sociology, anthropology, and cultural studies we identify three distinct but interrelated perspectives that provide a theoretical and programmatic framework for studying travel journalism. These three perspectives are discussed as issues of periodization, power and identity, and finally experience and phenomenology.

In the current hyper-commercialized, technology-driven, and entertainment-saturated postmodern media landscape when many scholars lament the "end of journalism" (e.g., Hardt, 1998), it seems inadvisable to rely on the term journalism for our framework. We agree that public communication is in transition and journalism has increasingly become "part of an entertainment package that transnational corporations sell to audiences across the globe" (Chalaby, 2000, p. 32). Nevertheless, we consider it an important category for defining our area of analysis. We understand journalism in Hartley's sense as a "textual system." As he explains:

> The most important *textual* feature of journalism is the fact that it counts as true. The most important component of its *system* is the creation or readers as publics, and the connection of these readerships to other systems, such as those of politics, economics, and social control. (1996, p. 35)

Thus, what we consider for analysis is an often-privileged position in public discourse. Yet, we do not identify journalism exclusively by the medium or technology used (print, broadcasting, or Internet) nor by its professional intention (inform or entertain) nor by a job description (travel journalist, producer, or content provider).[1]

WHY IS IT IMPORTANT TO INVESTIGATE TOURISM AND TRAVEL JOURNALISM?

A number of reasons support the argument for a closer scholarly engagement with travel journalism.

1. Tourism and Its Impact Remain Understudied

The majority of the research on tourism is based on industry perspective and the focus has been on generating economic information for the formulation of corporate or government tactics. Similarly, communication research on tourism has been primarily limited to evaluation of promotional strategies. Located within the fields of marketing and advertising/public relations, these studies are aimed at maximizing financial returns by handling the various publics in an effective way. A number of studies have used the notions of tourist demand, marketing, forecasting, planning, and development in their studies (Martin and Witt, 1988). Most of these studies see tourism primarily as an economic fact, characterized by its effects on the financial balance, and ignore its social and cultural role in contemporary society.

2. Leisure as a Significant Social Practice

Tourism and travel writing are often seen as a frivolous topic, not worthy of serious research. In general, tourism is considered "a recreational activity devoid of social and political meaning" (Chang and Holt, 1991, p. 102) since it seems to involve the private sphere and thus, to lack public relevance. Until recently most scholars shared this attitude. Anthropologists, for example, buried their data on tourism in field notes and only occasionally published peripheral articles, as if tourism were not a scientific subject (Smith, 1989, p. 1). For many fieldworkers, tourists did not fit their framework, "like weeds in the garden plot, tourists spoil the character of the researchers carefully cultivated community" (Pearce, 1982, p. 1). Literature produced by travelers was considered limited, in the words of Levi-Strauss, little more than "the exact number of packing cases required and misdemeanors of the ship's dog" (1970, p. 16). Even if anthropologists had been aware of the impact of tourism on indigenous societies, argues Nuñez (1989, p. 27), they would have "refrained from publishing their observations in systematic form because the study of tourism was somehow not considered 'proper' or within the traditional purview of the discipline." Similarly, a "political scientist with a scholarly interest in tourism might be looked upon as dabbling in frivolity not as a serious scholar but an opportunist looking for a tax-deductible holiday" (quoted in C. M. Hall, 1994, p. 5).

This lack of critical attention to tourism and travel journalism may lie in deeply embedded values in Western society about play and work. Protestant ethics have emphasized the value of hard work—effectively devaluing play and leisure as cultural pursuits not worthy of serious theoretical engagement. However, we suggest that it is precisely the significance of leisure in contemporary society that makes the study of tourism and of travel journalism so crucial.

3. Travel Journalism as Important Site for International Communication Research

Paralleling the growth of tourism as a global industry has been the exponential growth of travel journalism. In addition to the traditional travel section in most major national and regional dailies, a large number of general travel magazines are published, along with a prodigious number of specialized travel publications dealing with interests as diverse as rock climbing or cruise vacations. The broadcast media offers specialized travel programs, celebrity travel shows, and in various countries entire cable channels (e.g., in the United States and the United Kingdom the Discovery Communications, Inc.-owned Travel Channel, or in France Voyage) devoted to the subject. The Internet is another highly successful outlet for travel-related information. Travel sites of online services and travel related web pages are among the most accessed websites on the Internet.

The growing international tourism industry affects the media industry in two ways. First, international travel is no longer mostly a one-way stream from the West to other countries, but affluent groups from an increasing number of countries are traveling for pleasure or business. This makes international person-to-person contact more likely and generates audience interest for travel-related journalism and information as a global media topic. Potential travelers will be interested in this kind of journalism for advice and entertainment. Moreover, a growing global "middle class" will understand travel, especially international travel, as a desirable private goal while using mass-mediated travel as *ersatz* experience as long as they cannot afford actual trips. Second, the growing tourist industry will generate an increasing market for travel advertising and public relations looking especially for media outlets that promise a targeted and receptive audience. These two trends are very likely to stimulate a bigger market for specialized travel journalism on a global scale.

Clearly, the increased prominence of travel journalism has relevance for scholars of international communication. This is especially evident when we consider how travel journalism functions much like international news to provide both information and cultural frames for "others." But so far, international communication research has focused either on the spread of news, entertainment, or advertising in a global market (e.g., Reeves, 1993); when looking at the way national media represent foreigners and foreign cultures, studies normally analyze international news content in newspapers or on television. However, audience interest in "hard" international news is waning while media representations of "others" remain decisive factors in this era of globalization. Therefore, a research agenda of international communication studies should refocus by evaluating other media genres. Examining travel journalism is an important strategy for analyzing the ongoing dynamics of media globalization.

4. The Special Contingencies of Travel Journalism

Travel journalism needs to be closely evaluated for its tacit allegiance to both advertising and the travel industry. In fact, travel journalism is a highly charged discourse beleaguered by public relations efforts of the private travel industry and by government-sponsored tourism departments. In addition to the public relations saturation, travel journalism exists in symbiotic relationship with advertising. Travel is mostly covered in special sections of newspapers, in magazines, or on television shows, which almost exclusively find their advertisers within the travel industry itself. Moreover, free trips and other inducements for travel journalists are common—only a few publishers are willing to finance the trips of the journalists. This places many travel journalists in a difficult position between major interest groups. A travel writer, for example, commented—

after confessing to the fine line between gifting and bribes—that "the fact remains that most travel writing simply dishonors our free press" (Weir-Alderson, 1988, p. 28).

Considering all the above delineated factors, we argue that instead of examining travel journalism as trivial cultural celebration we need to ask in the context of international communication research what discourse is created within media representations of travel? What are the cultural and ideological assumptions upon which such constructs are based?

A FRAMEWORK FOR THE STUDY
OF TRAVEL JOURNALISM

Following transnational cultural studies, we want to establish a research agenda for the study of travel journalism broadly rather than narrowly. To that end, we suggest examining both issues of encoding (here we include both studies of journalistic work routines and media practices and the textual analysis of travel journalism) and those of decoding or reception.

Based on the literature on tourism in the fields of sociology, anthropology, and cultural studies, we have identified three different perspectives that can inform the study of travel journalism. The first approach deals with the issue of periodization, the second with issues of power and identity, and the last with issues of experience and phenomenology. Under each of these headings we first map the various conceptual issues that might frame our understanding of tourism and travel journalism and then identify research questions that studies of travel journalism might address. The research questions in each case deal with both aspects of encoding and decoding.

ISSUES OF PERIODIZATION

Modernity

Several studies have tried to locate tourism within the historical development of Western societies. Cohen (1972) suggests that the coining of the terms "tourist" and "tourism" corresponds to a novel category of traveler, separate from historically known travelers such as warriors, crusaders, or pilgrims. Historically, the word "tourist" is linked to the travel of English gentlemen on a tour as part of their education and entertainment. Etymologically, the word "tourist" first appears in English, with the Oxford English Dictionary dating the word "tourist" from 1800 and "tourism" from 1811. It appears in the French Robert Dictionary (as "touriste") in 1816, while "tourisme" appears in 1841, both derived from English.

While it is relatively easy to track the word's etymology, it is more difficult to identify the cultural frameworks that have made tourism the enormous sociological fact that it is. For some, the answer lies in the emergence of tourism as an offshoot of modernity. Four issues peculiar to modernity can be seen as underlying the growth of tourism: first, the creation of work and leisure as separate spheres of social activity; second, the importance of issues of authenticity; third, the division of the social environment into discrete units of experience; and fourth, the impact of technology on everyday life.

Urry argues that tourism's location within leisure time (rather than labor) makes it a truly modern enterprise:

> Tourism is a leisure activity which presupposes its opposite, namely regulated and organized work. It is one manifestation of how work and leisure are organized as separate and regulated spheres of social practice in "modern" societies. *Indeed acting as a tourist is one of the defining characteristics of being "modern"* and is bound up with major transformations in paid work. (1990, pp. 2–3; emphasis added)

Modernity also is characterized by transformed cultural dynamics, as rural communities—with their strong association with traditional sources of cultural coherence (e.g., religion and patriarchy)—were replaced by large urban centers characterized by a search for alternate sources of cultural coherence. At the heart of this search was the desire for authenticity. As MacCannell explains:

> For moderns, reality and authenticity are thought to be elsewhere: in other historical periods and other cultures, in purer, simpler lifestyles. . . . [T]he concern of moderns for "naturalness," their nostalgia and their search for authenticity are not merely casual and somewhat decadent, though harmless, attachments to the souvenirs of destroyed cultures and dead epochs. They are also components of the conquering spirit of modernity—the grounds of its unifying consciousness. (1976, p. 3)

McCannell sees the artificial preservation, reconstruction, or the museumization of traditional sociocultural forms (for example, the "primitive" or the "exotic") as the ultimate sign that modernity has succeeded. Tourism becomes the "spirit" of modernity. Moreover, the cultural logic of modernism is tied into the development of industrial rationalism and a collective bureaucratic vision that divides the social environment into discrete units of experience. While traditional communities had little sense of rigid boundaries between different spheres of life, the modernist isolates and transcribes discrete spheres of influence and control. This makes it possible to isolate "nature" from "culture," the "environment" from "history," or "body" from "mind."

Finally, any modernist approach to analyzing travel cannot overlook how modern technology, travel, and tourism are intrinsically linked. The tourist gaze is often mediated through a camera (first photography and later video) as Urry explains. In its extreme, "travel is a strategy for the accumulation of photographs" (1990, p. 139). This photogenic logic structures tourist locations (vistas) and social experience. Professional travel photography and television travel shows can be theorized as an extension of this motivation. Similarly, advancements in modern transportation technology initiated modern mass tourism. Prato and Trivero elucidate how the cultural history of the car, train, and the plane has structured the ideological aspects of travel and tourism, up to a point when motion and transport "ceases to function as a metaphor of progress or at least of 'modern' life, and becomes instead the primary activity of existence" (1985, p. 40).

Each of these issues resonates with scholarly interest in travel journalism. At the level of production and textualization, it would be useful to ask questions about the exact conjuncture of the development of travel journalism with the rise of modernity. In the West, this would entail an examination of the early development of travel journalism from perhaps older narrative forms such as the colonial travelogue and the diaries of adventurers. The history of the newspaper is tied into the development of modern industry and the notion of work itself. Concomitantly, it would be interesting to see the development of notions of leisure and recreation within early newspapers. Since colonial narratives usually endorse travel as an educational activity, one should analyze how the modernist notion of leisure as an activity in and for itself develops in relation to its colonial origins.

The issue of authenticity is one that lends itself well to the study of both the historical and contemporary texts of travel journalism. What are the constructs of authenticity that travel journalism has predominantly used in the past and now? Why are some topics (such as nature, ethnicity, and religion) used more than others? What are the specific institutional forces that foster and develop these modes of authenticity in travel journalism (for example, national and state governments, environmentalist groups, park authorities, religious groups, etc.)? In what ways have the workings of these institutions helped to perpetuate the structuring of social experience (and consequently tourism)? At the level of reception, one can ask to what extent have travelers internalized the structuration of touristic experience along the lines of the structuration of social experience? What are the modes of authenticity that travelers as (subjects of modernity) most subscribe to? How does the reading of travel journalism help to relate to those constructs of authenticity? What textual strategies work best to further issues of authenticity and leisure? How does actual travel reflect the experience of authenticity? Is there a tension between the textualization of authenticity and the actual experience?

Postmodernism

While the literature on postmodernism connects with tourism in a number of ways, one issue has direct relevance for scholars of tourism and travel journalism: the hybridity of cultural forms in postmodernity. Leong, for example, argues:

> Tourist culture in effect is a showcase of postmodernism: a concoction of something "native," something borrowed, something old and something new. . . . In such a melange, authenticity is somewhat eclipsed by estrangement: dance and other rituals, organized for tourist consumption, become performances rather than integral parts of the social life of participants. They are something to be watched by others rather than something to be lived by themselves. (1989, p. 371)

Urry calls the "tourist gaze" a symbol of postmodernity. Like Leong, he sees typical aspects of postmodernism (pastiche, kitsch, the hyper-real, copies without original, dissolution of boundaries) represented in tourism. For him, "being a tourist" is *the* typical stage of postmodernity.

> [T]he era of mass communication has transformed the tourist gaze and many of the features of postmodernism have already been partly prefigured in existing tourist practices. What I have termed the tourist gaze is increasingly bound up with and is partly indistinguishable from all sorts of other social and cultural practices. This has the effects, as "tourism" per se declines in specificity, of universalizing the tourist gaze—people are much of the time "tourists" whether they like it or not. The tourist gaze is intrinsically part of contemporary experience, of postmodernism. (1990, p. 82)

Analyzed from the prism of postmodernity, several research questions emerge. Is travel journalism a modernist text that reinforces rather than blurs traditional forms of authenticity or do postmodern travel texts blur the boundaries? Textual analyses can examine the different subjectivities portrayed in the range of tourist periodicals, newsletters, television shows, and Internet sites. What authority does travel journalism provide in postmodern societies? At the level of reception, researchers can ask what is the role of mass tourist periodicals in a postmodern age that encourages the development of differentiated and hybrid identity forms? How do different populations based on age, ethnicity, gender, and locality deal with postmodern travel texts? What is the range of specific cultural (and subcultural) mediations of these already fragmented texts?

Nationalism

Modernity is inextricably linked to nationalism and the formation of the nation-state (Giddens, 1990). To become "modern" is often seen as a goal by emergent nation-states. Within this context, tourism is often seen as fulfilling the goals of economic development of the nation-state, that is, modernizing it (DeKadt, 1979). However, tourism has more than just an economic function. In many cases, tourism's function is symbolic, working to create a map of the nation for both internal and external consumption. In the United Kingdom, for example, the tourist industry "sells" the royalty and Britain's imperial legacy as prime tourist attractions along with the "pristine" English countryside with its village inns and cricket greens. Such tours construct an image of England and the English that essentializes a certain narrowly prescribed notion of nationhood based on a particular ethnicity (white, male, and upper class). As Stuart Hall (1989) points out, such a discursive rendering of culture is implicitly ideological and has been less reflective of England's multiculturalism than it is of the cultural ideology of Thatcherite conservatism.

Tourism works in similar ways in other parts of the world. Leong (1989) shows how states, in his case Singapore, manufacture traditions for tourism by choosing certain areas of the past in the process of nation building. National tourism becomes a site where unified national symbols are constructed, even if this involves the cultural "cleansing" of cultural practices that are thought of as non-attractive to tourists. Instead of presenting existing exotic lifestyles, Singapore creates a new "exotic" that—combined with Western amenities and facilities—becomes the travel package "Instant Asia": "Since most visitors stay no more than three days in Singapore, marketers of cultural meanings try to show and sell those messages quickly in a condensed form" (p. 366).

Yet, as the tourist industry (public or private) generates "national traditions" and constantly refers to past nostalgic sites, the modernization process may be thwarted in counterproductive ways. Chang and Holt discuss the dilemma facing Taiwan:

> Forcing a culture into the straitjacket of a defined "past" serves to fix cultural Others in a "timeless present," confining them to a place that cannot change, or cannot change as easily as the representer's culture. This may prevent Taiwan (in the eyes of Western tourists, at least) from achieving full modernization as long as it continues to respond to the West's demand for traditionality and authenticity—two conceptions that usually conflict only when the tourist transaction brings them forcibly together. (1991, p. 116)

This dilemma is not limited to Asian or European countries. Rowe (1993), for example, points to the Australian travel industry's juxtaposition of a nostalgia for nature ("the bush") and the past against modern urban life ("the city")—a construction that does not work smoothly. Comparing it to British travel images, he concludes: "[W]hereas Britain is romanticizing its past as civilization, Australia is marketing the timelessness of nature. This is ironic for a nation allegedly seeking to modernize itself" (p. 264). This irony is intensified, as Rowe points out, by the fact that tourism always brings about major changes in infrastructure and therefore threatens the very existence of undisturbed nature.

The entire process of nationalism and its discursive construction provides an important site for studying travel journalism. At the level of production and textualization, the questions are numerous: Where does travel journalism fit into agendas of nationalist construction and reconstruction both historically and in contemporary times? And how do formal institutions (such as state and national government, travel agencies) construct the boundaries and characteristics of nations? How do travel services (agencies, newspaper sections, television shows, public relations) articulate those concerns? Whose vision of nation is being served by each of these institutions? How do the texts of travel literature and travel journalism in developing nations reconcile the paradoxes between modernization, authenticity, and change? At the level of reception analysis one can look at how the vision of the nation and its discursive "destinations" in travel journalism direct actual tourists. How do tourists experience the national gazing at monuments (such as the Vietnam Memorial or India Gate)? How do hosts in mass tourist locations (such as Hawaii and the Caribbean) sustain earlier (or develop new) authenticities as they become "tourist nations"?

POWER AND IDENTITY

Studies of international communication and culture have emphasized issues of power through two main approaches—cultural and media imperialism on the one hand and ideology and identity formation on the other. Both these approaches are useful for understanding tourism and travel journalism in its cross-cultural context.

Cultural Imperialism

C. M. Hall (1994) has suggested that the tourism research in marketing and economics, with its "value-free" approach to science, has failed to consider the political context of tourism. He contends, "tourism is a central element of some of the critical economic and political issues of the contemporary era: the internationalization of capital; industrial and regional restructuring; urban redevelopment; and the growth of the service economy" (p. 197). Hall questions the naive approach of seeing tourism as a "force of peace" and a nonpolluting industry that many policy makers try to promote.

Instead, theorists working from a dependency framework have argued that tourism performs economic functions for the "rich tourist-generating super powers . . . it reinforces rather than undermines the structures of dependency and underdevelopment upon which the world system exists. Active encouragement of tourism by developing countries has led to an enmeshment in a global system over which they have little control" (Britton, 1982, p. 331). And, as Bryden (1973) shows in an economic analysis of Caribbean economies, it often does not produce the expected dividends. Hence, "tourism is only another manifestation of the existing economic and political [inequalities]" (Geshekter, 1978, p. 57).

However, while a tremendous transfer of money, labor, and goods occurs within this largest industry in the world, its impact goes well beyond monetary implications. As MacCannell (1976) writes: "[N]ot only our old favorite, 'the profit motive,' operates unambiguously in the development of [tourist] attractions. Some attractions are developed and maintained at great expense, though there are no economic returns" (p. 162). MacCannell's work suggests that tourism should not be reduced solely to a form of economic and political dependency but also be considered with regard to its cultural/ideological aspects. Thus, tourism becomes a form of cultural domination constructed by the Western countries—that is, tourism as a new form of imperialism (e.g., Nash, 1989). Travel journalism in turn can be seen as a form of cultural imperialism that perpetuates what Shome calls "discursive imperialism":

> [I]n the present times, discourses have become the prime means of imperialism. Whereas in the past, imperialism was about controlling the "native" by colonizing her/him territorially, now imperialism is more about subjugating the "native" by colonizing her/him discursively. (1996, p. 42)

A similar vision for understanding the representational practices of travel journalism also underlies the work of Pratt, who has studied nineteenth-century travel writing. She asks:

> How has travel writing produced "the rest of the world" for European readerships at particular points in Europe's expansionist trajectory? How do such signifying practices encode and legitimate the aspirations of economic expansion and empire? How do they betray them? (1992, p. 5)

We can extend Pratt's questions to contemporary travel journalism. At the level of textual analysis, one can ask what are the dominant modes of representation in Western travel writing? What is the range of these frames and what are the discursive categories that they draw on? Who benefits from such frames and who does not? Do certain kinds of tourism present different modes of representation or is a cultural homology evident in their representation? What are the changes that take place in travel representations with changing geopolitical interests of Western nation-states? Can travel journalism be seen as an ongoing expression of cultural transgression and reinvention that reflects the current inequalities between the First and Third worlds? At the level of reception, however, any theorizing of tourism as one-sided dominating ideological transfer overlooks the complexity of this cultural practice. The idea of complexity derives from Foucault's notion of discourse. As he puts it, "discourses are tactical elements or blocks operating in the field of force relations; there can exist different or even contradictory discourses within the same strategy . . . [Power is] a multiple and mobile field of force relations wherein far-reaching, but never completely stable, effects of domination are produced" (1980, p. 100).

Spivak draws on this notion of discourse and argues that postcolonial power is incorrectly defined in a static binary opposition of colonizer and colonized. This typology does not explain the "heterogeneity of 'colonial power' and . . . discloses the complicity of the two poles of that opposition" (quoted according to Parry, 1987, p. 29). Understanding processes of cultural colonization then is not limited to the constitutive powers of colonizers over the colonized (by the articulation and rearticulation of culture), but expands to processes of culture and colonization that are diversely structured, localized, and articulated within and across groups in the relationship.

Pratt applies these themes to travel writing. She develops two concepts ("contact zone" and "transculturation") useful for our purposes. "Contact zones" refer to the

> space of colonial encounters . . . a contact perspective emphasizes how subjects are constituted in and by their relations to each other. It treats the relations between colonizers and colonized, or travelers and "travelees" not in terms of separateness or apartheid, but in terms of co-presence, interaction, interlocking understandings and practices, often within radically asymmetrical relations of power. (1992, p. 7)

With the term "transculturation" Pratt highlights the general process of cultural mediation of this relationship and, specifically, to the cultural texts produced by such encounters. These texts are not only the Eurocentric text of the Western (or First World) travel writer but equally the texts of the Third World (or historically of the colonized). She asks

How are metropolitan modes of representation received and appropriated by the periphery? How have Europe's construction of subordinated others been shaped by those others? By the constructions of themselves and their habitats that they presented to the Europeans? In what terms do colonized subjects represent themselves in ways that engage with (and resist) the colonizers' own terms? (1992, p. 5)

Transforming these questions to the level of reception, we must identify the different strategies that Third World citizens bring to First World texts about the Third World. In other words, to study how the images of a Western "other" are incorporated by the "others" themselves. We need to also investigate what is the range of travel journalism texts produced in the Third World? What are the indigenous models for framing travel? What are the kinds of oppositional strategies for constructing travel destinations that do not adhere to the discursive strategies of Western texts? How is domestic tourism different from international tourism? How have indigenous traditions for travel transmuted into more modern forms of travel? Finally, we need to recognize that tourism is not a one-way flow from the First to the Third World. A growing number of the middle class (not just elites) travel to the First World as tourists, students, and workers. The question is how these new tourism constituencies and their associated journalism construct travel experience.

Ideology and Identity Formation

Issues of ideology and identity formation and maintenance have been at the forefront of cultural studies and have relevance for the study of tourism and travel journalism. Generally speaking, ideology formation from a cultural studies perspective is seen as a symbolic process. Like metaphors for language, ideologies are indispensable for the construction of meaning. They provide a framework for action and for understanding complex and incomprehensible realities—in the case of tourism the contact with the "Other." Like a road map, ideologies provide a model of and a model for reality at the same time (Geertz, 1973). Therefore, the analysis of the ideological dimension of tourism must involve all aspects of symbolic processes. From such a perspective, travel journalism must be considered a key site of ideological formation, one that functions through contrasting practices. As Urry, for example, writes:

[T]he gaze in any historical period is constructed in relationship to its opposite, to non-tourist forms of social experience and consciousness. What makes a particular tourist gaze depends upon what it is contrasted with; what the forms of non-tourist experience happen to be. . . . By considering the typical objects of the tourist gaze one can use these to make sense of elements of the wider society with which they are contrasted. (1990, pp. 1–2)

Contrasting travel journalists' constructs with underlying assumptions of the opposite allows for an understanding of what is taken for granted. Recent debates in the field of cultural anthropology illuminate this point. Chang and Holt explain how closely connected the experiences of ethnographers and tourists are.

> Just as the culture is selectively manifested to the ethnographer, so is it selectively manifested to the tourist. Both ethnographers and tourist engage in cultural *in*scriptions (not *de*scriptions) that lead them to fixate the host culture in a certain way. (1991, p. 103)

These ideas provide an importing starting point for evaluating travel journalism. At the level of encoding, we can ask what ideological work do travel journalists perform? It appears that travel journalists, even more than "average" tourists, are trying to fix the "Other." Their professional purpose is to come up with a narrative, a well-told story about other cultures, the past or distant places—in short, to package culture. This places travel journalists in a *liminoid* situation in society. They operate at the border between the foreign and the familiar. This situation makes their discourse especially charged. Studies of travel journalism need to consider the complexity of *how* this narrative is created. Moreover, at a time when globalizing trends in business and media have resulted in a "global identity crisis" (Morley and Robins, 1995, p. 10), this situation "on the border" puts travel journalists in the critical position of cultural translators, trying to define identity. The process of defining identity takes place across many sites. As Rowe explains:

> National, racial-ethnic as well as metaphysical mythologies are constructed and selectively mobilized in the act of consumer persuasion. These images are not, therefore, mere inventions or devices, nor can their ramifications be limited to the tourist cash nexus. They form part of the ensemble of cultural, economic, social and political relations in play in the constitution of society. (1993, p. 261)

Travel journalism, much like tourism, is a multifaceted cultural practice with many players involved: government, private travel industry, travel writers/journalists, tourists, public relations agencies, and advertising firms. Research needs to address how these agencies—all with different and even contradictory interests—collectively shape an image of the "Other." It needs to be examined at what level all these versions of reality are connected. Numerous reception issues can be addressed: What kinds of "identity work" do cultural industries (such as the travel industry) perform for audiences? To what extent do the texts of travel journalism construct common boundaries of cultural and identity formation across social categories such as class, race, and gender? Given that travel journalism is about selling destinations and cultures, are "positive" identities replacing "negative" images of the "Other"?

EXPERIENCE AND PHENOMENOLOGY

A third body of research in sociology, anthropology, and cultural studies has examined the specific experiences and dynamics of tourist and host interactions and formulated typologies of tourists/tourism and tourist experiences. Smith (1989), for example, divides tourism into five varieties (ethnic, cultural, historical, environmental, and recreational) while Cohen (1973) provided a typology of four tourist roles—the organized mass tourist, the individual mass tourist, the explorer, and the drifter. The first two were categories of institutionalized tourist roles that prefigure greater social distance between tourists and natives, and the latter two are noninstitutionalized roles and reflect meaningful cross-cultural interaction. Cohen (1979) also distinguishes between five modes of tourist experiences. Based on a phenomenological classification of tourist motivations, he distinguishes between recreational, diversionary, experimental, experiential, and existential modes.

Other researchers in this tradition include Boorstein, with his early classification of tourism as a "frivolous activity" (Cohen, 1979, p. 184) and of the tourist thriving on "pseudo-events" and not authentic experiences. In a similar vein, MacCannell (1976, p. 1) drawing on the work of Durkheim and Goffman examines tourism as a form of "staged authenticity" and "touristic spaces." Tourism, MacCannell argues (as opposed to Boorstein), is a modern form of the essentially religious quest for authenticity but tourists are often robbed of that experience. The hosts create "tourist spaces" in which spurious attractions are presented as if they were "real." In other words, purveyors of culture "stage authenticity" for tourist consumption. The hosts create tourist spaces when tourists encroach on the "back" regions of the culture. Such staging of roles is especially evident with mass tourism, where tourists become dehumanized objects to be tolerated for economic gain (Pi-Sunyer, 1977) and subject to excessive familiarity or hostility because of a failure to understand social roles within respective cultures (Smith, 1989).

In contemporary times, tourists themselves tend to distance themselves from "tourism." MacCannell calls this the dilemma of *anti-tourism versus pro-tourism*, and suggests that:

> The modern critique of the tourist is not an analytical reflection on the problem of tourism—it is part of the problem. Tourists are not criticized . . . for leaving home to see sights. They are reproached for being satisfied with superficial experiences of other people and places. . . . [T]ouristic shame is not based on being a tourist but on not being tourist enough, on a failure to see everything the way it "ought" to be seen. (1976, p. 10)

Instead of successfully challenging the shortcomings of mass tourism, anti-tourists present a reified version of "modern" tourism as unachievable model. One group of anti-tourists which has not given up on travelling but contests the standards of traditional mass tourism is introduced by Corrigan (1997) called *untourists* after an Australian travel network established in the early 1990s. These untourists are analogous to "eco tourists, green tourists, cultural tourists, alternative tourists, educational tourists" (according to an activist quoted in Corrigan, 1997, p. 144). These tourists often travel with an environmental mission as reaction to the problem of mass tourism. They still are searching for authenticity (beyond the impossibilities of the postmodern age) but it is an elite construct of authenticity high on cultural capital and distinctively class defining. Quite a few untourists deliberately reject luxury at their vacation places after spending a large amount of money to reach the location in the first place (e.g., wilderness trek on the Amazon). "They reject 'luxury' for what is presumably a more sophisticated way," explains Corrigan (1997, p. 145).

Tomaselli adds a semiotic perspective to the problematic of tourism to indigenous people in Africa (by Western tourists, filmmakers, or anthropologists). He uses the term cultural tourism to distinguish this form of tourism as the "commodification of difference" (2000, p. 4). In several case studies, Tomaselli shows the symbolic work of western tourists, tour guides, and native populations in Africa while creating the tourist experience. Often locals actively "reinvent their authenticity" (1999, p. 188) to create a tourist experience. All parties together seem to develop agreed upon representations of the tribes that are accepted by the tourists as authentic experience but often have nothing to do with the actual more westernized lives of these tribes. Certain moments in Tomaselli's case studies even hint at more postmodern forms of tourism similar to what Feifer (1985) elucidates. *Post-tourists*, according to Feifer, actively play with the inauthenticity of the modern tourist experience. They "know that there is *no* authentic tourist experience, that there are merely a series of games or text that can be played" (quoted in Urry, 1990, p. 11). Corrigan evaluates the different new types of tourism from the perspective of class and Bourdieu's cultural capital and anticipates:

> It seems likely that post-tourists and untourists will be the elite tourist categories of the future, the former representing the postmodern strand of culture . . . and the latter growing out of the environmental strand. Ironic players with appearance and earnest seekers after "authentic" reality: the two poles of philosophical approaches to the world hardly ever seem to change. Perhaps the "traveller" is an uncertain mixture of both, while mass tourism will continue to serve those with lower levels of various types of capital. (1997, pp. 145–146)

Rojek reaches a step further and argues that the "quest for authenticity is a declining force in tourist motivation" (1997, p. 71). Instead, he sees tourists actively create meaningful experiences in processes of symbolic "indexing and dragging." In a media-saturated world being a traveler and mobility becomes a standard state of mind—no longer a distinction from everyday life. As the media make everything seem familiar, difference needs to be culturally and artificially created: "[D]rift, as opposed to division, is a more appropriate characterization of tourist attitudes and practices" (1997, p. 71).

The research questions linking travel journalism to issues of phenomenology and experience could consider questions of how travel journalists construct tourist experience. What concept of ideal tour and preferred traveler are created? How is their travelling different from those of the tourist? In what terms does their engagement with the hosts construct their understanding of tourism? In which forms of tourism do most travel journalists engage (based on Cohen, Smith's, Corrigan, or Feifer's typologies)? At the level of reception, one can study the specific dynamics between travel journalism and tourist institutions. This would entail examining the range of "cultural brokers" that mediate tourism sites (such as priests at pilgrimage sites). Joseph (1994), for example, found that local hosts in an Indian tourist town knew all the major travel writers and actively cultivated them, thereby actively structuring the tourist experience. Another branch of research should investigate what concepts of authenticity are manifested in travel journalism. Is there a trend toward presenting post-tourism and the postmodern state of mind of "traveling" in accounts that reflect the contemporary travel situation?

BEYOND TRAVEL AS CULTURAL METAPHOR

Recently metaphors of travel have become popular as a vocabulary for cultural theorists to analyze methodological and epistemological issues of cultural analysis. One of the seminal contributions is Clifford's article *Traveling Cultures* (1992) in which he questions the dichotomy between dwelling and traveling. Several theorists argue that cultural analysis that invokes the position of the traveler can better reflect the hybridization of culture and challenge the traditionally privileged position of researchers. They urge scholars to see culture as antiessentialist and fluid category. Thus, the position of "subjects" as well as of researchers should be constructed in the new position of unsettled normads (e.g., Grossberg, 1988; Morris, 1988; Said, 1993). Wolff (1993) criticized this theorizing as a gendered discourse based in a vocabulary that privileges male travel experiences. She argues "that the use of that vocabulary as a metaphor necessarily produces androcentric tendencies in theory" (p. 224). Loshitkzky (1996) problematizes travel metaphors in cultural analysis as overly celebratory stylistic elements that often ignore actual power inequalities. As an example, she shows how the cultural impact of global television is shaped by postmodern "traveling" moments but also by actual colonizing forces.

We add to this criticism that cultural theory has to go beyond using often romanticized notions of travel as metaphors and engage with actual travel practices. To briefly summarize, our aims here have been primarily programmatic—to map a theoretical framework (from a cultural studies perspective) for studying travel journalism. To that end, we have reviewed cross-disciplinary sets of literatures in cultural studies, sociology, and anthropology and made connections from that literature to specific questions for mass communication research. Especially postcolonial studies (e.g., Pratt, 1992) and sociology (e.g., Urry, 1990, 1995; Rojek and Urry, 1997) have begun to embrace travel and tourism as topics for academic inquiry. We argue that it is time for communication scholars to follow suit and interrogate contemporary practices of travel journalism. The analyses of travel journalism we have suggested should not narrowly focus on any one aspect of this global discourse but equal attention should be paid to both the encoding and decoding dimensions. This research places travel journalism within the broader context of international communication and media globalization. We see it as an institutional site where meaning is created and where a collective version of the "Other/We" is negotiated, contested, and constantly redefined. By calling attention to and theorizing this understudied genre, we hope to encourage media scholars to begin the empirical analysis of travel journalism globally.

NOTES

This is a reworked version of an earlier publication by Elfreida Fursich and Anandam P. Kavoori, Mapping a critical framework for the study of travel journalism, *International Journal of Cultural Studies*, 4(2), 149–171.

1. We understand that there is a blurring of boundaries between travel journalism and travel writing. It is not unusual for travel journalists to move from print journalism (newspapers and magazines) to publishing books. Notable examples are Pico Iyer (2000), Paul Theroux (1985), or P. J. O'Rourke (1988). Overall, we don't find it necessary to establish extremely exclusive categories when defining our area of study. But in general, travel writing in our category are non-fictional accounts echoing Hartley's imperative (1996) that journalism "counts as true."

REFERENCES

Britton, S. (1982). The political economy of tourism in the Third World. *Annals of Tourism Research, 9*, 331–358.

Bryden, J. (1973). *Tourism and development: A case study of the commonwealth Caribbean*. Cambridge: Cambridge University Press.

Chalaby J. K. (2000). Journalism studies in an era of transition in public communications. *Journalism, 1*(1), 33–39.

Chang, H., & Holt, G. R. (1991). Tourism as consciousness of struggle. *Critical Studies in Mass Communication, 8*, 102–118.

Clifford, J. (1992). Traveling cultures. In L. Grossberg, C. Nelson & P. Treichler (Eds.), *Cultural studies* (pp. 96–116). New York: Routledge.

Cohen, E. (1972). Toward a sociology of international tourism. *Social Research, 39*(1), 164–182.

Cohen, E. (1973). Nomads from affluence: Notes on the phenomenon of drifter-tourism. *International Journal of Comparative Sociology, 14*, 89–102.

Cohen, E. (1979). A phenomenology of tourist experiences. *Sociology* 13, 179–201.

Corrigan, P. (1997). *The sociology of consumption: An introduction*. London: Sage.

De Kadt, E. (1979). *Tourism: Passport to development?* Oxford: Oxford University Press.

Excite, Inc. and Preview Travel, Inc. forge 5-year, multi-million dollar web alliance; comprehensive service creates leading market reach in travel with key content and advertising partners. (1997, September 10). *PR Newswire*.

Feifer, M. (1985). *Going places*. London: Macmillian.

Foucault, M. (1980). *Power/knowledge: Selected interviews and other writings, 1972–77* (C. Gordon, Ed.). New York: Pantheon Books.

Geertz, C. (1973). *The interpretation of cultures*. New York: Basic Books.

Geshekter, C. (1978). International tourism and African underdevelopment: Some reflections on Kenya. In V. Sutlive, et al. (Eds.), *Tourism and Economic Change: Studies in Third World Societies, 6*. Williamsburg, VA: College of William and Mary Press.

Giddens, A. (1990). *The consequences of modernity*. Stanford, CA: Stanford University Press.

Grossberg, L. (1988). Wandering audiences, nomadic critics. *Cultural Studies, 2*, 377–391.

Hall, C. M. (1994). *Tourism and politics: Policy, power, and place*. Chichester, UK: John Wiley.

Hall, S. (1989). New ethnicities. In K. Mercer (Ed.), *Black film, British cinema*. London: ICA.

Hardt, H. (1998). *Interactions: Critical studies in communication, media, and journalism*. Lanham, MD: Rowman & Littlefield.

Hartley, J. (1996). *Popular reality: Journalism, modernity, popular culture*. London: Arnold.

Herbote, B., & Goldberg, M. (Eds.) (1995). *World tourism directory '95/96. Part 2: The Americas*. Munich: K. G. Sour.

Iyer, P. (2000). *The global soul: Jet lag, shopping malls, and the search for home*. New York: Alfred A. Knopf.

Joseph, C. (1994). Touts, tourists, and tirtha: The articulation of sacred space at a Hindu pilgrimage. Unpublished doctoral dissertation. The University of Rochester, New York.

Leong, W. (1989). Culture and the state: Manufacturing traditions for tourism. *Critical Studies in Mass Communications, 6*, 355–375.

Levi-Strauss, C. (1970). *Tristes tropiques*. New York: Atheneum.

Loshitzky, Y. (1996). Travelling culture/travelling television. *Screen, 37*, 323–335.

MacCannell, D. (1976). *The tourist: A new theory of the leisure class*. New York: Schocken.

Martin, C., & Witt, S. (1988). Substitute prices in models of tourist demand. *Annals of Tourism Research, 15*, 255–268.

McDowell, E. (1998, May 6). Jumping on America's hospitality bandwagon: Foreign students choose U.S. for studying tourism. *New York Times*, C1, C3.

Morley, D., & Robins, K. (1995). *Spaces of identity: Global media, electronic landscapes and cultural boundaries*. London: Routledge.

Morris, M. (1988). At Henry Parkes motel. *Cultural Studies, 2*, 1–47.

Nash, D. (1989). Tourism as a form of imperialism. In V. L. Smith (Ed.), *Hosts and guests: The anthropology of tourism* (2nd ed., pp. 37–52). Philadelphia: University of Pennsylvania Press.

Nuñez, T. (1989). Touristic studies in anthropological perspective. In V. L. Smith (Ed.), *Hosts and guests: The anthropology of tourism* (2nd ed., pp. 265–279). Philadelphia: University of Pennsylvania Press.

O'Rourke, P. J. (1988). *Holidays in hell*. New York: Atlantic Monthly Press.

Parry, B. (1987). Problems in current theories of colonial discourse. *Oxford Literary Review, 9*(1/2), 27–58.

Pearce, P. (1982). *The social psychology of tourist behavior*. New York: Pergamon Press.

Pi-Sunyer, O. (1977). Through native eyes: Tourists and tourism in a Catalan maritime community. In V. L. Smith (Ed.), *Hosts and guests: The anthropology of tourism* (1st ed.) Philadelphia: University of Pennsylvania Press.

Prato, P., & Trivero, G. (1985). The spectacle of travel. *Australian Journal of Cultural Studies, 3*(2), 25–42.

Pratt, M. L. (1992). *Imperial eyes: Travel writing and transculturation*. London: Routledge.

Reeves, G. (1993). *Communications and the "Third World."* London: Routledge.

Rojek, C. (1997). Indexing, dragging, and the social construction of tourist sights. In C. Rojek & J. Urry (Eds.), *Touring cultures: Transformations of travel and theory* (pp. 52–74). London: Routledge.

Rojek, C., & Urry, J. (Eds.) (1997). *Touring cultures: Transformations of travel and theory.* London: Routledge.

Rowe, D. (1993). Leisure, tourism, and "Australianness." *Media, Culture & Society, 15,* 253–269.

Said, E. W. (1993). *Culture and imperialism.* New York: Alfred A. Knopf.

Shome, R. (1996). Postcolonial interventions in the rhetorical canon: An "other" view. *Communication Theory, 6*(1), 40–59.

Smith, V. L. (1989). Introduction. In V. L. Smith (Ed.), *Hosts and guests: The anthropology of tourism* (2nd ed., pp. 1–17). Philadelphia: University of Pennsylvania Press.

Theroux, P. (1985). *The great railway bazaar: By train through Asia.* New York: Pocket Books.

Tomaselli, Keyan G. (1999). Psychospiritual ecoscience: The Ju/'hoansi and cultural tourism. *Visual Anthropology, 12,* 185–195.

Tomaselli, Keyan G. (2000). The semiotics of anthropological authenticity: The film apparatus and cultural accommodation. In W. Schmitz (Ed.), *Sign processes and complex systems.* Conference Proceedings of the Seventh International Congress of the International Association for Semiotic Studies, Dresden, Germany.

Urry, J. (1990). *The tourist gaze: Leisure and travel in contemporary societies.* London: Sage.

Urry, J. (1995). *Consuming places.* London: Routledge.

Waters, S. R. (1997). *Travel industry world yearbook: The big picture—1996–1997* (Vol. 40). New York: Child and Waters.

Weir-Alderson, J. (1988, July/August). Confessions of a travel writer. *Columbia Journalism Review,* 27–28.

Wolff, J. (1993). On the road again: Metaphors of travel in cultural criticism. *Cultural Studies, 7,* 224–239.

Appendix B

India Night in Georgia: Why the Dancing Diasporic Desi[1] Men Cross-Dressed

Anandam Kavoori and Christina Joseph

PRELUDE

*A*nnouncer *(walks to center of stage)*: Good evening, ladies and gentlemen. We have a special treat for you. It's a first. The first research paper written as a performative text[2] (pause for sense of exaggeration). A research play, if you will. If you know of others, we suggest you keep that knowledge to yourself (pause for humor). It's a multimedia play—auto-ethnographic, self-reflexive, bilingual, and perhaps humorous.

Its narrative is structured through conversations between three sets of protagonists. The first are two anthropologists/authors (referred to as A1 and A2—this rhymes with R2 and D2, if you know what I mean) who discuss the text of a Hindi film called *Laawaris*, which means "orphaned" and was made by the Bollywood director Prakash Mehra in 1981, and a dance by Indian film superstar Amitab Bachchan in the film where he dresses up as five different women. (Pause.) Yes, five.

The dialogue between the anthropologists/authors is interspersed with extracts and interpretations of interviews with the second set of protagonists, three Indian students at a southern American University who performed a version of the dance. Two Indian members of the audience who watched the performance make up the third set of protagonists. (They are referred to as R1 and R2, for respondent.)

Finally, two narrators named "Made-to-Marcus" and "Vivid Mani" provide commentary, context, and framing at different points in the play. You are probably wondering what the names "Vivid Mani" and "Made-to-Marcus" mean. Well, you'll need to wait until the end of the play. When I come back. Don't worry about it right now. What's important (and what you came to see anyway) is this research play, which begins with the discovery of a mystery. Enjoy the show.

ACT 1: THE MYSTERY

A1 and A2 stand under two spotlights at two ends of the stage. Projected on the screen between them are three images of billboards. The first has the words "Laawaris" emblazoned on the top with a picture of Amitab Bachchan dancing in a white suit, his chest open to midriff and his eyes hostile. The second billboard is for a show called India Night in Georgia,[3] *with a picture of four cross-dressing men in the foreground. The third billboard reads simply "Crises of Representation" with blood dripping dramatically from the letters.*

MADE-TO-MARCUS: "The popular Hindi film proves a considerable element of commonality to Indian communities, even among those where Hindi is not spoken, a profound homage to the Hindi film's rooted-ness in the deep mythic structures of Indian civilization. Across the globe, the popular Hindi film commands an extraordinary allegiance from Indians."[4]

VIVID MANI: "The borderline work of culture demands an encounter with newness that is not part of the continuum of past and present. It creates a sense of the new as an insurgent act of cultural translation. Such art does not merely recall the past as social cause or aesthetic precedent; it renews the past, refiguring it as a contingent 'in-between' space, that innovates and interrupts the performance of the present. The 'past-present' becomes part of the necessity, not the nostalgia of living."[5]

(Stridently) Ladies and gentlemen, it's India Night from Georgia. (Ends lamely.) Well, people talking about it anyway.

Lights fade from the billboards. A1 picks up a chair next to him and moves to the middle of the room. R1 and R2 join in from the other side of the stage. They hug each other, exchange abuses in Hindi, open cans of Budweiser and light cigarettes. Behind them the screen shows a concrete block of buildings with the words "Graduate Housing" written on it. An old Honda with a smashed headlight is superimposed on the building. A2 stands on one side of the stage.

A1: So what do you think of these guys cross-dressing and dancing?

R1: I actually found it quite crass.

A1: Were you surprised to find out who was playing Amitab Bachchan's role?

R2: I mean, if you know the guy, it's hard to believe it.

R1: Yeah, especially given that he was doing it. He's a *seedha*[6] guy and it was just a surprise to see him do it.

R2: Actually, the guy's family is you know really part of the community and well regarded. It was just the contrast . . .

R1: You know it reminded me of *Hijras*. Just the whole thing was a turn off. Just can't understand why they chose to do that dance.

A1: Yes, they did remind me of *Hijras* in India.

A2: "There is in India a community of people known as *Hijras* described variously as eunuchs, transvestites, homosexuals, bisexuals, hermaphrodites, androgynes, and transsexuals. *Hijras* dress in women's garments. They imitate a woman's swaying walk, take female names upon being initiated into the community and affect in a comical way, women's mannerisms."[7]

A1 walks over to A2.

A1: So, the mystery is simply this: why did four middle-class, good Indian American boys, raised to behave properly, cross-dress and dance lewdly in front of their families?

MADE-TO-MARCUS: "Men have cross-dressed for what have been considered erotic reasons deriving from psychopathological drives. In most western societies being a man and demonstrating masculinity is more highly prized than being a woman and displaying femininity. Some non-Western societies however are more tolerant and even encourage men to behave like women and women to act like men."[8]

A2 (POINTING TO R1 AND R2): You know, for audience members like these two students from India, this may be crass but I am sure that the performers didn't have hijras on their mind. I mean they grew up in America.

A1: Well, let's talk to them. But they did watch the original dance by Amitab Bachchan in *Laawaris*. First let's see what that's all about. What do you think, Made-to-Marcus?

MADE-TO-MARCUS: "Identity groups are about themselves, for themselves, and nobody else."[9]

ACT 2: THE MOTIVE

R1 and R2 pick up their chairs and leave. A1 and A2 move to two ends of the stage. The screen at the center of the stage now shows a medley of Amitab Bachchan shots from his various film magazine covers between the 1970s and 1990s.

MADE-TO-MARCUS: "Among the constituting elements of the Hindi film industry, the single most dominant group is the film's stars. With a powerful grip on people's imagination, 'star texts' compromising narratives of the film stars' lives, are a constant preoccupation of film magazines."[10]

VIVID MANI: Amitab was not just a creation of film magazines. "Amitab introduced the motif of the angry young man to Indian cinema. This is at a time in the mid 1970s when domestic politics was in a period of great turmoil, student unrest was at its height, and the employment prospects for educated young men were bleak at best."[11]

A1: He articulated a sense of unrest and paradoxically of community. I will always remember the time Amitab almost died during the making of the film *Coolie*. I can't think of anything else that drew India together—besides the assassination of Indira Gandhi—than those hours when we all thought that he was dead.

The screen turns to a somber image of Amitab with his hands folded. A ticker tape at the bottom of the image runs the following statement as somber classical Indian music is played as background: "The passionate affection of the people in this country through prayers, are moments that I will carry as a huge debt on me, to my grave. There are no words to substitute this feeling of the extent of affection of my fans and well wishers and the awareness toward the potential that one human body possesses."[12]

A2: What I can't figure out is what possessed him to cross-dress in *Laawaris*.

A1: Well, you got to see it in terms of the movie itself. *Laawaris* is a humdinger of a class conflict movie. It's got all the redemptive pathos of *The Wizard of Oz* with its reiteration of the mythical centrism of the American farm.

A2: Where is the American farm in *Laawaris*? You're stretching it.

A1: No, of course, it's not the American farm, but it is about redemptive pathos Bollywood-style where culture and class are unproblematically gendered.

The screen shows a sequence of scenes from the movie Laawaris with commentary from Made-to-Marcus and Vivid Mani. A1 and A2 move to different corners of the stage.

MADE-TO-MARCUS: *Laawaris* literally means "without an heir" but it can also signify "orphaned" more generally, somebody who has not been claimed by anybody, somebody whose parents do not want to acknowledge or accept. Somebody, in short, that society rejects. The movie *Laawaris* tells the story of one such boy.

VIVID MANI: Here is how his story begins. A famous woman singer and a rich man are lovers.[13] It is the rich man's birthday (also India's Independence Day). After performing one of her songs, she rushes into the arms of her lover backstage eager to tell him that this was a special song for him and to give him a special message—that at the end of the year there will be three of them and not just two. The rich man withdraws from her and rejects her. She slaps the rich man, who then mocks her by telling her to shout from the top of the Red Fort[14] of the child she is carrying; of the disgrace she will bring to his name.

Film excerpt of the above scene plays on the screen.

VIVID MANI: The baby is given away to a drunk who beats the boy whenever he is drunk or so inclined. The boy grows up into a strong, insolent, aggressive, and self-confident hero. Amitab Bachchan plays the hero. In the opening scene showing his coming of age, Amitab shouts insolently at the factory supervisor where he works.

Film excerpt of the above scene plays on the screen.

MADE-TO-MARCUS: Amitab Bachchan displays a "contraction between detached stability into explosive force and back into self-enclosure. A device employed by other hero figures such as Clint Eastwood but in Bombay cinema it has become a distinctive marker of Amitab Bachchan. It is this behavior coupled with a distinct physical appearance that has been harnessed by Bachchan and the film makers in a series of roles that have inscribed him into contemporary Indian culture as a disruptive modern force that cannot be ignored."[15]

VIVID MANI: The young man goes to work and makes money. On his way home, his father asks him for money for alcohol. Amitab refuses and says he will beat him up if he asks him again. His father turns to him angrily and tells him that he is not his son, rather he is a bastard, without a heir, much like the garbage that rich people (a reference to the young man's father) throw away.

Film excerpt of the above scene plays on the screen.

MADE-TO-MARCUS: This paradigmatic scene in the film throws Amitab's already embittered life completely off balance. He goes into a shouting and raving fit, which culminates in his going to an *adda*[16] and drinking himself into an aggressive somnolence.

VIVID MANI: Amitab turns to drinking and womanizing. In a whore house he meets a rich man's son who employs him as a hired thug. He earns the respect of the rich man's father (who happens to be his own father) and through a complex series of incidents finds validation and affection from the rich man's sister and gains approval from the father. In a climactic scene these relationships are established through the bonds of *raakhi*.[17]

Screen shows the above scene and then flickers off. A1 and A2 walk to the middle of the stage.

A1: Let's talk about this last scene. I think it's important for understanding the cross-dressing dance.

A2: Yeah, it's paradigmatic in a number of ways. First, it brings to a close the basic premise of the film—that society only values those who belong. Amitab does not belong at birth; he does not belong to his drunken father; he does not belong to the workplace where he works. He only begins to belong when he is acknowledged by the class structure that he fights against. Specifically, the film seems to be saying that the vehicles which establishes his new identity are those of class excess (those of the rich man's son repeating the sexual and moral compromise of the father) but equally those of upperclass magnanimity. The fact that Amitab's salvation comes at the hand of the rich man's daughter speaks to the inherent displacement of a lowerclass person like Amitab who can only be rehabilitated financially through the son and humanistically through the fictive bonds of brotherhood bestowed by the daughter and the blessings of an unacknowledged paternity.

A1: I couldn't have put it better.

A1 and A2 move to their corners of the stage. The screen lights up again.

MADE-TO-MARCUS: And what follows is important. Because soon after the *raakhi* is tied, Amitab realizes it's his sister's birthday. He then proceeds to sing the same song that years ago on his birthday his mother the singer had sung to his unacknowledged father. Each verse of this song shows Amitab in a different set of women's clothes. The song is called "Mere Angane Mein" (In My Home).[18]

The screen shows Amitab Bachchan's cross-dressing song and dance. A1 and A2 pull out TV remotes from their pockets and pause the tape after each verse to offer analysis in shorthand by listing concepts that occur to them.

Screen shows first verse which speaks of who should be allowed into one's home? An insider joke about the role of women—in their proper place, at home.

A1 AND A2 (SPEAKING TOGETHER AFTER THE FIRST VERSE): Class consciousness, over determined discourse, and notion of home as moral center/agency and class/lower class as moral agent/discursive disruptions of class relations.[19]

Screen shows the second verse, which speaks of the virtues of having a tall wife— she is somebody you can use as a ladder!

Screen shows the third verse, which speaks of the virtues of having a fat wife— she can be used as a mattress!

Screen shows the fourth verse, which speaks of the virtues of having a dark skinned wife—she can be used as eyeliner?

Screen shows fifth verse, which speaks of the virtues of having a fair wife—she can be used as a light bulb!

Screen shows sixth verse, which speaks of the virtues of having a short wife— she can be treated as a child!

A1 AND A2 (TOGETHER): Gendered functionalities/bodies and visual regimes/male agency in patriarchy/femininity and normalcy/bodies and domesticity/gender roles and class formation/hybrid sexualities/ *hijra* sexualities.

A1 AND A2 (TOGETHER): Discursive constructions of femininity/patriarchal agency and feminine beauty/racialized norms of femininity/beauty and functionality/beauty and domesticity/color and female agency/ color and functionality/body form and domesticity/femininity and childhood/gender and agency/*hijra* and hybrid sexualities.

A1 and A2 walk to center of stage.

A2: I'm lost in those words. We are at the end of this act. (Pause for pun.) So, what is the motive?

A1: Well, simply put, I guess it's this. If what is being looked at is why a bunch of Indian American men cross-dressed, then we needed to see what legitimated that act. Now, we have at least two answers: to understand the act, we first had to look at the overall discursive space that Amitab Bachchan occupies and then at the specific narrative space that this film and dance occupy. In both cases, the space is sociologically contingent on a number of historical and cultural forces. Amitab's case rests on a specific model of masculinity and in the case of the film, that masculinity articulates an unambiguous vision of community. In the case of community in the Indian context, the song reifies through a *hijra* performance (i.e., with humor at a distorted femininity/masculinity) the racial, class and gender politics of the Indian middle-class mainstream viewership and their concept of community.

A2: In other words, the young men chose this song because it would sell and it made fun of women?

A1: Well, it's never that simple, or maybe it is. I mean there is a lot more going on. It's performed in Georgia, remember. Let's find out.

ACT 3: REVELATION

The screen in the center of the stage shows a bar with the words "The Blind Pig Tavern" on top. The TV shows a football game from the South Eastern Conference. A1 and three participants in the cross-dressing dance sit down. They open bottles of beers and start to drink.

A2: (STANDING ON ONE SIDE OF THE STAGE): In the India Night version of Amitab Bachchan's dance there were six participants in all. Five of the men dressed up as one of the women from each verse: tall (lambi), fat (moti), dark/black (kali), fair/white (gori), and small (chhoti). Amitab was played by the sixth man.

All six men are students. They met in college and were drawn to each other because of their Indian heritage. They visit each other frequently. Beer and football is usually involved. Their friendship was also built through other dances they have taken part in over their four years of college. Their cross-dressing dance was performed in their senior year.

The three students present tonight are Moti, Gori, and the student we can call "American Amitab."

MADE-TO-MARCUS: "Men form their gender identities by relating to the dominant values in the culture."[20] However, "masculinity also varies within any one society by the various types of cultural groups that compose it. In the contemporary United States, masculinity is constructed differently by class culture, by race and ethnicity, and by age. The resulting matrix of masculinities is complicated and often the elements are cross-cutting, but without understanding this, we risk collapsing all masculinities into one hegemonic version."[21]

A1: What made you decide on this act?

AMERICAN AMITAB: The thing was that we had done a *bhangra*[22] before and one last year, and we wanted to do something for laughs in place of something serious. And then Gori came up with the idea that let's dress up and cross-dress and we were like cool, let's do that. Let's do meera angane mey.

MOTI: Gori came up with the idea. And since none of us was going to be here after this year, since this was our last time together, we were like let's do something different. This was the last time we could do something together.

GORI: It was pretty much the last time we could be together and we wanted to leave with a blast. We decided to something drastic actually, to do something different.

VIVID MANI: The ideology of male friendship-loyalty, affection, and trust has never gone out of style. Urbanization and bureaucratization, social and geographical mobility, all may foster instrumental and expedient relationships, but they surely induce a sense of individual isolation.[23]

A1 walks over to A2.

A2: So is this is what it's about—a way for Indian American men to bond, to remove the individual isolation they live under in postindustrial America. What do you think, Vivid Mani?

VIVID MANI: Well, you may have something there. "One of the most interesting phenomena at present is the appearance of so-called crises of masculinity in advanced industrial nations. There is a widespread popular and academic agreement that something is troubling men."[24]

A1: Not just any men, but specifically Indian men raised in the United States.

A1 walks back to the group, sits down, and asks a question.

A1: Why do most Indian men raised in America not want to dance at these cultural festivals?

MOTI: In India, guys go and do *garba* and *raas*[25] and they already have skills to dance, but in America they grow up as guys so they cannot dance at all while the girls, since they are feminine, they can pull it off. That's the reason why. I mean even when we dance, that is the problem: there is an overflow of girls but there are no guys to dance with.

AMERICAN AMITAB: There are no open-minded guys who would come to the dance like we would. The girls want to be the center of attention on the stage. Guys here seem so uninterested. Usually the guys are not into cultural stuff, they just want to look good, show off, hang out, and drink. They are not into the show. They will still go to garba, to hang out and look at the girls.

A2: The real issue it seems is that dancing is culturally prescriptive for women and not for men. Hindi films reiterate these concerns by locating the female body as the central source of performative pleasure. In other words, film culture provides a vocabulary for dance performances for women in the Indian diaspora and not for Indian men. What do you think, Made-to-Marcus?

MADE-TO-MARCUS: I think you are on the right track. "The relationship between the male body and the dominant discourses of masculinity converges upon the issue of desire. Consumer culture stimulates men's desires to be attractive, intelligent, and effectual individuals; the pleasure/desire axis thus sustains social forms which keep relationships as they are."[26]

A1 gets up from his chair and walks over to A2.

A1: It still leaves the all-important question unanswered. If they did it out of a need for the articulation of a desi masculinity in the diaspora, how did they traverse the gendered/sexualized terrain of the performance in the film itself?

Moti, Gori, and American Amitab walk off stage.

A2: Well, lets look and compare.

The center of the stage has now has two screens. On one screen, there is the India Night dance which is screened and on the other Amitab Bachchan's version.

A1 AND A2 (TOGETHER AT THE END OF THE SCREENING): I see differences in sequence, structure, and costume, but this is part of the same discursive formation—similar narrative interpretation, similar sexualization of performance, similar male agency, similar sexual politics.

VIVID MANI: Huh. That's surprising. I thought under current conditions of globalization "history becomes spacialized out, aesthetic hierarchies and developments are collapsed with the mixing of genres and high art, popular and commercial forms."[27]

MADE-TO-MARCUS: Yes, but "entertainment forms come to have the emotional significance they do: that is, by acquiring their signification in relation to the complex of meanings in the social-cultural situation in which they are produced."[28]

A1: Well, let's go back to what we do know: that men in the Diaspora don't dance and women do. The issue must of necessity return to sexual politics. To women and how they are seen to dance.

Moti and Gori walk back on stage.

MOTI: Look at Indian dances like *Bharatnatyam* and compare them to rock and pop videos on MTV. Do you see any of the *Bharatnatyam* dances mixed into dances by women? They are probably trying to improvise a little, but the movement that is coming out is more focused on an area of their body. Look at their outfits, look at the jhumka[29] in their hips. They are trying to make something more conspicuous than the art itself. That's exactly what American culture is making them do.

GORI: Girls have a tendency to become slutty. I have noticed this. I know many of these girls personally. They actually do the dance to be slutty and attract more guys. Most of the girls want to be the solo. Teamwork might be significant, but they really want to go solo.

A2: So the issue of motive remains that for these Indian men, their performance is not about being slutty or going solo but about their own participation in a collective act. They assume both agency and priority in their performance.

A1: It is about what we knew all along. The revelation as, we properly foreshadowed at the end of Act 1, is about identity groups, about community.

VIVID MANI: "While Europeans were intent on claiming lands for their sovereigns and for cartography, transforming land into space, Indians sought to render space into place, localizing spaces into habitats for communion with self. In so doing, they also cherished memories of the ancestral land."[30]

A2: Yes, it's about the ancestral land and its sexual politics and reification of community. The cross dressing dance is also about creating a space for identity in the Diaspora—a move to address *desi* contestedness by claiming unambiguously an affiliation with a mythical rendering of *desi* identity. In the case of the cross-dressing *desi* men, they locate themselves in direct opposition to both new Indian International students and younger second-generation Indian students (to which they belong) and instead place themselves in allegiance with older Indian immigrants who mainly subsist on a mythical/essentialist rendering of Indian identity.

MOTI: I consider myself as *desi*. The new Indian students are hardcore *desi*. But they are trying to be westernized and that does not suit them at all. And with the second generation Indians, they are trying to be *desis* which they are not. Their thinking is not *desi*.

GORI: When you see the Indian international students you see people that have been brought up not only by Indian parents but in India and you see the Indian culture that has been brought with them. Their thoughts are all Indian. They know what culture is all about.

AMERICAN AMITAB: I have seen all sides of society. I have sort of had this pressure ever since elementary and middle school, having the American way of life being pushed on me. I owe it to my parents. Because of them I was able to be, I guess it's not much, but who I am right now. I don't mean to be really Indian in my thoughts but deep down inside I am more Indian than anybody else, as far as my family.

A1: So the revelation is that the community made them do it?

A2: Well, paradoxically yes. The videotape of the dance is very popular in the Indian community now. It's put on in various homes when people want to watch something funny.

A1: So the Indian students in Act 1 were wrong. Instead of embarrassing their community, the cross-dressers actually celebrated it. It was equally a dance of celebration and control, of masculine destiny in the Diaspora.

A destiny that resurrects a discourse very familiar to them—those from their immigrant parents. Listen to the American Amitab.

AMERICAN AMITAB: Even if you are, pardon my language, fucked up, you have your parents to rely on. That has put this feeling inside me that, look, I need to do what makes them happy to at least until their lifetime.

Stage lights go out.

POSTLUDE

Announcer (walks onto the stage):

And so you have it. The first research play in the history of the world. (Pause.) Well, as you go home, we hope it will allow you "further exploration around the weighty issues surrounding culture, gender, and performance."[31] (Pause.) Or you could get Indian takeout and curl up with a good Bollywood movie. At any rate let me get our big thoughts out of the way. We have three big thoughts. So please stay in your seats and don't worry, the refreshment stands will be open for an hour after the show is finished.

The first has to do with those awkward names: Vivid Mani and Made-to-Marcus. The names are tongue in cheek references to two influential scholars in the field of ethnography and postcolonial studies. George Marcus is well known for his work in rethinking ethnographic discourse and writing and Lata Mani is well known in the field of postcolonial studies. The term "Made-to-Marcus" (read, "made to mark us") refers to the enthusiastic spirit in which postmodern ethnography has been embraced by many anthropologists from the developing world, a turn itself worthy of examination in looking at the link between academic discourse and the politics of placement. The term "Vivid Mani" (read, "vivid money") is meant equally to refer to an author and to the purchase that postcolonial theory has had on many scholars from the developing world.

It goes without saying that the terms are not used in any way to criticize or provide commentary on the work of these fine scholars. What we do criticize and want to emphasize in this research play is that this attention to the act of construction should not make us forget the connection implicit in the title of Margery Wolf's book, *A Thrice Told Tale: Feminism, Postmodernism and Ethnographic Responsibility*. It's a message that Jane Flax warned us about over a decade ago, but it seems to have been forgotten. It's worth repeating and if you'll indulge me, I'll read it in its entirety:

> A problem with thinking about (or only in terms of) texts, signs, or significa-
> tion is that they tend to take on a life of their own or become the world . . .
> such an approach obscures the projection of its own activity onto the world
> and denies the existence of the variety of concrete social practices that enter
> into and are reflected in the constitution of language itself . . . This lack of at-
> tention to concrete social relations including the distribution of power results
> in the obscuring of relations of domination.[32]

I can see you shifting in your seats and wondering if the next point is going to be as long-winded. I promise you it won't be. In fact, I am done with four simple words: "Places changing, times unchanging." In the terminological blizzard that is postmodern and postcolonial inter-rogation of the contemporary world, the nature of the unproblematic is often seen as unworthy of consideration. This research play points to the simple truths that often may underlie the complex apparatus that we bring to reality and research. It does this, in one place, by letting the anthropologists pause the video of Amitab's performance and in stac-cato fashion provide the complex analytical grid that can underlie a sin-gle performance.

In the end, the revelation that does emerge is simple. The dance by the diasporic men, whatever else it may be about, is in the end about relations of domination in the Diaspora, a diaspora that is startlingly similar to other spaces—dare we say, immigrant spaces in the original homeland. What is important is not difference, disarticulation, or hybridity but the reiteration of an unproblematic gendered ideology across all the spaces of the contemporary Diaspora, whether a village in Baroda, Gujrat, or in Al-pharetta, Georgia.

Finally, if you are still in your seat, the research play is about you. It in-terrogates the relations that you have brought to it. If life is a text—an overused analogy, if I ever heard one—then texts too have their own lives. Mary Bateson's wonderful book *Composing a life: Life as Work in Progress* looks at the complex imbrication of life as text and text as life. This re-search play is we hope, one such complex mediation where the inter-twining of fieldwork, writing, performance (life as text) are related to what is happening right now (you in your seats, me rattling on, in other words, text as life). It is that understanding, that manifestation of the pos-sibility of transformation of every moment of life.

Thank you, ladies and gentleman. Good night. And we'll see you at the movies.

NOTES

1. "Desi" is the Hindi word most commonly used among Indians in the Diaspora for people from South Asia or of South Asian origin.

2. In writing our paper as a performative text, we are drawing on recent trends in ethnographic writing that have focused on issues of "exploring various intersections, various blendings of genre and voices" (Reed-Danahay, 1997, p. 3). The important issues have been those of providing alternate ways for ethnographic expression including those of "real fiction," poetry, plays, life histories, personal narratives (Archetti, 1994; Benson, 1993; Gullestad, 1996; Lavi et al., 1993). Theoretically the focus on writing is reflected in anthropology's literary turn and the development of a postmodern ethnography (Atkinson, 1992; Fischer, 1994; Strathern, 1987; Van Maanen, 1995) with its concomitant focus on issues of native identity, postcolonialism, and gender (Narayan, 1993; Chow, 1993; Brettell, 1997).

3. This paper is part of an ongoing ethnographic study of South Asians in the U.S. South. The performance analyzed here was done at India Night, an annual celebration of Indian culture, arts, and identity at a Southern U.S. university. The celebration brings together three populations: international students from India, first-generation Indian American students, and the local Indian community, consisting of older immigrants. Our study has focused on media use (films, websites, videos) across these populations and on the actual text of the annual program. We argue that India Night has become a site for the struggle to define cultural identity, authenticity, and agency among the three populations. This paper examines some of the dynamics around masculinity, film, diaspora, and performance for the first generation Indian American students.

Fieldwork and interviews for this project have been conducted across all three communities. This paper uses transcripts from interviews with three students (the dancers) representing the first generation Indian American students, with one caveat. Two of the three students were born in India but their parents immigrated to the United States soon after. The two respondents in the first act are Indian international students. The cultural milieu the first generation Indian American students grew up in is of a specific Indian ethnicity called "Gujarati" (i.e., from the Indian state of Gujarat). They described their community as cohesive, tied by bonds of language, commensality, food, and frequent cultural celebrations such as dances, religious gatherings, and family events around birthdays, marriages, and so on. All three of the dancers had been to India numerous times, and their understanding of India was more contextual than others of their generation who had only been there once or twice in their life. All three dancers anticipated marrying within their ethnic and religious community.

4. Lal, retrieved on November 12, 2000, from www.sscnet.ucla.edu.

5. Bhaba, 1994, p. 7.

6. Honest, likeable.

7. Lal, 1998, pp. 60, 68.

8. Bullogh and Bullogh, 1993.

9. Hobsbawm, 1996, p. 44.

10. Virdi, 1997.

11. Retrieved on November 12, 2000, from www.sscenet.ucla.edu.

12. Interview with Amitab Bachchan, *Cine Blitz*, 2000, p. 27.

13. Played by the well-known character Bollywood stars, Raakhee and Amjad Khan.

14. The Red Fort is where India's prime minister gives his annual Independence Day speech.

15. Mishra, Jeffrey, and Shoesmith, 1989.

16. Adda is a cheap drinking establishment frequented by the poor.

17. Raakhi is a ceremony establishing a fictive sibling kinship between a man and a woman. It is symbolized by a thread, which a woman puts on a man's wrist.

18. Translations of these songs were done by the authors for the purpose of analysis but are not being reproduced here.

19. This rhetorical strategy can be seen as a kind of analytic shorthand that signals the contexts of interpretation without laying out a predetermined path for all readings to follow. We follow Denzin's (1997) rationale and Kohn (1998, 1994) example in assuming this strategy.

20. Harris, Torres, and Allender, 1994, p. 704.

21. Kimel and Messner, 1992, pp. 9–10.

22. A popular dance from the Indian state of Punjab. It's very popular among South Asians in the Diaspora.

23. Hammond and Jablow, 1987, p. 256.

24. Mcdowell, 2000, p. 201.

25. *Garba* and *Raas* are dances from the Indian State of Gujarat.

26. Coward, 1985, p. 13.

27. Featherstone, 1991, p. 69.

28. Dyer, 1993, p. 275.

29. *Jhumka* can be roughly translated as style. Here it refers to what the respondent thinks is an overly sexual style of women dancers.

30. Lal, retrieved on November 12, 2000, from sscnet.ucla.edu.

31. *Jump Cut* reviewer's comments.

32. Flax, 1987, p. 632.

REFERENCES

Archetti, E. (Ed.) (1994). *Exploring the written: Anthropology and the multiplicity of writing*. Oslo: Scandinavian University Press.

Atkinson, P. (1992). *Understanding ethnographic texts*. London: Sage.

Benson, P. (1993). *Anthropology and literature*. Urbana: University of Illinois Press.

Bhabha, H. (1994). *The location of culture*. London: Routledge.

Brettell, C. (1997). Blurred genres and blended voices: Life history, biography, autobiography, and the auto/ethnography of women's lives. In D. Reed-Danahay (Ed.), *Auto/ethnography: Rewriting the self and the social* (pp. 223–246). Oxford: Berg Publishers.

Bullogh, V., & Bullogh, B. (Eds.) (1993). *Cross dressing, sex, and gender*. Philadelphia: University of Pennsylvania Press.

Chow, R. (1993). *Writing diaspora.* Bloomington: Indiana University Press.

Coward, R. (1985). *Female desires.* New York: Grove Press.

Denzin, N. (1997). *Interpretive ethnography.* London: Sage.

Dirlik, A. (1994). The post-colonial aura: Third World criticism in the age of global capitalism. *Critical Inquiry, 20,* 328–356.

Dyer, R. (1993). Entertainment and utopia. In S. During (Ed.), *The cultural studies reader.* London: Routledge.

Featherstone, M. (1991). *Consumer culture and postmodernism.* London: Sage.

Fisher, M. (1994). Autobiographical voices (1, 2, 3) and mosaic memory: Experimental sondages in the (post)modern world. In K. Ashley et al. (Eds.), *Autobiography and postmodernism* (pp. 79–129). Amherst: University of Massachusetts Press.

Flax, J. (1987). Postmodernism and gender relations in feminist theory. *Signs, 12*(4), 621–643.

Gullestad, M. (1996). *Everyday life philosophers: Modernity, morality, and autobiography in Norway.* Oslo: Scandinavian University Press.

Hammond, D., & Jablow, A. (1987). Gilgamesh and the Sundance Kid: The myth of male friendship. In H. Brod (Eds), *The making of masculinities.* New York: Routledge.

Harris, I., Torres, J., & Allender, D. (1994). The response of African-American men to dominant norms of masculinity within the United States. *Sex Roles, 31*(11/12), 703–719.

Hobsbawm, E. (1996). Identity politics and the left. *New Left Review, 217,* 39–48.

Kimel, M., & Messner, M. (Eds.) (1992). *Men's lives.* New York: McMillan.

Kohn, N. (1994). Messing: Information, liminality, dread. *Cultural Studies: A Research Annual, 4,* 243–275.

Kohn, N. (1998). Wonder never seizes. *American Communication Journal, 1*(2), 1–36.

Lal, V. Reflections on the Indian Diaspora. Retrieved on November 12, 2000, from www.sscnet.ucla.edu/south asia/diaspora.

Lal, V. (1998). Hijras in India: Gender bending and the cultural politics of sexuality. *Suitcase, 3,* 60–73.

Lavi, S., Narayan, K., & Rosaldo, R. (Eds.) (1993). *Creativity/anthropology.* Ithaca, NY, and London: Cornell University Press.

McDowell, L. (2000). The trouble with men? Young people, gender transformations and the crises of masculinity. *International Journal of Urban and Regional Research, 24*(1), 201–209.

Mishra, V., Jeffrey, P., & Shoesmith, B. (1989). The actor as parallel text in Bombay cinema. *Quarterly Review of Film and Video, 11,* 49–676.

Narayan, K. (1993). How native is a native anthropologist. *American Anthropologist, 95,* 671–686.

Reed-Danahay, D. (Ed.) (1997). *Auto/ethnography: Rewriting the self and the social.* Oxford: Berg Publishers.

Strathern, M. (1987). The limits of auto-anthropology. In A. Jackson (Ed.), *Anthropology at home* (pp. 59–67). London: Tavistock Publications.

Van Maanen, J. (1995). An end to innocence: The ethnography of ethnography. In J. Van Maanen (Ed.), *Representation in ethnography.* London: Sage.

Virdi, J. (1997). Film text: Symbolic worlds of real/fictional histories in the culture of popular Indian films. Paper presented at the Couch Stone Symposium, College Park, Maryland, 1997, available at www.bsos.umd.edu/css97.

Index

About the Author

Anandam Kavoori is associate professor in the Grady College of Journalism and Mass Communication at the University of Georgia, Athens. He is the author of *Thinking Television* and the novel *The Children of Shahida*.